The Microgenre

The Microgenre

A Quick Look at Small Culture

Edited by
Molly C. O'Donnell and Anne H. Stevens

BLOOMSBURY ACADEMIC
NEW YORK • LONDON • OXFORD • NEW DELHI • SYDNEY

BLOOMSBURY ACADEMIC
Bloomsbury Publishing Inc
1385 Broadway, New York, NY 10018, USA
50 Bedford Square, London, WC1B 3DP, UK

BLOOMSBURY, BLOOMSBURY ACADEMIC and the Diana logo are trademarks
of Bloomsbury Publishing Plc

First published in the United States of America 2020

Volume Editor's Part of the Work © Molly C. O'Donnell and Anne H. Stevens

Each chapter © of Contributors

For legal purposes the Acknowledgments on p. xiv constitute an extension
of this copyright page.

Cover design by Eleanor Rose

Library of Congress Cataloging-in-Publication Data
Names: O'Donnell, Molly C., editor. | Stevens, Anne H., 1971- editor.
Title: The microgenre : a quick look at small culture / edited by
Molly C. O'Donnell and Anne H. Stevens.
Description: New York : Bloomsbury Academic, 2019. | Includes
bibliographical references and index.
Identifiers: LCCN 2019025882 (print) | LCCN 2019025883 (ebook)
| ISBN 9781501345807 (paperback) | ISBN 9781501345814 (hardback)
| ISBN 9781501345821 (epub) | ISBN 9781501345838 (pdf)
Subjects: LCSH: Culture–Philosophy. | Literary form. | Art genres.
Classification: LCC HM621 .M5255 2019 (print) | LCC HM621 (ebook) |
DDC 306.01–dc23 LC record available at https://lccn.loc.gov/2019025882
LC ebook record available at https://lccn.loc.gov/2019025883

ISBN: HB: 978-1-5013-4581-4
         PB: 978-1-5013-4580-7
         ePDF: 978-1-5013-4583-8
         eBook: 978-1-5013-4582-1

Typeset by Integra Software Services Pvt. Ltd.
Printed and bound in the United States of America

To find out more about our authors and books visit www.bloomsbury.com
and sign up for our newsletters.

Contents

List of Figures   vi

Contributors   x

Acknowledgments   xiv

1   Introduction *Molly C. O'Donnell and Anne H. Stevens*   1

2   The Myron's Cow Epigram *Paul Hay*   9

3   The Premature Ejaculation Poem *Christopher Vilmar*   15

4   Prostitute Narratives of Ancien Régime France *Alistaire Tallent*   25

5   The Neoclassical Plague Romance *Matthew Duques*   31

6   Anesthesia Fiction *Jennifer Diann Jones*   39

7   Magic-Portrait Fiction *Diana Bellonby*   47

8   Topographical Reports of the American Frontier *John Hay*   61

9   Grangerism *Megan Becker-Leckrone*   71

10   Shirley Temple's "Baby Burlesks" *Nora Gilbert*   81

11   Nudie-Cuties *Cynthia J. Miller and Thomas M. Shaker*   93

12   Giallo *Gavin F. Hurley*   103

13   Nuclear Realism *John Carl Baker*   113

14   Anti-Sitcom Video Art *Susanna Newbury*   121

15   Home Depot Art *Danielle Kelly*   133

16   The Mommy Memoir *Mary Thompson*   147

17   *Minecraft* Fiction *Michael T. Wilson*   155

18   Heavy Metal Microgenres *Heather Lusty*   163

19   Mexican Neo-Surf Microgenres *Aurelio Meza*   171

20   Fanfiction Microgenres *Elyse Graham and Michelle Alexis Taylor*   181

21   Machine-Classified Microgenres *Jonathan Goodwin*   189

Index   196

List of Figures

5.1 Michael Sweerts, *Plague in an Ancient City* (1650–52) [Courtesy of the Los Angeles County Museum of Art]   32

5.2 Thomas Cole, *Destruction*, from five-painting series *Course of Empire* (1833–36)   35

7.1 Illustrated title page of D. G. Rossetti's "Hand and Soul" (1850; Chicago: Way and Williams, 1895) [Newberry Library, Chicago (Wing ZP 845.K331)]   52

7.2 Illustrated final page of Ouida's "The Adder" (in *Arts and Letters: An Illustrated Review* (July 1888), 272) [British Periodicals Database (ProQuest)]   54

7.3 Illustrated page from Frances Forbes-Robertson's "Jotchie: A Sketch" (in *The English Illustrated Magazine*, October 1895, 42) [British Periodicals Database (ProQuest)]   56

7.4 Film stills with portrait from *Portrait of Jennie* (Dieterle, 1948)   57

7.5 Film still featuring Kim Novak from Alfred Hitchcock's *Vertigo* (1958)   58

7.6 Film still featuring Kate Winslet from James Cameron's *Titanic* (1997)   58

8.1 *Col. Fremont Planting the American Standard on the Rocky Mountains* (New York: Bake & Godwin, 1856) [Library of Congress: LC-DIG-pga-03521]   65

8.2 From J. W. Powell, "The Cañons of the Colorado" (*Scribner's Monthly* 9.3 (January 1875), 305) [Image courtesy of the University of Arizona Library]   67

9.1 *A Collection of Portraits to Illustrate Granger's Biographical History of England, and Noble's Continuation of Granger; Forming a Supplement to Richardson's Copies of Rare Granger Portraits. Volume E, Containing Twenty-Four Portraits* (London: T. and H. Rodd, 1820) [Archive.org]   74

9.2 Image/Engraving: *The Destruction Room* advertisement (Peltz, "Facing the Text," 92) [Woodcut vignette from *A Complete Set*

of Prints, Cuttings, and Pamphlets, from the Gentleman's
Magazine, from 1831–1847 (London, *c*. 1847), 17] 75

9.3 Portrait of Leo Tolstoy, 1897 [Library of Congress]; Colorized
frontispiece to Leo Tolstoy, *What Is Art?* (trans. Aylmer Maude
(New York: Thomas Crowell, 1899)) [Archive.org]; Beerbohm's
"improved" portrait of Leo Tolstoy [Mark Samuels Lasner
Collection, University of Delaware] 78

10.1 *The Runt Page* (1932) 82

10.2 *Kid in Hollywood* (1933) 84

10.3 *The Kid's Last Fight* (1933) 85

10.4 *War Babies* (1932) 85

10.5 *Polly Tix in Washington* (1933) 86

10.6 *Wee Willie Winkie* (1937) 87

10.7 *Susannah of the Mounties* (1939) 87

10.8 *The Pie-Covered Wagon* (1932) 88

10.9 *Glad Rags to Riches* (1933) 88

10.10 *Kid 'in' Africa* (1933) 89

10.11 *Kid 'in' Africa* (1933) 90

11.1 Film poster for *Mr. Peters' Pets* (1963) 95

11.2 Film poster for *Nude on the Moon* (1961) 96

11.3 Film poster for *The Immoral Mr. Teas* (1959) 97

12.1 In *Bloodstained Shadow* (1978), Count Pedrazzi (Massimo
Serato) hears a killer in his house as he drinks several glasses
of prominently displayed J+B Scotch 105

12.2 A killer stalks Vanessa Matthews (Claudie Lange) in *Death
Walks on High Heels* (1971) 106

12.3 First-person "killer cam" angle in *Seven Blood-Stained Orchids*
(1972); Elena Marchi (Rossella Falk) stares into the camera as
she is pursued by her killer 108

12.4 Surrounded by fashion magazines, music, artistic décor, and
bottles of alcohol, Minou (Dagmar Lassander) washes down
some pills with whiskey in *The Forbidden Photos of a Lady
Above Suspicion* (1970) 109

14.1 Still from Michael Smith, *It Starts at Home* (1982) [Courtesy
of Electronic Arts Intermix (EAI), New York] 122

15.1   Cady Noland, *Untitled* (Exhibition: Mattress Factory, October
        14–December 22, 1989) [Courtesy of the Mattress Factory
        Museum, Pittsburgh, PA]   134
15.2   Jessica Stockholder, *Assist #1: A Cyst* (2015) (© Jessica
        Stockholder) [Courtesy of the artist; Kavi Gupta, Chicago and
        Mitchell-Innes & Nash, New York]   137
15.3   Jessica Stockholder, *Lay of the Land* (2014) (© Jessica
        Stockholder) [Courtesy of the artist; Mitchell-Innes & Nash,
        New York, and Galerie nächst St. Stephan, Vienna]   137
15.4   Rachel Harrison, *Alexander the Great* (2007) (Photograph:
        Jean Vong) [Courtesy of the artist and Greene Naftali,
        New York]   138
15.5   Rachel Harrison, *The Spoonbender* (2011) (Photograph:
        John Berens) [Courtesy of the artist and Greene Naftali,
        New York]   138
15.6   Phoebe Washburn, *Nothing's Cutie* (Exhibition: LFL Gallery,
        September 2–October 2, 2004) [Courtesy of the artist]   139
15.7   Phoebe Washburn, *True, False, and Slightly Better* (Exhibition:
        Rice University Gallery, January 24–March 24, 2003)
        [Courtesy of the artist]   139
15.8   Kate Gilmore, *Beat It* (2014) (Commissioned by
        H&R Block Space at Kansas City Art Institute) [Courtesy of
        the artist]   140
15.9   Kate Gilmore, *Between a Hard Place* (2008 video stills)
        (Commissioned by ICA Philadelphia) [Courtesy of the artist]   140
15.10   Seth Price, *Wrok Fmaily Freidns* (2016) (Exhibition
        view at 356 S. Mission) [Courtesy of the artist]   142
15.11   Mark Bradford, *Pickett's Charge* (2017) (© Mark Bradford)
        (Exhibition: Hirshhorn Museum and Sculpture Garden,
        Washington D.C.; photographer: Cathy Carver)
        [Courtesy of the artist and Hauser & Wirth]   143
15.12   Mark Bradford, *Pickett's Charge* (2017) (© Mark Bradford)
        (Exhibition: Hirshhorn Museum and Sculpture Garden,
        Washington D.C.; photographer: Cathy Carver) [Courtesy of
        the artist and Hauser & Wirth]   144

15.13   Mark Bradford, *Pickett's Charge* (2017) (© Mark Bradford)
        (Exhibition: Hirshhorn Museum and Sculpture Garden,
        Washington D.C.; photographer: Cathy Carver) [Courtesy
        of the artist and Hauser & Wirth]   144

17.1   Sample *Minecraft* scene (Mojang © 2009–19. © 2019
        Microsoft) ["Minecraft" is a trademark of Mojang
        Synergies AB]   156

19.1   Lost Acapulco, *Acapulco Golden* (Mostrissimo Records,
        Mexico, 2004) [Courtesy of the artist/designer Dr. Alderete]   172

19.2   First LP by Fenomeno Fuzz, *Martinis y Bikinis* (Ctentaydos
        Records, Mexico, 2004) [Courtesy of the artist/designer
        Dr. Alderete]   172

19.3   Daddy-O Grande poster for Danny Amis benefit night,
        featuring some of the most recurrent motifs for surf bands:
        wrestling masks, Rapa Nui figures, Mexican pyramids,
        and sci-fi imagery (Club Mayan, Los Angeles, 2011)
        [Courtesy of the artist/designer Dr. Alderete]   173

19.4   *Spaguetti & Chili Western: A Collection of Western Instros*
        (Isotonic Records, Mexico, 2005) [Courtesy of the artist/
        designer Dr. Alderete]   176

19.5   Poster for the second edition of Wild O'Fest (Carpa Astros,
        Mexico City, 2017) [Courtesy of the artist/designer
        Dr. Alderete]   177

19.6   Twin Tones, *Nación Apache* (Grabaxiones Alicia, Mexico,
        2005) (©Andrés "Huracán" Ramírez) [Courtesy of the record
        producer]   178

19.7   "Zócalo Surf," photograph by Ernesto Muñiz (Mexico, 2004).
        An improvised luchador dances on a surfboard across the
        audience during a rainy concert in Mexico City's
        downtown Zócalo square (©Ernesto Muñiz, https://www.
        ernestomuniz.com/) [Courtesy of the photographer]   179

Contributors

Molly C. O'Donnell is an instructor in the Department of English at James Madison University. She was the recipient of the *Gaskell Journal* Joan Leach Memorial Prize (2016), and her work has appeared in publications like *Victoriographies* and the *Norton Anthology*.

Anne H. Stevens is Professor of English and Chair of the Department of Interdisciplinary, Gender, and Ethnic Studies at the University of Nevada, Las Vegas. She is the author of *British Historical Fiction before Scott* (2010) and *Literary Theory and Criticism: An Introduction* (2015).

Paul Hay is Visiting Assistant Professor in the Department of Classics at Case Western Reserve University. His research interests include the intellectual and social history of ancient Rome, ancient sexuality, and ancient Greek and Roman literature.

Christopher Vilmar is Professor of English at Salisbury University. His research interests focus on intersections of satire, political writing, and philology in eighteenth-century English literature. In addition to publications on Samuel Johnson, satire, and pedagogy, he is an associate editor of *The Encyclopedia of British Literature, 1660–1789* (2015).

Alistaire Tallent is Associate Professor at Colorado College in the Department of French and Italian. Her research interests focus on libertine fiction, gender in eighteenth-century French fiction, and intersections of science and the novel. Her publications include "Intimate Exchanges: The Courtesan Narrative and Male Homosocial Desire in *La Dame aux camélias*" (2014) and "Female Friendship and *Fraternité* in the Prostitute Memoir Novels of Eighteenth-Century France" (2009).

Matthew Duques is Associate Professor at the University of North Alabama in the Department of English. His current research focuses on the role of water in early American captivity narratives. He is the coeditor of the forthcoming *Brill Companion to Classical Reception in Early America*, and he has published articles and book chapters on John Dennis, Lydia Maria Child, Fanny Wright, and William Apess.

Jennifer Diann Jones specializes in nineteenth-century literature, culture, and medicine; narrative theory; and aesthetic theory. She works on both canonical (George Eliot and Charles Dickens) and popular fiction (L. T. Meade and Arabella Keneally). Her current work in progress is a book-length study of the representation of anaesthesia in Victorian literature and culture; also, she is coediting a volume on literary orphans with Dr. Diane Warren and Dr. Laura Peters. Jennifer has work published or forthcoming in *Studies in the Novel, Victoriographies, The George Eliot Review*, and *Peer English*.

Diana Bellonby is Visiting Scholar in the English Department at Vanderbilt University and President of the Fringe Foundation. Her research focuses on Victorian fiction, aesthetic philosophy, and histories of gender and sexuality. She has published on Henry James and theories of influence and intertextuality. Currently, she is working on two books: the first traces a Victorian literary history of toxic masculinity, and the second examines the relationship between British aestheticism and magic-portrait fiction.

John Hay is Associate Professor at the University of Nevada, Las Vegas, in the Department of English. His research interests focus on nineteenth-century American literature, the history of science, narratology, and intellectual history. He is the author of *Postapocalyptic Fantasies in Antebellum American Literature* (2017).

Megan Becker-Leckrone is Associate Professor of English at the University of Nevada, Las Vegas, where she specializes in critical theory, late Victorian studies, and medical humanities. She is the author of *Julia Kristeva and Literary Theory* (2005). Her essay on Oscar Wilde's "Critic as Artist" appears in *Wilde's Other Worlds* (2018), edited by Michael Davis and Petra Dierkes-Thrun. Forthcoming publications include essays on Walter Pater in *Reading Victorian Literature: Essays in Honour of J. Hillis Miller* (2019), edited by Julian Wolfreys and Monika Szuba; and on Max Beerbohm's extra-illustrated books, in *Extraordinary Aesthetes* (2020), edited by Joseph Bristow.

Nora Gilbert is Associate Professor of English at the University of North Texas, where she co-specializes in Victorian literature and classical Hollywood film. She is the author of *Better Left Unsaid: Victorian Novels, Hays Code Films, and the Benefits of Censorship* (2013) and has published articles on a broad range of subjects, including the fiction of Thackeray, the Brontës, and Aphra Behn and the films of Preston Sturges, Alfred Hitchcock, and Fred Astaire.

Cynthia J. Miller teaches in the Institute for Liberal Arts at Emerson College in Boston, MA, and is the editor or coeditor of numerous scholarly volumes focused on the horror genre and cult films. A cultural anthropologist specializing in visual media, Cynthia is the recipient of the Peter C. Rollins Prize for a book-length work in popular culture and the James Welsh Prize for lifetime achievement in adaptation studies. She serves on the editorial board of the *Journal of Popular Television* and also edits the Film and History book series for the Rowman & Littlefield Publishing Group.

Thomas M. Shaker is an independent scholar and filmmaker. He recently retired from teaching after thirty years, directing the Communications Department at Dean College in Franklin, MA, and lecturing at Northeastern University in Boston and WPI in Worcester, MA. His research interests include music history, pop culture, and film and television. He is the coauthor of *A Treasury of Rhode Island Jazz & Swing Musicians* (2015) and coproducer of the award-winning documentary *Do It Man! The Story of the Celebrity Club* (2018).

Gavin F. Hurley is Assistant Professor of English at the University of Providence. His research interests include philosophy of communication, religious rhetorics, and the rhetorics of horror. He has published in *The Journal of Communication and Religion, The Journal of Religion and Popular Culture, Horror Studies*, and a variety of essay collections.

John Carl Baker is Nuclear Field Coordinator and Senior Program Officer at Ploughshares Fund. He manages the organization's North Korea portfolio, develops strategy for grassroots investment, and works to increase collaboration among foundations in the nuclear policy field. He writes regularly on nuclear weapons issues and US-North Korea relations.

Susanna Newbury is Assistant Professor of Art History at the University of Nevada, Las Vegas. Her research focuses on the social history of twentieth- and twenty-first-century art, histories of photography and of the image, urban studies, and economic geography.

Danielle Kelly is the Creative Arts and Communication Pathway Leader at Lake Forest College and Lecturer in studio art and art criticism. As an arts administrator, she has served as the executive director of the Las Vegas Neon Museum and Surface Design Association, as well as publisher of the *Surface Design Journal*. Her visual art has been featured in solo and group exhibitions in Los Angeles, Seattle, Las Vegas, San Francisco, and Portland, OR. Her writing ranges from essays and art criticism to arts and cultural reporting.

Mary Thompson is Associate Professor of English and Coordinator of the Women's, Gender and Sexuality Studies program at James Madison University. Her scholarship examines literary and popular representations of reproductive justice issues. She has published on gender, motherhood, and race in *GENDERS, Frontiers*, and *Feminist Media Studies*. Her most recent work is the coedited volume *The Politics of Reproduction: Adoption, Abortion and Surrogacy in the Age of Neoliberalism* (2019).

Michael T. Wilson is Associate Professor in English at Appalachian State University. His recent publications include "'We know only names, so far':

Samuel Richardson, Shirley Jackson, and Exploration of the Precarious Self," coauthored with Jennifer Preston Wilson in *Shirley Jackson: Influences and Confluences* (2016), and "'Absolute Reality' and the Role of the Ineffable in Shirley Jackson's *The Haunting of Hill House*" in *The Journal of Popular Culture* in 2015. His current research interests include violence and masculinity in the detective novel and adolescent psychology and food imagery in the work of Shirley Jackson.

Heather Lusty is Assistant Professor of English in the Honors College at the University of Nevada, Las Vegas. She works on nationalism and national identity in literature, print mediums, music, and rhetoric. She has edited a collection of essays on James Joyce and D. H. Lawrence titled *Modernism at Odds* (2015) as well as *Lawrence's Stories, The Border Line: D.H. Lawrence's Soldier Stories* (2018). She is currently working on a manuscript exploring spectacle in heavy metal music.

Aurelio Meza is a doctoral candidate in Humanities at Concordia University in the Centre for Interdisciplinary Studies in Society and Culture. His writings on decolonization, border studies, and the intersection of sound and literature have been published in Spanish and English. His most recent book is *Sobre Vivir Tijuana: Textos Mutantes Fronterizos* (2015).

Elyse Graham is Assistant Professor at Stony Brook University in the Department of English. Her research interests focus on digital humanities, the history of the book, and the future of texts. Her most recent book is *The Republic of Games* (2018).

Michelle Alexis Taylor is a doctoral candidate in English at Harvard University. Her book project focuses on modernist coterie consumption, production, and circulation, and her research focuses on twentieth-century literature, book history, and television.

Jonathan Goodwin is Associate Professor at the University of Louisiana at Lafayette in the Department of English. He is writing a book about statistics and probability in twentieth-century literature. His website is https://jgoodwin.net.

Acknowledgments

For both editors, our interest in the small culture of microgenres began with our research into popular fictional genres in the eighteenth and nineteenth centuries. For Stevens, a curiosity about weird clusters of novel titles like *A Winter in London* (1806), *An Autumn at Cheltenham* (1808), *A Summer at Weymouth* (1808), *I Says, Says I* (1812), *Thinks-I-to-Myself* (1811), and *Says She to Her Neighbour, What?* (1812) led to conference presentations and panels at the American Society for Eighteenth-Century Studies annual meeting. Thanks to David Mazella for co-organizing a panel with Stevens on "New Theories and Histories of Eighteenth-Century Genre" for the 2018 meeting and to panelists Rachael Scarborough King, Leah Orr, Manu Samriti Chander, Emily Friedman, Jonathan Sadow, and Michael Edson; to the participants in the "Microgenres in the Eighteenth Century" panel Stevens organized for the 2015 meeting: Mazella, Marcie Frank, Gretchen Woertendyke, and Alistair Tallent; and to Stephanie Insley Hershinow for organizing a pair of panels on "Novel Experiments" for the 2013 meeting.

For O'Donnell, research into the publishing histories and influences on and of early works by Elizabeth Gaskell and Charles Dickens sparked an interest in niche genre studies. Contextualizing strange novels as tales novels, a new microgeneric descriptor, made for a fruitful exploration of the work of these and other canonical and noncanonical literary figures. Versions of that larger study were presented at the Pacific Ancient and Modern Language Association Convention and Northeast Modern Languages Association Convention in 2014, as well as the North American Victorian Studies Association Conference and International Conference on Narrative in 2013. Thanks to the organizers, panel participants, and attendees, as well as to Kelly J. Mays, Megan Becker, David L. Hardy, and coeditor Anne H. Stevens for invaluable input.

We also thank Nicholas Rinehart for inviting us to join a seminar on "The Return of Generic Criticism" for the 2018 American Comparative Literature Association annual meeting and to Dabney Bankert for securing O'Donnell's funding to attend. These ongoing conversations about genre helped shape the initial idea for this collection.

We are grateful to Joshua Wolf Shenk and Hayden Bennett of the *Believer* magazine for publishing an earlier version of Aurelio Meza's chapter on Mexican neo-surf music on the *Believer Logger*, to Gary Totten for publishing advice, to Howard Carrier for assistance in securing image permissions, and to the many folks who submitted fascinating and delightful proposals in response to our call for papers. We didn't anticipate the number of submissions we'd receive, and we definitely have enough material for several additional volumes of essays.

Finally, the editors would like to thank Bloomsbury for believing in our project and allowing it to see the light of day, in particular Katie Gallof, Samantha Caveny, Erin Duffy, Leah Babb-Rosenfeld, and the six anonymous readers who reviewed our proposal.

Introduction

Molly C. O'Donnell and Anne H. Stevens

Everybody knows, and maybe even loves, a microgenre, though we might not know it by this exact name. Like one-hit wonder musicians, microgenres can be overnight sensations that vanish as quickly as they appear, or they can develop gradually, collecting ever-nuanced attributes only to be folded into broader and more recognizable categories later on. "Microgenre" as a term associated with the digital age has come to popularity in describing television streaming algorithms, digital musical phenomena, and self-published fiction available on Amazon. In this context *microgenre* refers to the classification of increasingly niche-marketed worlds in popular music, fiction, television, and the internet. Netflix has highlighted our fascination with the ultra-niche genre with hilariously specific classifications—"independent dramedy featuring a strong female lead"—that can sometimes hit a little too close to home. The streaming giant has identified 76,897 different microgenres in its algorithms and has used them to great effect in developing hit new series like *House of Cards* and *Orange Is the New Black*.[1] On Amazon you can find categories as microscopic as dinosaur erotica (sample title: *Ravished by the Triceratops*) and quilting cozy mysteries (sample title: *Quilt or Innocence: A Southern Quilting Mystery*), while the worlds of electronica and metal can be parsed into dozens of sub-sub-subgenres.

Usages of the term predate the digital age, however. In many ways, popular culture has always relied on hyper-specific formulas and subgenres. Jonathan Goodwin asserts in his contribution here on machine-classification that microgenres are inherently digital, but he does identify several usages of the term "microgenre" in critical works of the 1980s and 1990s, where writers use it as a way to characterize subgenres of a high degree of specificity. Even earlier, a French article about historical fiction from 1975 distinguishes "microgenre" and "macrogenre": a microgenre is a more narrowly defined group of texts connected in time and space, whereas a macrogenre is more diffuse and thus harder to generalize about, for instance, historical novels of the era of Walter Scott versus historical novels more broadly construed or the female gothic novels of the 1790s as compared to the long-ranging and multifaceted tradition of the gothic writ large.[2] Many if not most of the chapters in this collection focus on microgenres that also participate in larger macrogenres—from Paul Hay's look at a subset of the epigrammatic tradition to Mary Thompson's focus on a small slice of the larger world of memoirs.

While the chapters in this collection testify to the fact that the concept of the microgenre, though it has gained prominence in the digital age, can be applied fruitfully to all eras of cultural production, what *has* changed in the world of the twenty-first-century microgenre perhaps has to do with speed and familiarity. The rapidity of classification, as contributors Elyse Graham and Michelle Taylor note in their treatment of fanfiction, means "readers and writers arrive at new sets of generic expectations ... not over the course of years, but over the course of months or even days." Genre becomes a function of classification where "constraint is not a limitation ... But rather a core characteristic." The creation of post hoc genres based on more random or less familiar elements is, as Goodwin observes, "not necessarily the type of observation that could have come to mind before computerized classification was done." So although the concept of the microgenre as a highly specific generic phenomenon is not new, the unique iterativeness of microgeneric formation means we are more keenly aware of them in our era of cultural supersaturation.

This awareness has sparked those like digital humanities scholar Ted Underwood to observe that "the concept of the 'microgenre' is one of the salient critical innovations of the twenty-teens."[3] Microgenres offer unique frameworks for thinking about classification and historical organization in formally, historically, and theoretically nuanced ways. Pinpointing the existence of highly specific categories helps bring to the forefront relations of resemblance, the role of imitation, and the role of genres as marketing categories. Smallness allows us to see the effects of genre in all their glorious iterations: authors trying to "get in" and "get out," readers with little time on their hands enjoying the shorthand that generic specificity provides, readers with too much time on their hands reveling in the familiar, scholars becoming more aware of the process of experimentation in its failures and victories.

"There is such a thing as being too seamless," writes Wai Chee Dimock, "wrapping up too soon, and missing out on the unsettled vitality of rough edges."[4] Rough edges can be valuable, in considering both what is particular and what might be generalizable. Rough edges are, however, also often difficult to square with the human tendency to classify into neat categories. There is no place where this difficulty is more observable than in the study of genre. That the hyper-specific is often unsustainable is a fact that fails to either prevent attempts at classification or stop the niche from influencing longer and larger trends.

Yet one question comes to mind more than any other when we think of genre: What is the utility of thinking about works from novel generic perspectives? Or as Goodwin puts it, "What use is [the microgenre] as a critical category?" As Ralph Cohen writes in *Genre Theory and Historical Change*, "The problem ... is not whether genre hypotheses are useful, but what uses they serve."[5] In other words, the question isn't whether a critic has gotten to the "true" definition of a genre or properly categorized a work. Genres can function as archetypes, transhistorical categories, or macrogenres like Northrop Frye's comedy, tragedy, romance, and satire. By contrast, microgenres are flexible, provisional, and temporary, used by each of the chapters in this collection as a means to make micro-connections among cultural artifacts, drawn from a range of historical periods and from literature, film, music, television, and the performing and fine arts. Here, the chapters reflect the wide range of uses to which the concept of the microgenre can be applied. We've arranged the chapters in this collection in a rough chronological order and also sometimes grouped them by medium (film, music, art). Though most of our pieces come from U.S.-based scholars, the topics covered include some geographic range, from the United States and Mexico to Britain, France, and Germany and from the ancient Mediterranean world to our contemporary globalized society. It is our hope that future work on microgenres would expand upon this range to include even more diverse and global perspectives.

The most useful thing about examining the small in this way is something it's easy enough to lose sight of: complexity. Cultural history looks different depending on the degree of granularity of the genre-systems investigated. The terrain of the nineteenth-century novel takes on new contours if one focuses not on the broad and well-established categories of realism, the gothic, the sensation novel, but instead more closely scrutinizes literary clusters like the tales-novels, anesthesia fiction, or magic-portrait fiction. In order to demonstrate a bit of the complexity that scale affords small genre studies, this survey brings together small-scale areas of cultural production that serve different cultural purposes. As our first contributor Paul Hay observes of his microgenre, "The survival of these [works] into the modern period ... is made possible by the transmission of anthologies." The micro is, by its very definition, small in scale and hence under the radar of grand narratives of cultural history. Without inclusion in a work of this type, these creations of cultural production would be lost or at least forgotten. While this may not be seen as a tragic circumstance, with the loss of a microgenre comes a loss of nuance. The oversimplification of generic classification neglects forces of influence as it negates unexpected and fruitful interpretation with the potential to dash readerly expectations, as contributor Christopher

Vilmar points out that the premature ejaculation poem confounds readers accustomed to thinking of "back in the day" solely in prudish terms.

Explorations of microgenres can help to fill out the picture of a particular historical moment, while at other times they help to show lines of influence or to trace an under-regarded stage of development in a larger genre. In some cases the study of the forgotten works of a microgenre helps to shed light on the horizon of expectations for a more canonical work. Contributor Alistaire Tallent's discussion of prostitute memoirs places Sade's *Juliette* at the end of a long and female-centric tradition; Diana Bellonby's careful tracing of magic-portrait fiction highlights the subversive ways Oscar Wilde plays with the tropes of the microgenre in *The Picture of Dorian Gray*; Gavin Hurley's treatment of the Italian giallo films demonstrates their connection to American slasher films of the 1970s and 1980s. Other explorations of microgenres help to make sense of forgotten corners of the archive that don't necessarily link up to more canonical works or genres, such as John Hay's discussion of American topographical reports: the aesthetic and literary in the unexpected area of government reports. These types of generic explorations tell alternate tales of microgeneric making. Megan Becker-Leckrone points out how "Terry Gilliam's cut-out animation drove the antic absurdism of *Monty Python's Flying Circus*" that "draws deeply from familiar signs of Englishness—grangerism for a new century," another example of a forgotten microgeneric history.

So what causes other microgenres to arise and coalesce? Some microgenres are established labels: Nora Gilbert's chapter discusses how "Baby Burlesks" is the self-designated title of a series of Hollywood shorts; "Nudie-Cuties," the subject of Cynthia Miller and Thomas M. Shaker's chapter, similarly appears on the marketing poster for one of the earliest films discussed; fanfiction and musical microgenres (as treated by Graham and Taylor and Heather Lusty and Aurelio Meza, respectively) serve as identificatory markers, as metadata on fanfiction sites or as markers of particular musical scenes.[6] In other cases our contributors are themselves inventing categories as a way to make connections. Danielle Kelly is tentative in her use of the term "Home Depot Art" but convincingly shows lines of connection among artists who work primarily with materials from big-box hardware stores. Likewise, Goodwin talks about the ways digital algorithms could help to identify new microgenres.

Some microgenres consist of creators responding to each other or to established templates, creating variations on a theme. In Paul Hay's chapter, for example, epigrams describing a particularly realistic statue of a cow function as the ancient world equivalent of an internet meme. Similarly, premature ejaculation poetry and prostitute narratives offer us creators who seem to know what their genre "ought" to be, as Paul Hay observes, and "thus were perceived and shaped by a ... tradition ... consciously responding to the efforts of their predecessors."

While it's perhaps obvious how a creator might have mercenary motivations for participating in an established microgenre, there are other factors related to competition and community observable in the surveyed works. Writers of fanfiction, for example, talk about the nonmonetary rewards offered in the form of likes and views. Similarly, Becker-Leckrone's discussion of the practice of cutting and pasting into printed books offers a portrait of the destruction of books as commodities, whereby we get an early example of the material equivalent of fanfiction, participants remixing and repurposing others' creations. This stands in contrast to the idea of genre labels used merely as marketing categories. Even Paul Hay's classical epigrams speak to noncommercial motivation and form, as there was no market for these works per se. Tallent's discussion of prostitute memoirs reveals "a sense of community among producers and consumers ... each one complementing the other," just as Michael T. Wilson's treatment of *Minecraft* fiction demonstrates the informal writing competition as incentive enough. Genre is often a means of continuing a conversation, either rapidly online or over time through "the use of intertextual signifiers," as Paul Hay notes, "add[ing] additional nodes of connection."

Other microgenres seem to be less fluid, tethered to particular moments of cultural anxiety or technological innovation. Exploring the possibilities and perils of new technology offers new distribution networks, as Matthew Duques discusses in his exploration of the neoclassical plague romance. Microgenres are sometimes means of coping with the present by learning from the past. Author Lydia Maria Child's plague romance, for example, gives her nineteenth-century readers the historical setting of the final days of golden-age Athens as a means for antebellum America to consider its own cataclysmic moment in history in terms of the perils of both slavery and war. Jennifer Diann Jones talks about the ways Victorian writers imagined the dangerous possibilities of anesthesia in fictional form, "shortly after its discovery," with the phenomenon disappearing "after the professionalization of medicine in the late nineteenth and early twentieth centuries." A similarly "of the moment" microgenre, video art is tied to the new technology of the camcorder and the new platform of cable access TV. Artists, writes Susanna Newbury, "inhabit[ed] television to leverage it to their own imaginative ends, as video art ... not to see art on TV, but how to see TV, through art, as constructed medium." Like many other microgenres presented in this collection that reflect particular historical circumstances, anti-sitcom video art is an example of medium inspiring message, a link between artistic possibility and consumable goods. John Carl Baker explores a perhaps less domesticated memory of the early 1980s when the threat of nuclear war seemed imminent and several made-for-television movies responded to this anxiety. Mary Thompson links the rise of the mommy memoir in the mid-1990s to a similar moment of contemporary concern, this time about motherhood in the context of third-wave feminism.

Themes of gender, sex, and sexuality arise in our contributors' explorations of microgenres long before the late twentieth-century account offered in Thompson's chapter, however. Many of the chapters discuss microgenres that revolve around erotic material, sometimes thinly disguised political metaphor and sometimes not. Vilmar's discussion of poems about premature ejaculation and Tallent's investigation of prostitute memoirs both point out the direct reference being made within the works to real historical figures. Here, sex is used as the less scandalous mode of critique in times where overt engagement in political intrigue often resulted in decapitation. Miller and Shaker's tracing of the "nudie-cutie" film, on the other hand, and Gilbert's discussion of the troubling "Baby Burlesks" series are more direct treatments of sex in the service of comedy. "Sex," as Miller and Shaker observe of these films, "is a laughing matter." Microgenres like "baby burlesks" seem to reveal a much more scandalous past, though, than general conceptions account for. Starring an, at the time, unknown Shirley Temple, "Baby Burlesks" depict explicit sexism and racism that is presented in more subtle ways in later Hollywood blockbusters featuring Temple. Yet sometimes what an exploration of microgenre reveals meets our expectations about time's forward march toward the libertine perspective. Nudie-cuties and giallo films seem tame when set beside the graphic sexuality and violence of their successors in grindhouse pornography and slasher horror film.

Moving from the worlds of literature, film, and art to music, we are offered counterpoints. While Lusty outlines some of the key developments in fifty years of heavy metal, Meza looks more closely at a single musical movement. These chapters, once again, remind us that in popular media the term "microgenre" is most often associated with recent trends (think "witch house," "seapunk," and "vaporwave").[7] Both heavy metal and Mexican neo-surf also again offer us a contemporary illustration of communities of practice: fans and groups of creators making myriad microworlds within already niche areas that represent conversations between actors.

On a larger scale, we hope that this collected presentation of diverse microgenres reveals conversations like these. Our aim was to present previously untreated points of cultural curiosity in an effort to reveal the profound truth—that humanity's desire to classify is often only matched by the unsustainability of the obscure and hyper-specific. This survey also affirms, in colorful detail, what most people suspect but have trouble fathoming in an increasingly homogenized and commercial West: that imaginative projects are just that, imaginative, diverse, and sometimes completely and hilariously inexplicable.

Notes

1 Alexis C. Madrigal, "How Netflix Reverse-Engineered Hollywood," *The Atlantic*, January 2, 2014, https://www.theatlantic.com/technology/archive/2014/01/how-netflix-reverse-engineered-hollywood/282679.

2 Jean Molino, "Qu'est-ce que le roman historique?" *Revue d'Histoire Littéraire de la France* 75 (March–June 1975): 195–234.

3 Ted Underwood, "Genre Theory and Historicism," *Journal of Cultural Analytics*, October 25, 2016, http://culturalanalytics.org/2016/10/genre-theory-and-historicism.

4 Wai Chee Dimock, "Weak Theory: Henry James, Colm Tóibín, and W. B. Yeats," *Critical Inquiry* 39 (Summer 2013): 745.

5 Ralph Cohen, *Genre Theory and Historical Change: The Theoretical Essays of Ralph Cohen*, ed. John L. Rowlett (Charlottesville: University of Virginia Press, 2017), 37.

6 On musical scenes as a particular type of microgenre, one that helps communities coalesce, see Jennifer C. Lena, *Banding Together: How Communities Create Genres in Popular Music* (Princeton: Princeton University Press, 2012).

7 See, for example, Emilie Friedlander and Patrick D. McDermott, "A Recent History of Microgenres," *Fader*, October 8, 2015, https://www.thefader.com/2015/10/08/timeline-history-of-music-microgenres-chillwave-cloud-rap-witch-house.

2

The Myron's Cow Epigram

Paul Hay

The Myron's Cow epigram is a microgenre of ancient literature that can be described, at the simplest level, as a group of poems all describing a statue of a cow by the Greek sculptor Myron. The cow statue (unfortunately now lost) was created in the fifth century BCE in Athens, but Greek and Latin poets can be found from the third century BCE until the sixth century CE who tackled the statue as a subject for short, playful poems. Some thirty-six examples survive of this ancient microgenre, including epigrams that not only describe the hyperrealistic bronze cow with increasingly exaggerated and humorous claims but dive more deeply into the nature of the literary and plastic arts' ability to capture the truth of natural objects and into the meaning of artistic representation in their contemporary world.

Understanding the nature of these epigrams first requires an understanding of the wider genre of the ancient epigram. The Greek epigram originated with inscriptions that appeared on or near monuments, funerary sites, or religious venues, or with inscriptions made on objects to say what they were and to which god they were dedicated. Thus, many epigrams feature deictic words, such as "here" or "this," or a speaking subject ("I"). By the beginning of the third century BCE, Greek epigrams had shifted from real-life inscriptions on objects and monuments to a wider range of subjects: love, lampoons, the world of elite drinking parties (sympotic contexts), but also fictitious dedications and detailed verbal descriptions of objects (ekphrastic poetry). The dedicatory inscription, with its familiar meters (chiefly elegiac couplets) and language (such as the deictic vocabulary), was thus liberated from its connection to actual objects and became a site for poets to play with generic expectations and tackle unconventional subjects. Modern scholars sometimes refer to the "epigraphic fallacy" of treating such epigrams as evidence of real-life objects, since the poets may be describing objects that they had never actually seen or that had never existed.

The survival of these short epigrams into the modern period in manuscript form was made possible by the transmission of anthologies (collections of epigrams and other poems) such as the Palatine Anthology and the Planudean

Anthology. The anthologists arranged the epigrams in a variety of ways, often thematically, with the effect of presenting a single corpus of epigrams combining different authors and time periods into one body. Thus, it is often difficult if not impossible to determine who wrote any particular epigram (sometimes a name is all we know about a given epigram's alleged author), when any particular epigram was written, which authors were familiar with which predecessors (and might be responding to earlier poems with their own works), and how the poems were arranged in their original publications or in earlier collections of anthologies from which later compilers drew. The silver lining to such difficulties of historical contextualization is that we are forced to observe more closely the texts of the epigrams themselves, and from such analyses we can identify the rise of poetic microgenres within the epigram tradition, such as the Myron's Cow epigram.

Who was this Myron, whose Cow inspired so many poems? Myron was a sculptor from Athens active in the fifth century BCE who achieved a high level of fame in antiquity. His sculptural technique was characterized by close attention to movement and heightened dramatic moments as well as an intense realism. His range of subjects went from the typical gods and heroes to more everyday figures such as animals or athletes. Perhaps his most famous work that survives (though only via later Roman copies) is the Discobolus, or Discus Thrower, whom Myron depicted precisely at the moment when his backswing is shifting to his throw. Other works by Myron (and other notable sculptors such as Praxiteles) also received poetic tributes in the corpus of Greek epigrams, but it is only his Cow that activated poets' imaginations to such an obsessive level.

The poets who composed Myron's Cow epigrams are a motley bunch, covering a long stretch of time and space in the ancient Mediterranean world. At the latest end are two politically powerful figures: Julian of Egypt and Ausonius. Julian of Egypt was a praetorian prefect in Egypt during the sixth century CE who composed a series of eight Byzantine-inflected epigrams on Myron's Cow. The famous and prolific late Roman poet Ausonius, whose works are characterized by their wit and refined literary sensibility, composed entries in the microgenre while cultivating influence in the imperial court in various French cities in the fourth century CE.[1] We know much less about the careers of the earlier contributors beyond what we can read in the poems themselves, though some figures are more than just names to us. For example, Philippus of Thessalonica was a poet and editor under the emperor Nero who had compiled his own collection of epigrams arranged alphabetically by first word. The Greek mathematician Geminus, a contemporary of Philippus, seems also to have contributed an epigram to the microgenre. During the Hellenistic period (roughly 323 BCE–31 BCE) of Greek literature, a compositional high point for the surviving epigrams, many poets composed Myron's Cow epigrams, including two of the most famous poets: Antipater of Sidon, a prolific epigrammatist who had spent time in Rome, and Leonidas of Tarentum, a highly influential early epigram master whose works were imitated by later Greeks and Romans on a number of topics. But some of the authors of the poems are little more than names in the manuscripts, and many other contributions come down to us anonymously. Ultimately, we can see that the microgenre attracted a mixture of savvy litterateurs and poetastic dabblers, in various areas of the Greek world and beyond, for almost a millennium of ancient literature; we also have evidence, from Roman writers such as the elegist Propertius and the encyclopedist Pliny the Elder, that others were aware of the microgenre even if they did not write such poems themselves.

The Myron's Cow poems make up a highly specific fraction of the immense corpus of ancient epigrams. Unlike poetic topics such as death, love, or nature, the Myron's Cow epigrams focus their subjects on one highly specific object. And while other specific objects were the subject of multiple poems from multiple authors (even some other statues), none comes close to the scale of the Myron's Cow epigram in terms of contributions or contributors. This scale is all the more noteworthy in consideration of the wide range of time periods, from early Hellenistic epigrams to Imperial and Late Antique contributions. The generic expectations of what a Myron's Cow epigram "ought" to be (or could be) thus were perceived and shaped by a long tradition of poets, and many poetic successors clearly are consciously responding to the efforts of their predecessors.

The surviving body of Myron's Cow epigrams features multiple iterations of similar themes and verbal formulae. Consequently, the microgenre itself became a fertile site for poetic explorations of tropes and themes, some of which appear in the contributions of multiple poets. For example, many selections comment on the deceptive power of the cow's lifelike quality captured by Myron. "A calf died beside your heifer, Myron," writes one anonymous contributor, "tricked into believing that the bronze had milk within." Others pursued a different direction, instead insisting that Myron did not actually sculpt the cow but simply convinced a real cow to stand on the statue base. The Imperial poet Marcus Argentarius writes: "Stranger, if you see my herdsman, give him this message, that the sculptor Myron bound me here."[2] The statue activates a variety of thematic explorations and gives the poets a wide range of topics to discuss in even a two-line epigram.

My identification of the Myron's Cow epigram as a microgenre of classical literature is further justified by the ancient awareness of a vaguely similar category. We are told by Pliny the Elder that the cow statue sculpted by Myron had made him particularly famous, as it was praised in celebrated verses, and it is difficult to interpret this reference as anything other than a mention of the corpus of epigrams composed by Greek poets before Pliny's time in the late first century CE (though perhaps not yet compiled into a standard manuscript group). In fact, the classicist Irmgard Männlein-Robert has read the Pliny passage to say that Pliny "traces the fame of the Cow back to the epigrams themselves."[3] Additionally, the Roman poet Propertius (writing at the end of the first century BCE) records that the emperor Augustus had erected a set of twelve copies of the cow statue at his Temple of Apollo on the Palatine Hill in Rome, and Propertius refers to the cows by referencing a trope familiar from the poems of the Myron's Cow epigram microgenre: "Myron's herd ... lifelike statues."[4]

Of course, the very appearance of the poems grouped together in the manuscript tradition also speaks to an ancient understanding that the poems, despite being composed by multiple hands and in differing places and times in history, should be categorized together: not as a narrative sequence, not as a poetic cycle, but as a unique subcategory of epigram. (And most ancient literary critics had only vague theories of genre, usually relying on formal characteristics or thematic material, which further suggests that they noted the literary affinity of these poems.) The transmission of the poems together through manuscripts would then further reinforce this perception among subsequent ancient readers. In her book-length study of the Greek epigram, Kathryn Gutzwiller has suggested, based on the Pliny passage, that "the fame of the statue continued to increase just because of its fame, not through genuine appreciation of its merits."[5] As more poets composed Myron's Cow epigrams, then, more readers (and writers) became aware of the microgenre itself.

In treating the Myron's Cow epigram as a distinct microgenre of ancient literature, one complication can be raised. There was no "market" for this kind of ancient poetry composition, so epigrams were never really "commodities" in the way we often think of when reflecting on microgenres in literature and, especially, film and music in the twentieth and twenty-first centuries. But the categorization of these poems as a microgenre is perhaps valuable nonetheless because it demonstrates how recognizable microgenres do not have to be bound to contemporary economics and market forces; instead, a certain kind of literary milieu (in this case, the hyperliterate Alexandrian library strivers of the Hellenistic era and the medieval/monastic world of compilers and manuscript transmitters) can present another viable context for a given microgenre to flourish.

The Myron's Cow epigram, thus identified as a distinct microgenre, is a fascinating segment of ancient literature. As many scholars have argued, the Myron's Cow epigrams are not simply descriptions of a statue with humorous exaggerations about its realism, but in fact they comment more deeply on sophisticated artistic themes. One such theme is the dual function of art as both a revealer and a deceiver. In achieving the ultimate stage of sculptural realism, Myron has reached the zenith of mimetic art, such that he has captured every aspect of life. Ausonius insists that "the bronze cow of Myron could moo, but it is afraid to detract from the talent of the artist."[6] At the same time, no matter how successfully Myron has achieved this mimesis, his cow is not a living thing but only a bronze copy. Julian writes, "Endure it, Myron: art overpowers you—the work is lifeless."[7] Thus the poems engage with both the ability and impossibility of art to reflect the truth of reality. Männlein-Robert has demonstrated that many examples from the microgenre use heavily loaded terminology, familiar to the realm of literary theory, to engage with these debates over the force of verisimilitude in the arts.[8]

Similarly, the Myron's Cow epigram microgenre demonstrates, with its multiple variations on the same physical subject, the limitations of ekphrastic poetry. Simon Goldhill, in an analysis of ekphrasis in poetry, has suggested that poets have adopted this technical vocabulary of literary criticism because they ultimately are responding "not to art but to the tropes of verisimilitude."[9] Goldhill rejects the reductive analysis that the poets are simply toying with different ways to express the lifelike qualities of the statue and instead argues that they can only be describing the power of description itself. It is unclear, and probably unlikely, that all the poets had seen the original statue at Athens (or later at Rome), so they cannot actually describe an object they have seen in these epigrams but must meditate on the act of description through the microgenre.

A further salient feature revealed when considering the Myron's Cow epigrams as a single microgenre is the extent of competition among poets through intertextual references and common literary traditions. Like Marcus Argentarius, one of the earliest entries by Leonidas of Tarentum imagines Myron not actually sculpting the statue but stealing an actual cow away and attaching it to a statue base. Gutzwiller has argued that the series of Myron's Cow epigrams of Antipater of Sidon (in which other calves and shepherds gullibly approach the statue) not only paraphrase the Leonidas original but also can be read as "an extended working out of the possibilities set up by Leonidas' clever poem."[10] The use of intertextual signifiers, at the verbal level, adds additional nodes of connection (and competition). Michael Squire reads two poems by Antipater and one by the later Demetrius of Bithynia as consciously adopting the Greek verb *mukēsetai* ("it will moo") in order to explore not only the realism of the poem but the potentiality of mimetic arts to capture all sensory aspects, such as sound (with the onomatopoetic verb punning on this very feature, with its initial "moo" syllable).[11] Read as a single poetic corpus, the microgenre reveals multiple generations of poets responding to each other in a growing discursive contest.

The social disorder that accompanied the dissolution of the Roman Empire in the fifth century CE contributed to the loss of most of Myron's works (including the original Cow) and the diminution of his fame, and as a result the Myron's Cow epigram is unattested after the entries by Julian of Egypt. Epigrammatic material on classical (or rather, "pagan") themes also saw a sharp decline during the rise of Christianity in the late Empire and Medieval periods; thus, we can declare the end of the microgenre roughly 800 years after it began. Nonetheless, the thirty-six surviving Myron's Cow epigrams provide us with a robust exploration of poetic and artistic capability through a focus on a single bronze statue.

Notes

1   Ausonius writes in Latin instead of Greek, but as an epigrammatist he is otherwise indistinguishable from his Greek peers.

2   Various authors, *The Greek Anthology, Volume III: Book 9: The Declamatory Epigrams* (Cambridge: Harvard University Press, 1917), 400, 398, author's translation.

3   Irmgard Männlein-Robert, "Epigrams on Art: Voice and Voicelessness in Hellenistic Epigram," in *Brill's Companion to Hellenistic Epigram*, ed. Peter Bing and Jon Bruss (Leiden: Brill, 2007), 266n75.

4   Propertius, *Elegies* (Cambridge: Harvard University Press, 1990), 198, author's translation. On the presence of the later copies at Rome and their significance in Roman coinage, see Hadrian Rambach and Alan Walker, "The 'Heifer' *Aurei* of Augustus," *Schweizerische Numismatische Rundschau* 91 (2012): 41–57.

5   Kathryn J. Gutzwiller, *Poetic Garlands: Hellenistic Epigrams in Context* (Berkeley: University of California Press, 1998), 246.

6   Ausonius, *Volume II: Books 18–20* (Cambridge: Harvard University Press, 1921), 196, author's translation.

7   Various authors, *Greek Anthology*, 430, author's translation.

8   Männlein-Robert, "Epigrams," 266.

9   Simon Goldhill, "What Is Ekphrasis For?" *Classical Philology* 102 (January 2007): 17.

10   Gutzwiller, *Poetic Garlands*, 247.

11   Michael Squire, "Making Myron's Cow Moo? Ecphrastic Epigram and the Poetics of Simulation," *American Journal of Philology* 131 (Winter 2010): 611–12.

3

The Premature Ejaculation Poem

Christopher Vilmar

During the seventeenth century, ten poems in French and English dealt with the sticky subject of premature ejaculation. Every year during a British literature survey, I teach two of them at a regional Maryland university to students from all majors and backgrounds. These poems discuss sex so frankly and openly that the students are by turns amused and horrified. The explicit detail of these poems—not only kisses and caresses but penises and vaginas in various states of arousal, mutual desire, and forceful seduction— is surprising, mainly because students tend to expect that serious authors from "back in the day" write in dignified language, and these gory sexual encounters frustrate these expectations. In Rochester's "The Imperfect Enjoyment" (c. 1680), words like "fuck" and "cunt" are part of his blitzkrieg against pretty much everything that is dignified: the sentiments of romantic love, the heroic language of John Dryden's tragedies, and plain common decency. Even now, readers are offended to find a writer of Rochester's talent writing such a nastily delicious poem.

What students don't know is that serious authors have been writing about boners since *way* "back in the day." There is a lengthy tradition of literature about impotence. In *Amores* (c. 16 CE), Ovid describes a sexual encounter foiled by his lack of erection. The hapless woman attempts to stiffen his resolve without success, then reproaches him with illness or having come from another woman's bed—a possibility the poet confirms when he brags to have lately had other escapades where he got it up as many as "nine times" in "one short night."[1] Ovid leaves the reader to decide on the veracity of these claims. In Petronius's *Satyricon* (late first century CE), Encolpius is solicited by the servant of an alluring Roman matron. But he cannot get erect even after lavishing kisses on her. She then pays a sorceress to sodomize Encolpius in a ritual designed to restore his ability to perform and later flogs him herself. He is therefore not only disappointed but relieved to escape from her bed without success. Fifteen centuries later, Montaigne develops this tradition by relating a story about "a friend" whose impotence occurs simply because "the friend" heard of another man who was unable to perform.

In this gossipy, possibly autobiographical account, anxiety and self-doubt prevent "the friend" from getting it up.[2] Montaigne draws on these classical accounts, but makes physical incapacity the product of psychological issues: the mind has become more important than the body.

During the next century, the Cartesian shift from body to mind occurs in premature ejaculation poetry as it transforms the impotence tradition: impotence prevents intercourse, while premature ejaculation only shortens it uncomfortably. Here the mind gains primacy over the body. The tangible relief Encolpius feels when he escapes a situation that is unpleasant and even shameful requires later poets to innovate as well as copy if they want to capture the frustration of being unable to finish what you started. This change has an analogy in seventeenth-century politics as well, where confident monarchs were nevertheless often frustrated as they sought to exercise increasingly limitless power. In France and later in England, kings who felt that their divine appointment gave them absolute authority sought to exercise this power in the face of considerable opposition. As a result the emotional discomfort of the premature ejaculator who fails to fulfill himself or his partner becomes tacitly similar to the psychological consequences of political defeat. The initial embarrassment spirals quickly into anguish, shame, and regret. Or such is the argument of Hannah Lavery; Leo Braudy, however, disagrees. In his highly theorized account, sexual experience changes over time, and these poems mainly reveal how much sexual response has changed with changing cultural contexts: sexuality is not static but dynamic, and the sexual experience of these poems is shaped by norms determined by their historical context.[3]

Such debates may occupy a lazily contemplative afternoon, but deciding between their competing conclusions does not change historical fact: the first premature ejaculation poem was "Impuissance," by the French poet Rémy Belleau, written during the late sixteenth century and published in 1618. Its title alone negates military prowess (or "puissance") and ironically undermines the analogy that relates cocksmanship and swordsmanship. According to Richard E. Quaintance, the poems that follow were: in French, Mathurin Régnier's "Impuissance" (1613), Charles Beys's "La Jouissance Imparfaite. Caprice" (1651), Payot de Morangle's "L'Occasion Perdue. A Cloris" (1652), and Jean Benech de Cantenac's "L'Occasion Perdue Recouverte" (1660); and in English, Sir George Etherege's "The Imperfect Enjoyment" (1672) (which imitates Beys), the anonymous "Fruition" (1674), Rochester's "Imperfect Enjoyment" (1680), Aphra Behn's "The Disappointment" (1680) (which paraphrases part of Cantenac), and a final anonymous "The Lost Opportunity Recovered" (1682) (which again translates Cantenac). John H. O'Neill argues for an eleventh anonymous poem in manuscript, written before Rochester.[4]

The French poems precede and influence the English ones, of which several are free translations from the French. English laws against obscenity likewise made it difficult to publish explicit poems. Many of the English examples circulated in manuscript, sometimes for years, before being published by booksellers willing to assume the risk of publishing smut. Indeed, the French texts are not readily available except in the renditions of the talented English poets above, which afford glimpses of their earlier French models. Instead of analyzing rare translations, therefore, I will examine their historical context and explain how they disguised political satire as erotic verse during the reign of Louis XIV in France. This context will be valuable as we look at English poets who adapted this microgenre when Charles II returned from exile in France to become king of England in 1660.

Four-year-old Louis XIV ascended to the throne of France in 1643. Once he reached adulthood, he inherited a nation threatened by religious antagonism for several generations: his grandfather was murdered by Protestant zealots, and his father struggled to prevent further religious and political disintegration. On the throne, Louis began an unprecedented consolidation of power. His belief in the divine ordination of his power buttressed his ambition to rule France without peers or rivals, and this ambition was embodied in the architecture of the palace he began to build at Versailles. The finished structure would eventually symbolize his subjection of the ancient noble families of France, whom he forced to abandon their estates and attend to him at Versailles. But when Charles arrived in Paris as an exile in 1651 following the execution of his father after the English Civil Wars, Louis's dreams were as yet unrealized. The grandeur of this unfulfilled ambition formed the background for the French premature ejaculation poems, so that their critique of the sexual performance of a powerful man immediately suggests a political subtext. Indeed, to criticize the one was to criticize the other. Louis had many mistresses and treated sexual conquest as simply another display of royal authority. Rochester similarly equivocates between the two in the following lines about Charles: "Nor are his high desires above his strength, / His scepter and his prick are of a length, / And she that plays with one may sway the other."[5] Charles was exiled in Paris during the time when most of the French poems were written, and it would have been impossible to avoid their *double entendres* with regard to sex and power. The later English poems, therefore, would have had an obvious political subtext.

The anonymous English poem discovered by O'Neill, "Bless me you stars!," does not redeem its vulgarity with any reflective or philosophical development:

Her legs stretcht wide, her C—t to me did show ...
I cou'd by no means make him Raise his Head,
I kiss'd, I toy'd, I clapt her Cheeks & Tail,
And Fingerd too, yet I cou'd not prevail,
Yea, tho' she took it in her warm moyst hand,
And Cramm'd it in, (dull Dog) it cou'd not Stand.[6]

These crass images—spread legs, sadistic "claps" on "her Cheeks & Tail," fingering, and even cramming the limp penis into the vagina, all in a vain attempt to stimulate an erection—merely shock or titillate. Indeed, the only thing they accomplish is to reveal a fundamental error: the confusion of premature ejaculation with impotence.

Such confusion is not just present in O'Neill. Much of the scholarship on these poems, like Lavery's fine book, conflate the two sexual states. As satire, however, the two are obviously different. When Charles II was in exile and prevented from ruling England, impotence may have been a suitable metaphor. Once restored to the throne in 1660, however, premature ejaculation probably seemed more apt to describe the likelihood that he would unite a nation divided by over a century of religious contention and decades of civil war.

And the first English premature ejaculation poem was, in fact, published two years after Charles was restored: Etherege's "The Imperfect Enjoyment" (1662). Etherege trims the ninety-two lines of Beys to a mere fifty; his editor James Thorpe dates the poem to the years 1660–62, at the beginning of Charles's reign, describing it as "more witty and mannerly, less crude and bawdy" than the French original.[7] Unlike the crude pornography of "Bless me you stars!" Etherege is unfailingly decorous, always oblique or periphrastic in reference to sex. For example, the untimely ejaculation is described thus:

Come to the temple where I should implore
My saint, I worship at the sacred door.
Oh cruel chance! the town which did oppose
My strength so long now yields to my dispose
When, overjoyed by victory, I fall
Dead at the foot of the surrendered wall.[8]

The metaphorical conceit of the devotee worshipping at her sexuality is consistently developed. The woman is the "town," her vagina a "temple" dedicated to a "saint" the poet "should implore." Once his "strength" is "overjoyed by victory," it "falls / Dead at the foot of the surrendered wall": at the moment consent is given the penis ejaculates. This conceit is restrained and polite, especially compared with the spread legs and fingerbanging of "Bless me you stars!" or even the original text of Beys. The sexual tension between the urge to display and the need to disguise captures the licentious decorum of the Restoration. Charles II was able to flaunt his mistresses, provided that certain decorums were maintained; likewise Etherege could write verse that hinted at scandal so long as it was never openly discussed.

In this poem it is also noteworthy that the woman consents to sex. Her initial rejection of his advances notwithstanding, she is clearly torn between desire and the religious-cultural demand for chastity in seventeenth-century Britain: "Against her will she is my enemy." This ideological taboo on female sexuality outside of marriage prevents her from pursuing her desires at first, but in the following lines we see the torturous path that her desire must take in order to satisfy itself:

> Now she consents, her force she does recall …
> Her arms, which did repulse me, now embrace
> And seem to guide me to the fought-for place.
> Her love is in her sparkling eyes expressed,
> She falls on the bed for pleasure more than rest.[9]

And just as the "double standard" required even willing women to play various pro forma games before consenting to sex outside marriage, so did politics require its subjects to play games before giving in even to the most desirable demands of others. Behn, the only woman writing in this microgenre, would more fully explore the tension between desire, disguise, and consent. Yet even at the microgenre's inception in English, Etherege depicts female consent as essential to sexual pleasure, as would the pornographer writing "Bless me you stars!" In English premature ejaculation poetry, then, fornication becomes a symbol of the more permissive culture that followed the Restoration—for women as well as politicians—at least as long as everyone involved was satisfied.

Indeed, the backlash against the puritanism of the civil wars meant that fornication enjoyed a vogue in Restoration England. Even women were tacitly encouraged to undertake sexual adventure. But sexual freedom quickly teaches that desire is just as often frustrated as satisfied, and this is one of the themes explored by the premature ejaculation poem—and for women, particularly, in Behn's careful abridgment of Cantenac's poem in "The Disappointment." Her truncation of the original eliminates the possibility that a "lost opportunity" will be "recovered" by either the heroine Cloris or her suitor Lysander. By the end of the poem Cloris flees after touching his spent limpness, leaving him to curse "his Birth, his Fate, his Stars; / But more the *Shepherdess's* Charms."[10] But this desperate last-minute shifting of blame cannot mask her disappointment or his failure in an opportunity lost forever. As the only woman writing in the microgenre, it may seem inevitable that Behn highlights the question of Cloris's consent. The lovers seek a "lone Thicket made for love, / Silent as yielding Maid's consent."[11] Perhaps it is surprising that even Behn describes sexual consent as "silent," but patriarchal norms held their authority even over the secluded privacies of women. Cloris does say no, in the third stanza, but Lysander ignores her, and:

> His daring Hand that Altar seiz'd,
> That awful Throne, that Paradice,
> Where Rage is calm'd, and Anger pleas'd,
> That Fountain where Delight still flows,
> And gives the Universal World Repose.

The periphrasis here barely disguises the bald fact that Lysander has grabbed Cloris by the vagina. Despite her earlier refusal, she remains oddly receptive:

> Her Balmy Lips incountring his,
> Their Bodies, as their Souls, are joyn'd ...
> Cloris half dead and breathless lay ...
> And now no signs of Life she shows
> But what in short-breath'd Sighs returns & goes.[12]

Though Lysander has not attempted penetration, lips have met lips, and the lifeless and breathless Cloris seems to have had an orgasm. The adjective "balmy" may suggest the means: Rochester uses it in "The Imperfect Enjoyment," published originally in the same 1680 volume as Behn's poem: "My fluttering soul, sprung with the pointed kiss, / Hangs hovering o'er her balmy brinks of bliss."[13] Here "balmy" modified the "brinks of bliss," suggesting an aroused vulva. This proposes a reading of Behn's "Balmy Lips incountring his" where Lysander uses his tongue in a nonverbal means of persuasion aimed below the belt.

After this orgasm, Lysander finally obtains consent from Cloris: "Abandon'd by her Pride and Shame, / She does her softest Joys dispence, / Off'ring her virgin Innocence." But once Cloris abandons the constraints of patriarchal sexuality, Lysander comes too quickly. She flees, and Behn begins the final stanza with these lines: "The *Nymph's* Resentments none but I / Can well Imagine or Condole."[14] Whatever seeming solidarity between author and heroine, however, is lost when one remembers that Cloris is never able to defend herself or feel anything other than embarrassment. While Behn claims to understand Cloris, she does not exactly advocate for her. As a woman she may "Imagine or Condole … the *Nymph's* Resentents," but as a poet she makes no correctives and creates no alternatives.

In Rochester's "Imperfect Enjoyment," the willing consent of the woman is unencumbered by the patriarchal equivocations of Etherege or Behn. As in a classical tragedy, the poem begins in medias res: "Naked she lay, clasped in my longing arms, / I filled with love and she all over charms, / Both equally inspired with eager fire."[15] The equality of this desire does not last, however, and the sudden ejaculation leaves neither partner satisfied. Early in the poem the metaphors for sex are all heat, fire, and wetness, but these quickly dissolve into the "clammy joys" she wipes away after his early climax. She responds to this situation with genuine understanding:

> Smiling, she chides in a kind, murmuring noise …
> … "Is there then no more?"
> She cries. "All this to love and rapture's due,
> Must we not pay a debt to pleasure, too?"

But her sympathy does not help him achieve another erection. In the following lines, his chagrin quickly devolves into images of coldness, ice, and frigidity.

By the end of the poem the speaker seems utterly abject, and he curses his penis with disease and sexual humiliation for its betrayal of his eager desire:

> Worst part of me, and henceforth hated most,
> Through all the town a common fucking post
> On whom each whore relieves her tingling cunt
> As hogs on gates do rub themselves and grunt,
> May'st thou to ravenous chancres be a prey,
> Or in consuming weepings waste away,
> May straungery and stone thy days attend;
> May'st thou ne'er piss who didst refuse to spend
> When all my joys did on false thee depend.

The grotesque image that likens obtaining prostitutes with "hogs on gates" that "do rub themselves and grunt" divides the speaker's animalistic bedroom adventures from his failure to perform when "great Love the onset does command."[16] This paradox explores the division of sex and love, where great passion not only does not guarantee but in fact seems to prevent the height of physical satisfaction. To remain attached to love, the speaker must detach himself from his own body, regarding his penis as his "worst" part and condemning it to a series of urinary and sexual afflictions once its failure prevents the attainment of "all my joys." The extremity of this bodily dissociation satirizes earlier love poetry. Those Renaissance poets who imitated the love poetry of Dante and Petrarch, like the English writers Edmund Spenser and John Donne, characterize love as a sublime and ennobling passion. In Rochester's "Imperfect Enjoyment," sex and love flow in separate channels that rarely if ever meet, and his disappointment in this unpleasant state of affairs is palpable.

Throughout the ten seventeenth-century examples of premature ejaculation poetry, the sexual image almost always seems to expand to include other cultural issues where an untimely or unexpected ending leads to embarrassment, shame, and regret. Yet because these poems circulated in manuscript for an indeterminate time before publication, it can be very difficult to link them to specific historical events. It is not possible, for example, to tie Rochester's "Imperfect Enjoyment" to any of his friend and patron Charles II's political gambits with the kind of certainty that would pinpoint the political analogy of the poem's satire. Instead, the king's conflation of sexual conquest with political skill suggests the broad outlines of Rochester's political satire—and if the political context is not specific, its broad outlines help delineate the political dimension of the analogy. Finally, the fragile link these poems propose between body and mind in sexuality remains strikingly relevant. If the blatant sexual references of these poems cause modern readers to blanch, the ease with which the subconscious subverts sexual performance may well cause them to cringe—especially when we all confront the obvious shortcomings of erotic experience, or, still more alarmingly, as in the poetry of Rochester, the disparity between the limitless quality of desire and its all-too-finite satisfactions.

Notes

1   Ovid, *The Erotic Poems*, trans. and ed. Peter Green (Harmondsworth: Penguin, 1982), 150.

2   Michel de Montaigne, "Of the Power of the Imagination," in *The Complete Essays of Montaigne*, trans. Donald E. Frame (Stanford: Stanford University Press, 1958), 70.

3   Hannah Lavery, *The Impotency Poem from Ancient Latin to Restoration English Literature* (Burlington: Ashgate, 2014); Leo Braudy, "Remembering Masculinity: Premature Ejaculation Poetry of the Seventeenth Century," *Michigan Quarterly Review* 33, no. 1 (1994): 177–201.

4   Richard E. Quaintance, "French Sources of the Restoration 'Imperfect Enjoyment' Poem," *Philological Quarterly* 42, no. 2 (1963): 190–99; John H. O'Neill, "An Unpublished 'Imperfect Enjoyment' Poem," *Papers on Language and Literature* 13, no. 2 (1977): 197–202.

5   John Wilmot, Earl of Rochester, "A Satyr on Charles II," in *The Complete Works*, ed. Frank H. Ellis (Harmondsworth: Penguin, 1994), 3.

6   O'Neill, "Unpublished," 199.

7   Sir George Etherege, *The Poems of Sir George Etheridge*, ed. James Thorpe (Princeton: Princeton University Press, 1963), 77–78.

8   Ibid.

9   Ibid.

10 Aphra Behn, "The Disappointment," in *The Works of Aphra Behn: Vol. 1, Poetry*, ed. Janet Todd (London: William Pickering, 1992), 69.

11 Ibid., 65.

12 Ibid., 66.

13 Rochester, *Works*, 22.

14 Behn, *Works*, 67.

15 Rochester, *Works*, 28.

16 Ibid., 28–29.

4

Prostitute Narratives of Ancien Régime France

Alistaire Tallent

One of the benefits of organizing a group of texts into a smaller, more specific microgenre is the transformation of lesser-known works that individually have attracted little attention or interest into relevant and revealing cultural artifacts. The specificity of a microgenre shines a brighter light on certain recurring themes and tropes that are otherwise invisible in the dark forest of a genre. For instance, the eighteenth-century French libertine novel is a genre composed of a varied group of texts, from the witty innuendos of Crébillon *fils* to the brutal pornography of the Marquis de Sade. Libertine novels are sometimes epistolary and sometimes pseudo-memoirs with male or female narrators. Within this wide collection of styles and narrative voices, there exists a tiny collection of thirteen novels that share two key features: the heroines of these novels readily and unabashedly admit their profession as skillful and successful prostitutes, and they show women actively pursuing their own sexual desires while eschewing the path of monogamy, marriage, and motherhood.

The only well-known example of these prostitute narratives is Sade's *Histoire de Juliette, ou les prospérités du vice* (1797). But when we pull the other twelve texts out of the shadows, we recognize in their common features an important function of the libertine novel. In addition to articulating materialist philosophies, exposing immorality and hypocrisy, and undermining authority figures, the prostitute narratives also serve as expressions of frustration with and sites of resistance to the repressive social and political order of prerevolutionary France. These novels reveal a shared fantasy of a new France where personal merit is rewarded and individual freedoms lead to prosperity and satisfaction. The novels of this microgenre, then, so easily overlooked when tucked between Denis Diderot's *Les Bijoux indiscrets* (1748) and Choderlos de Laclos's *Les Liaisons dangereuses* (1782), are in fact a useful source for understanding the tensions that led to the overthrow of one of Europe's most powerful monarchies.

In each of these pseudo-memoirs, published clandestinely between 1739 and 1797, a female narrator describes her rise from humble beginnings to wealth and fame through some form of prostitution. Although these works somewhat resemble the British whore biographies written around the same time, the tone of these French tales is much less apologetic as each narrator relishes the naughty descriptions of her subversive sexual acts. These women speak openly and proudly about selling their bodies and feigning love for men they disdain. It is likely that the first of these texts was intended as a personal attack on the actress Claire Hippolyte Leris—known as Mademoiselle Clairon—a rising star in the Comédie française when the *Histoire de Mademoiselle Cronel, dite Frétillon* first appeared in 1739. The author is believed to be Gaillard de la Bataille, whose advances the young actress rejected the year before. Seeking revenge, Bataille penned a pseudo-memoir in which the narrator unabashedly admits to stringing along an array of lovers and attributes her success to her loose morals rather than any acting talent. After this first novel came twelve more, including the French abridged translation of John Cleland's *Memoirs of a Woman of Pleasure* (1751)[1] and Fougeret de Monbron's *Margot la ravaudeuse* (1750; recently translated by Édouard Langille), culminating with Sade's *Juliette*. All of the novels were published anonymously, although in most cases their authorship was discernable by writers and critics of the time.

Whoever they were, the authors of these texts clearly saw themselves as contributing to a coherent genre. The numerous intertextual references to other prostitute narratives signal at the least an awareness of the microgenre. For instance, the narrator of *La Belle Allemande, ou les Galanteries de Thérèse* (1745) compares herself to the narrator of the *Histoire de Mademoiselle Cronel*, using her nickname, Frétillon: "Already Frétillon's rival in the career of honor, I can imagine soon sharing with her the inseparable glory of being the heroine of a novel."[2] The "career of honor" here refers ironically to prostitution, but it is the use of the word "novel" that is the most audacious claim. Admitting to fictionality in a pseudo-memoir that otherwise observes the common practice of pretending to demonstrate verisimilitude is more than a coy wink to the reader. It is a deliberate subversion of respectable literary tropes as well as a quick nod to the other authors and readers of prostitute narratives. A sense of community among the producers and consumers of these prostitute narratives manifests in this declaration that even if she and Frétillon are rivals in their love lives—competing for the same wealthy patrons—they can "share" the glory of literary fame by starring in their own works, each one complementing the other.

When we place the stories of Frétillon, Thérèse, and the other eleven prostitute narrators side by side a common purpose emerges. These humorous and lewd fictions provide deeply subversive critiques of ancien régime society and hierarchies. Contemporaneous to the serious critiques of philosophes like Voltaire and Diderot, these "forbidden best-sellers" (to borrow a phrase from Robert Darnton) voiced similar complaints by ridiculing the wealthy and aristocratic men who enjoyed undeserved power and privilege.[3] More general than the satirical and obscene pamphlets and poetry mocking individual members of the royal family, these prostitute narratives undermined the entire patriarchal order—of which the abuses of the French nobility were the most obvious—in two key ways.[4] First, in these stories the men with the most power—the wealthiest bankers and tax farmers and aristocrats from the oldest noble families—appear as corrupt and degenerate fools. Second, the prostitute narratives offer a fictional alternative social and political hierarchy of ancien régime France where wealth and privilege are dispersed based on personal merit and in which, startlingly, women enjoy the same independence and agency as men.

Hyperbolic negative portraits of privileged men appear in every prostitute narrative. Over and over, we see the wealthiest and most noble clients spend enormous sums on the *filles entretenues* who secretly despise them. These men have physical appearances ranging from unattractive to hideous, as in this description by Thérèse of one of the wealthiest and most sought after men in Paris: "I was horrified after seeing him. What an abominable face: dark and wild-eyed, with a pallid and sallow complexion, truly the appearance of a reprobate! We all make allowances for ugly people, but it's just not permitted to have such a face! Oh, that nasty man!"[5] As we see in this description, the narrators of these novels are not simply repulsed by the unfortunate appearance of a man, or by older men, whose ugliness is a product of natural aging. Instead, words like "sallow" and "reprobate" associate the ugliness of these men with their immoral behavior. Thérèse's final epithet, that this man is "nasty" (in French, *vilain*), captures the nuances of the prostitutes' disgust for these men: *vilain* means both ugly and behaving badly.

In addition to their physical shortcomings, the clients these narrators disdain are also greedy. Even though they spend large sums of money on these prostitutes, among other pleasures, they often withhold necessary funds from members of their own family. As extreme examples of the injustice of primogeniture in this patriarchal society, these men of entitlement withhold inheritances and allowances from their (usually handsome) nephews and sometimes even force their wives and children to make do with tiny stipends. In these unfair situations, it is the indignant prostitute who acts as an avenging angel. One heroine describes overhearing the wife of her client begging him to give her more money to feed and clothe their children. After he refuses, the prostitute steps out of hiding and gives the distraught wife half of her earnings from the previous night. A more common occurrence in the novels is for the prostitute to squeeze as much money as possible from the older man then pass some of it on to the more deserving younger relative, with whom she is usually sleeping behind the official benefactor's back.[6]

Not only do these novels criticize specific characters representing the powerful classes, they also undermine the very system based on inherited privilege. In the mind of one prostitute narrator, women should care only about pleasure, not family lineage, as she explains:

> I know a lot of my dear and venerable comrades who give themselves a beautiful origin, without really being any nobler because of it. To hear them talk, it would seem that no girl could know how to wiggle her ass without being the daughter of a prelate, niece of a counselor, cousin of a duke and peer of the realm, etc. Such a genealogy is pure folly! A true whore must know only pleasure. She must scorn her birth and her family, and have no other ambition save that of quenching her passion and maintaining useful and agreeable acquaintances.[7]

These heroines also reject the social role assigned to women at the time, in particular the notion of a natural maternal instinct. The prostitute narrators have no desire to be mothers and are remarkably adept at remaining unencumbered. Throughout the thirteen novels filled with countless sexual encounters, we find only four heroines who ever get pregnant. Not one of the three narrators who carry to term raises her child; in fact, they never even give their babies names. These women are surely the opposite of Rousseau's Julie, who famously sacrifices her own life to save her child. These narrators instead display a lack of desire for any of the female virtues so vehemently lauded elsewhere. They eschew marriage and motherhood as hindrances to their pursuit of money and power, and they refuse to remain in the private sphere performing nurturing, domestic duties.

And yet these narrators are not the exceptions that prove the rule, the "bad" women who prove "good" women are maternal and docile. These narrators are admirable. They are talented, successful, and happy, and they perform generous and selfless acts such as helping other women in need while avoiding hypocrisy. As well as they feign love, attraction, and desire with their clients, the narrators of these memoirs are always honest and frank with their readers. Despite their defiance of church and secular laws against adultery and prostitution, these heroines embody a kind of virtue.

The fantasies of the prostitute narratives are not, however, the Republic of Virtue that the French revolutionaries praised and sought to establish, even though the world of this microgenre was just as much an alternative to the inequalities of the Ancien Régime. These authors were pushing back at the same problems: the unfair concentration of wealth and privilege in a hereditary aristocracy, the forced suppression of natural behaviors by hypocritical religious and secular authorities, and the many obstacles to the pursuit of personal liberty and happiness. The difference is that the model Rousseau and his followers depicted was a gendered utopia, with men working together in the public sphere to build a better nation, while women stayed in the home to raise its virtuous citizens. The microgenre of the prostitute narratives, on the other hand, articulates a very different fantasy— one that similarly rewards merit over birth, but also envisions freedoms for women as well as men. Yes, these novels—perhaps up until Sade—were comical and titillating, but to limit their purposes to amusement and arousal is to overlook the broader view of the microgenre. These novels gave a unique voice to authors and readers critiquing a social and political system that was on its deathbed.

Notes

1   The significant adaptation and abridgment to Cleland's *Memoirs of a Woman of Pleasure* warrant treating this novel as a separate work belonging to the French libertine novel tradition.
2   Antoine Bret or Claude Villaret, *La Belle Allemande, Part 2: Ou Les Galanteries de Thérèse* (Paris: Aux Dépens de la Compagnie, 1774), 3, author's translation.
3   See Robert Darnton's *The Literary Underground of the Old Regime* (Cambridge: Harvard University Press, 1982), *The Forbidden Best-Sellers of Prerevolutionary France* (New York: Norton, 1996), and *The Corpus of Clandestine Literature in France, 1769–1789* (New York: Norton, 1995).
4   The most common objects of the slanderous and often obscene pamphlets were Louis XV and his grandson's wife, Marie Antoinette.
5   Bret or Villaret, *Belle Allemande*, 70, author's translation.
6   The trope of the ugly older man competing unsuccessfully with (and often cuckolded by) a handsome young hero dates back well before even Molière's Arnolphe in *L'École des femmes* to the Italian *commedia dell'arte*. What these novels add is the story of a woman consistently getting the better of these powerful men.
7   Anonymous, *La Belle Cauchoise ou mémoires d'une courtisane célèbre* (1784), in *Œuvres anonymes du XVIIIe siècle 1: L'Enfer de la Bibliothèque Nationale*, 3 vols. (Paris: Librairie Arthème Fayard, 1985), 3: 389, author's translation.

5

The Neoclassical Plague Romance

Matthew Duques

Thucydides's short account of a plague that killed thousands of people living along the Mediterranean Sea during the fifth century BCE broke with tradition. By emphasizing the role that humans played in spreading and checking the illness, Thucydides suggested that people, not the gods, were the cause of such widespread death and misery. Modern writers have adopted a similar approach to Thucydides in their retelling of harrowing stories about the unanticipated spread of plague. Like Thucydides, writers of these neoclassical plague romances elaborate on the human causes and effects of actual historic epidemics. Their prose epics are historical fictions about plague in which the themes of sociopolitical decline and collective survival are prominent. Generally, such stories have been deemed lesser illustrations of the major written literary forms through which they are mediated—historical drama, poem, novel, short story—or they have been subsumed under contemporary genre categories, such as speculative fiction, post-apocalyptic horror, mystery, thriller, outbreak or climate-change narrative. Consequently, the evolution of the neoclassical plague romance as a minor genre in its own right has gone largely under the radar.

If one were to look for a visual model for the neoclassical plague romance, one could do little better than Michael Sweerts's *Plague in an Ancient City* (1650–52) (Figure 5.1). Sweerts depicts victims of a disease lying about a piazza while the living weep around them, look toward the heavens in desperation, express disgust. An infant suckles the breast of her dead mother; women nearby wail; a young man holds his nose.[1]

The majority of the dead appear at the front of the work, the lowest elevation point, and the most open space, suggesting that the illness likely spread through oceanic trade and/or cross-cultural contact. A dark woods, including a shady cave inhabited by the sick and the wicked, is set above the veritable ground zero for the disease and against a well-lit, symmetrical, sparsely populated piazza, all of which underscores the loss of not just people but morality as well. Meanwhile, a band of emigrants gather above the cave exit west into a wilderness, likely aiming to start a new life—

Figure 5.1 Michael Sweerts, *Plague in an Ancient City* (1650–52) [Courtesy of the Los Angeles County Museum of Art].

should they survive. With this painting, Sweerts aimed to do more than just convert troubling episodes from Greco-Roman antiquity into a spiritually uplifting Christian allegory, as many of his early modern predecessors had done. Instead, he tried to capture the story of a republic toppling due to a contagion, a story that reflects this political form's allegedly natural cycle: its rise, decline, and rebirth.[2]

A similar plot can be found over a generation later in a spate of writings about London's Great Plague of 1665–66, the last major epidemic of the bubonic plague in England. In 1672, English doctor Nathaniel Hodges wrote *Loimologia, or An Historical Account of the Plague in London in 1665*, an eyewitness account in which Hodges tells of elite citizens who fled when they should have stayed behind to stem the spread of the disease, "wretched nurses" who suffocated victims and willfully infected the healthy, ill patients who "broke out of their barr'd houses," and the "common people" who took no precautions to defend themselves since they believed London merely had to endure a plague every twenty years.[3] Daniel Defoe used Hodges's text as a guide in *Journal of the Plague Year* (1722).[4] Told from the perspective of a saddler named H.F., Defoe's semi-fictional book underscores how city residents of different socioeconomic backgrounds respond to the disease. Victims of the plague suffer from painful, visible buboes or hemorrhagic sores while their loved ones struggle to manage their grief and fear; conflict and crime ensue as local ordinances fail to stem spreading plague, much less help sick and dying people, and able-bodied, often wealthy Londoners flee to the English countryside. Defoe, like Hodges, describes a city community sensing that their way of life was ending. Both writers, though, use local perspectives to emphasize that this end is more apparent than actual. Modeling the deliberate opening up of sores as well as city spaces, rather than the rash closure of these contagions, Defoe's and Hodges's works illustrate how to heal London in a way that would make the city and the English republic more generally ready for future health crises.

Nineteenth-century American author Lydia Maria Child's neoclassical plague romance, *Philothea: A Grecian Romance* (1836), is largely forgotten today, though it was popular in the antebellum period with favorable reviews from the likes of Edgar Allan Poe. Child, a gifted storyteller and already a household name in American letters, gave readers, who felt that their country was more divided than ever, a story about a familiar and relevant epoch in ancient Greek history. Her novella is about the time period that Thucydides had first chronicled, which included the rise of the populist leader Pericles, the onset of war with neighboring Persia, the end of golden-age Athens, and, of course, the crippling spread of plague. Child related this well-known history of declension through the perspectives of two fictional friends, Philothea and Eudora, the former legally dependent, the latter legally enslaved. Philothea and Eudora's differing views on the health and morality of the downward-spiraling Athenian polity in which they were raised, their broken friendships and romances, and their forced family separations and joyous reunions, all allowed Child to show the complex of causes and the harmful effects of a declining Greek empire. Their stark visions speak to a fretful modern audience who worried that its own intransigent forms of inequity, regional division, and disease were signs of the end of their new American empire.

The middle of *Philothea* is entirely about the spread of plague in Athens and beyond its borders, which its protagonists and their associates glean from a relative distance. Philothea and Eudora learn that "men fall down senseless in the street" that becomes "heaped with unburied dead."[5] They hear male philosophers who speculate about the cause and implications of the disease. Plato, for instance, tells Philothea that he believes the disease to be "a manifested form of that inward corruption, which, finding a home in the will of man, clothed itself in thought, and now completes its circle in his corporeal nature." Hinting at the idea of divine intervention, Philothea's guardian, the philosopher Anaxagoras, wonders, "the pestilence has not been sent in vain, if the faith in images is shaken."[6] Ultimately, *Philothea* eschews such explanations and instead focuses on the survivors, those who avoided the disease and those who caught it yet managed to recover with exceptional powers, such as the son of Pericles and Philothea's betrothed, who lives on and now has "knowledge of the thoughts passing in the minds of those around him."[7] Philothea—the novella's main symbol of unchanging Athenian innocence and a stark contrast to the corrupted Athenian people—survives for a considerable period as she takes care of the survivors. Her post-epidemic death helps sound the idea that Athens, erstwhile beacon of the West, must amend its laws and institutions if it hopes to ever get well again and live on. Meanwhile, the concluding revelation that the survivor Eudora is a Persian princess, not a slave, helps establish the complimentary idea that reform must occur in the East too. Both Western and Eastern worlds are clearly tainted by the proto-capitalistic institution of slavery, which caused Eudora to be ripped from her homeland, sold as private property, and to be raised in Athens. With plague as its key topos— its morbid means of materializing other more figurative illnesses—Child warns her modern readers living in an increasingly divided American empire that the grandeur of antiquity came at tremendous costs. Child makes the case that political measures employed to shore up Greek and Persian global preeminence, including war, women's disenfranchisement, slavery, deportation, and the dissolution of social and political aid, have the potential to morally bankrupt their people and, therefore, to exacerbate their rapid decline.

The underlying political narrative of *Philothea* and virtually all neoclassical prose romances was arguably best exemplified by painter Thomas Cole in his ambitious five-painting series, *Course of Empire* (1833–36) (Figure 5.2). Each work in the series captures a distinct stage in the process of a generic ancient society's rise and fall, starting from its rudiments in the so-called savage state and followed by its idyllic character in a pastoral state, its zenith, its breakdown, and ultimately its return to ruins. His second to last piece, titled *Destruction*, highlights the people's responses to living in a war-torn and plague-ridden republic. Following Cole's course, mid-nineteenth-century fictions demonstrated how the historic spread of plague indexed a frightening end of empire. For instance, William Harrison Ainsworth's *Old Saint Paul's: A Tale of the Plague and the Fire* (1843) told of Londoners's discursive reactions to their infamous seventeenth-century plague. Poe's "The Masque of the Red Death" (1850), a bubonic plague–inspired short story, emphasized the futility of escaping from a mysterious illness in medieval times. These literary works, much like Cole's and Child's, reflect a pronounced interest in learning about how past republics endured a seemingly ineluctable tendency toward gluttonous self-destruction, surviving disasters, plague foremost among them. This interest in the handling of historic disasters can be read as an

Figure 5.2 Thomas Cole, *Destruction*, from five-painting series *Course of Empire* (1833–36).

early sign of a culture starting to recognize the catastrophic effects of modern industrialism on our bodies and our environments.

Popular neoclassical plague romances in the nineteenth and twentieth centuries reflect a growing interest in further specifying the human causes of epidemics, an interest reflected in the outpouring of historical fiction about similarly deadly epidemics. At the start of the nineteenth century, for instance, Charles Brockden Brown's novel *Arthur Mervyn, Or Memoirs of the Year 1793* (1799–1800) depicts the unprecedented yellow fever outbreak in Philadelphia. *Arthur Mervyn* is the tale of a rural farm boy who moves to the city in search of greater work prospects only to encounter yellow fever victims, grifters, and corrupt merchants. Like Thucydides, Brown got the very illness he wrote about, in this case while living in Philadelphia, which had branded itself as the Athens of America.[8] As with neoclassical plague romances, so too with Brown's *Arthur Mervyn*: the fever in this novel underscores related less literal maladies of prejudice and corruption, suggesting that all such illnesses reside at the core of the newly formed country, needlessly compromising equality and jeopardizing the lives of citizens and non-citizens.[9] The protagonist, for example, stumbles on "sheets tinged with yellow ... and gangrenous or black vomit" and presumes that the disease was caused by foreigners, exemplified by a victim he sees possessing "tawny skin," "brawny as Hercules."[10] With experience, Mervyn accepts the social or "miasma" theory of the disease. He speaks of "combat[ing] an opinion which I had casually formed, respecting the origin of this epidemic." The fever, he comes to think, was caused not, as he initially believed, by "infected substances imported from the east or west" but by "a morbid constitution of the atmosphere, owing wholly, or in part to filthy streets, airless habitations and squalid persons." In this way, *Arthur Mervyn* outs representative bias and unethical behavior because "of all the dangers, those allied to pestilence, by being mysterious and unseen, are the most formidable. Nurses and physicians soonest become intrepid or indifferent; but the rest of mankind recoil from the scene with unconquerable loathing."[11] Brown's novel also suggests that reform in the form of better urban planning and personal hygiene could temper these ghastly reactions by preventing urban epidemics from spreading.

Starting with the publication of Mary Shelley's speculative fiction *The Last Man* (1822), the plague and its modern variants became the main subject in a potential future, not just a possible past. Works such as Jack London's *The Scarlet Plague* (1912), George R. Stewart's *The Earth Abides* (1949), Stephen King's *The Stand* (1978), and Michael Crichton's *The Andromeda Strain* (1969) carried on what Shelley started. Meanwhile, Thomas Mann's *Death in Venice* (1912) and Gabriel García Márquez's *Love in the Time of Cholera* (1985) used actual historical diseases as the basis of their stories, capturing the destructive legacies of imperialism in their accounts of a once-grand republic beleaguered by disease. Mann's novella about the celebrated, aging writer Gustav von Aschenbach, who falls in love with a young boy while on vacation in Venice during a cholera scare, is not only a riff on the European grand tour narrative in which a man goes in search of culture in the home of antiquity only to find it sadly covered by corruption. It is also a romantic treatment of disease informed by advancements in germ theory. Mann follows a clear pathology of "Indian Cholera." He describes how cholera was "carried across the sea by Syrian merchants ... raising its head and show[ing] its mask ... in several Mediterranean ports simultaneously" until the "fearful vibrios had been discovered in Venice twice in the same day, in the emaciated, blackened corpses of a cargo-ship crewman and a female greengrocer."[12] Adopting the same modern scientific stance as was found in much speculative fiction animated by germ theory, *Death in Venice* exposes human failures to contain an epidemic as well as the specters of an exoticized, racialized other even as it assumes a precise identifiable course of a deadly, invisible pathogen across oceans, nations, and empires.

The neoclassical plague romance remains a significant yet minor form appearing principally in literary and filmic adaptations of earlier versions of the microgenre. Despite the knocks on Greco-Roman antiquity as outdated, interest in the original context for the plague is still strong as indexed by acclaimed historical fictions, such as Deanna Madden's *The World Beyond:*

A Novel of Ancient Greece (2017) as well as self-published fanfiction such as M. E. Wynne's "Athens Plague Series" (2017). Wynne's crudely constructed stories tell of the spread of the "Athens virus" through the perspective of a high school soccer player who has met his match in an airborne pathogen that he wonders may have been unleashed "in Greece or perhaps right here in Athens, Texas."[13] In more serious culture, Gabriel García Márquez's screenplay for the film *The Year of the Plague* (1979) and *Periwig Maker* (1999), a German short film narrated by Kenneth Branagh, have both adapted Defoe's *Journal.* Medieval plague narratives crop up with a similar broad range exemplified by Ken Follett's celebrated epic *World without End* (2007) and Peter Barnes's absurdist drama *Red Noses* (1985). Albert Camus's *The Plague* (1947), about a nineteenth-century epidemic in French Algeria, has inspired a host of more literal film, opera, drama, and fiction remakes, including Michael Grant's recent *Plague* (2011) and Kevin Chong's subtle, revealing novel, *The Plague* (2018). Meanwhile, numerous literary renditions of Philadelphia in 1793 by such authors as John Edgar Wideman and by YA phenom Laurie Halse Anderson have uncovered new perspectives about the historic outbreak, elaborating on the idea that the yellow fever episode was America's plague.

Accounts of the actual outbreak of rapidly spreading illness will likely continue to be a consistent draw no matter the medium and no matter how campy or avant-garde because, as Priscilla Wald argues, they foreground "the most basic of human narratives: the necessity and danger of human contact."[14] Since antiquity, plague narratives have introduced this critical plot as part of their focus on the role of people in causing and containing diseases. New spins on the plague have led to historical works that fictionalize a great deal for the sake of uncovering new information about what might have happened as an outbreak unfolds. Generally committed to representing an evolving science of pathology, these neoclassical plague romances contextualize the nature of human jeopardy while working to promote the kinds of contact that we as a species will always require.

Notes

1   Models for Sweerts's work include Italian painter Marcantonio Raimondi's engraving after Raphael, *Il Morbetto* (1515–16), and French painter Nicolas Poussin's *Plague at Ashdod* (1630).

2   William H. McNeill, *Plagues and People* (New York: Anchor, 1976).

3   Nathaniel Hodges, *Loimologia, or An Historical Account of the Plague in London in 1665* (London: James Street, 1672), 3.

4   Daniel Defoe, *Journal of the Plague Year* (New York: Penguin, 2003). John
     Quincy, a contemporary of Defoe's, translated Hodges from Latin to English
     a couple of years before Defoe published his quasi-fictional account.

5   Lydia Maria Child, *Philothea: A Grecian Romance* (New York and Boston:
     C.S. Francis, 1851), 94.

6   Ibid., 98, 97.

7   Ibid., 99.

8   Charles Brockden Brown, *Arthur Mervyn, Memoirs of the Year 1793*, ed.
     Steven Shapiro and Phillip Barnard (Indianapolis: Hackett, 2008). Most
     critics attribute the flurry of novel writing that Brown did at the tail end of
     the eighteenth century to the delirium caused by illness.

9   Shapiro and Barnard, for instance, rightly note that we must consider the
     fever's place in the novel in relation to the book's "underlying concerns with
     commercial corruption, Caribbean slave revolution, and abolition, and the
     larger social transformations of the revolutionary 1790s" (introduction to
     Brown, *Arthur Mervyn*, xxi).

10   Ibid., 113.

11   Ibid., 123, 127.

12   Thomas Mann, *Death in Venice*, trans. Stanley Appelbaum (New York:
     Dover, 2012), 52–53.

13   M. E. Wynne, *The Athens Plague Series* (n.p.: Something Else Publishing,
     2014), 4.

14   Priscilla Wald, *Contagious: Cultures, Carriers, and the Outbreak Narrative*
     (Durham: Duke University Press, 2008), 2.

6

Anesthesia Fiction

Jennifer Diann Jones

While anxieties about scientific and medical research are famously expressed in texts like Mary Shelley's *Frankenstein* (1818) and Robert Louis Stevenson's *The Strange Case of Dr. Jekyll and Mr. Hyde* (1886), there is one microgenre that addresses these concerns with particular reference to a nineteenth-century medical advance: anesthesia fiction. This microgenre, popular in the mid- to late nineteenth century, is typified by short stories such as Edmund Saul Dixon's "My Folly" (1854), Mary Elizabeth Braddon's "Good Lady Ducayne" (1896), and Arabella Kenealy's "A Human Vivisection" (1896), all of which are concerned specifically with the use and abuse of anesthesia.[1]

Such stories address mixed feelings about the use of anesthesia by doctors: on the one hand, the public welcomed not having to face the horror of surgery without anesthesia; on the other, anesthesia could be lethal and raised theological questions of what medical unconsciousness meant for the soul. Meanwhile, others worried that anesthesia would leave them open to abuses from unscrupulous surgeons looking to make money from unnecessary surgery, to use patients in their anatomical research, or to gather secret information from victims whose tongues are loosened by the drugs. Further, deaths occurring while the patient was under anesthesia were automatically subject to inquest, making its use of particular interest to writers of detective fiction. In addition to addressing the public's fears about medical unconsciousness, anesthesia fiction also responds to concerns about medical regulation; interestingly, this microgenre disappears after the professionalization of medicine in the late nineteenth and early twentieth centuries.

While there is no definitive list of works of anesthesia fiction, we can use databases to find rough numbers. For example, a search for the word "chloroform" in fiction in the British Periodicals Collection on ProQuest shows that between 1840 and 1859 there are thirty-five published works, but between 1860 and 1899 there are on average 125.[2] There is a sharp drop in the early twentieth century, with only forty-six hits for works published between 1900 and 1909, dropping off steadily from there. What this tells us is that the anxieties that led to the creation of anesthesia fiction were not primarily based on fear of the new and unknown. While some of the anxiety about medical overreach is owing to an underregulated medical profession, if this were the only cause, we would expect sharp drops following each of the Medical Acts. However, the issues raised in anesthesia fiction show that the public was concerned that regulation would do little to stop medical overreach. This is still the case today; we have extensive medical regulation (both by professional bodies and by the state), and yet we worry that doctors are playing God when they engage in practices like euthanasia and gene therapy.

Anesthesia and its possible abuses took hold of the public imagination shortly after its discovery (ether came into use as an anesthetic in 1846 and chloroform a year later), appearing in fiction from the mid-nineteenth century both in stories in which doctors use it benignly in surgery and in tales of criminal activity. Though anesthesia fiction deals with a variety of anesthetics (chloroform, ether, curare), it is chloroform that most captured the popular imagination. Chloroform is still popularly believed to render the victim or patient unconscious, for an indefinite period of time, in a matter of seconds after a chloroform-soaked rag is pressed to or waved in front of the face. In reality, it takes up to ten minutes to produce unconsciousness even in a willing patient, and this state is only maintained through regular, careful reapplication of chloroform. With an unwilling victim it would take longer, and only the weakest victims would not put up a struggle.

This mythic power of chloroform in (post)modern popular culture is an inheritance from the nineteenth-century anesthesia tale. Traces of the microgenre persist in twentieth- and twenty-first-century fiction, film, and television as writers and the public continue to come to terms with, and to mythologize, the extra-medical risks of anesthesia. Two recent examples are found in such diverse television series as *Castle* and *King of the Hill*: in "The Blue Butterfly," Clyde Belasco describes being instantly rendered unconscious by chloroform, and in "Now Who's the Dummy," Dale chloroforms himself to keep Hank from hitting him.[3] These examples demonstrate the afterlife of anesthesia fiction and the related anxiety over the use of chloroform.

In the nineteenth century, anesthesia appears in fiction in a variety of contexts. Tales in which anesthesia is used benignly rarely focus on anesthesia to any great extent and, therefore, cannot be considered examples of anesthesia fiction. For example, anesthesia is used benignly in 1895's "Creating a Mind" by L. T. Meade and Clifford Halifax.[4] But the story's main preoccupation is the health and mental development of the child character and the repercussions they have on his inheritance. Alternatively, in anesthesia fiction, the primary concern of the narrative is the power anesthesia gives to the surgeon who wields it. This power takes several forms: surgeons using it to perform procedures without their patient's consent, doctors using anesthesia to hide their own secrets or reveal those of their patient's, or doctors using it to gain control over their victims.

The fear that a doctor would use anesthesia to perform dangerous and medically unnecessary procedures inspired a lot of anesthesia fiction. The most well known of these is Braddon's "Good Lady Ducayne." In this story, Dr. Parravicini repeatedly chloroforms Lady Ducayne's companion, Bella, so he can take Bella's blood. He then transfuses her blood into Lady Ducayne in a bid to extend the older woman's life. It is made clear that Bella is just the latest companion to be used in this way—the others were dismissed when they became too weak to be bled. Bella is blissfully ignorant of what is happening to her; she simply thinks she is having strange dreams and waking with what Parravicini assures her are mosquito bites. As she weakens, a young doctor, Herbert Stafford, discerns the truth, puts a stop to the practice, and saves and marries Bella.

This story addresses a growing concern that young women were particularly vulnerable to being taken advantage of while under anesthesia. In the nineteenth century, several women accused medical men of violating them, with one of the most famous instances being Oscar Wilde's father, who was accused of violating Miss Travers while she was under chloroform in 1864. She later admitted, on the stand, that he had not chloroformed her but instead settled on saying chloroform was involved "because it had such a 'treacherous' reputation."[5] By "treacherous" she meant that it was a known aphrodisiac; it could make patients hallucinate sexual encounters.[6] For example, in 1877, Benjamin Ward Richardson described a young woman who had accused her dentist of sexual assault, but "fortunately for the dentist, her father and mother and two doctors" had been present during the procedure.[7] Often, though, there were either no chaperones present, or their contradiction of the patient's account was deemed insufficient. It was left to the courts to determine which claims of assault were real (some clearly were), which were made up by vengeful women, and which were hallucinations. Obviously, this left a lot of scope for the literary imagination, bound though it was by publishers seeking to appeal to the family market.

Kenealy's "A Human Vivisection" reveals an even darker fear about medical overreach. This story fails to offer a pretty young girl as a victim and an attractive young professional man who steps in to save her. Instead, only a poor man of indeterminant age who is a habitual drunkard is portrayed. In the absence of an obviously sympathetic character, this story highlights one of the greatest fears raised by the advent of chloroform. The victim is lured to the Professor's vivisection theatre on the promise that he will feel nothing as the Professor experiments on him; the victim's speech makes clear that though he is nervous, he expects to survive the ordeal. The

Professor reveals he has given his victim ten pounds to spend on alcohol in the week leading up to his vivisection by way of payment. What neither the victim nor the Professor's colleagues and students realize is that the Professor intends to let the chloroform wear off, so he can watch the effect of pain on his internal organs until he dies. Only the victim, who has no choice (he is strapped to the dissection table), and a colleague, who has drunken himself into a stupor, stay until the end. After the victim's death, the Professor's colleague raises a belated and weak objection, which the Professor dismisses by saying he is only objecting because of the shock of witnessing it for the first time, implying that his colleague and others like him will become habituated to such sights.

These stories offer extreme examples of people's anxieties about what was possible under anesthesia, but the other abuses of power are just as terrifying, if not always as lethal. In Dixon's "My Folly," Dr. Lemaire deviates from his usual practice of shouting to cover up his patients' incoherent ramblings as they went under anesthesia and uses a secret he learns about a patient against him. This is one of the earlier examples of anesthesia fiction. It is a story seemingly more concerned with the doctor's ungentlemanly behavior than with his abuse of the information that his patient had lied to a girl he took in as an orphan and hid her identity and right to the property he claimed as his own. Knowing what his patient would reveal, the next time Lemaire needs to anesthetize him, he takes his friend, the unnamed narrator, along to witness it. The narrator eventually marries the girl in question, thereby righting the wrong created by the patient, her guardian. Though the reader is expected to approve of these proceedings, the story raises the question of anesthesia's inherent risk to self-control and to patients' control over their own thoughts and feelings. This was a very real risk that was exploited by the military to detect malingering in France, Britain, and America.[8]

The fear that anesthesia could be used to violate a patient's trust grew over time. In an 1878 story called "Dr. Carrick," Braddon raises the issue as her eponymous doctor uses mesmerism to gain control over his wealthy patient in a bid to steal his property and then attempts to murder him by a chloroform overdose.[9] The patient, Squire Tregonnell, is saved by Hester, the doctor's cousin and housekeeper and later, the squire's wife. L. T. Meade and Robert Eustace's "Silenced" (1897), however, takes the threat even further.[10] In this story, a nurse is silenced by an unscrupulous surgeon, Mr. Hertslet, who does not want his beloved to learn that her long-lost fiancé is alive and under the surgeon's care. Hertslet chloroforms the nurse, makes a small hole in her skull, and destroys the part of her brain responsible for speech and writing. She is left an invalid incapable of communicating Hertslet's secret.

Meade and Eustace return to this issue in the Dr. Kort narrative in Parts III to VI of *Stories of the Sanctuary Club.*[11] Over the course of the four stories, it is revealed that Dr. Kort has chloroformed and then trephined his wife, who had also trained as a physician, to create a flap in her skull by which he can experiment on her and control her. If she is not kept in a pressure-controlled environment, she loses the ability to speak and would eventually die. Kort is found out and Drs. Cato and Chetwynd are able to save Mrs. Kort. As the century draws to a close, fear about the atrocities made possible by anesthesia shows no signs of abating.

For obvious reasons anesthesia made people feel more vulnerable than previous advances—they couldn't control what happened when they were unconscious. Anesthesia was poorly understood by the general public and, for much of the period, by medical professionals. Therefore, people quickly jumped to its possible criminal uses. All of this is exacerbated by the state of medicine in the nineteenth century. Anesthesia was discovered twelve years before the first medical reform bill (1858), and while that act went some way toward regulating medical practitioners and medical education, it would be decades before people could trust that doctors and surgeons were properly trained or their work regulated. Over the course of the nineteenth century, the regulation of medicine and especially medical qualification became more formalized. Medicine and medical training also became increasingly scientific. The nineteenth century sees the beginning of the practice of evidence-based medicine we have come to expect in the twenty-first century. Nevertheless, each scientific advance (then or now) brings ethical concerns about medical overreach. For the Victorians, these concerns were often expressed in the stories they read and wrote: experimentation on defenseless patients, unnecessary procedures, and exploitation of the poor. These are analogous to our current concerns over mitochondrial replacement therapy, gene therapy, and prenatal genetic screening. You only need to read Aldous Huxley's *Brave New World* (1932) or watch a film about genetic manipulation like *Blade Runner* (1982) to see concerns with genetic manipulation played out in narrative form.

How these fears are explored in popular media is shaped by the age in which they appear. Anesthesia fiction was published in some of the most popular family journals of the period. These include *Household Words* (1850–59) and *All the Year Round* (1859–95), both of which were founded by Charles Dickens, and *The Strand Magazine*, founded by George Newnes in 1891. In *Household Words*, Dickens famously sought to show the young and old the "Romance" of "all familiar things,"[12] while Newnes wanted to provide his readers with "[c]heap, healthful literature."[13] To be successful in these aims, such publications had to meet their readers' expectation that they were buying a magazine that would inform and entertain the whole family and that no parent need worry about leaving within reach of an impressionable child. In addition to publishing several examples of anesthesia fiction, these magazines published articles on the discovery and use of various anesthetics, as well as reports of their misuses and attendant dangers.

These publications' commitment to producing family-friendly fare has some effect on how potentially disturbing topics are dealt with within their pages. This effect is best illustrated by contrasting the treatment of anesthesia in these magazines with that found in Kenealy's story "A Human Vivisection" from *The Ludgate Magazine* (1891–1901). Also a journal that published general-interest stories along with fiction, *The Ludgate* often championed the cause of the antivivisectionists and was less inclined to shy away from the gruesome details of vivisection or give such narratives happy endings.

While the ways in which particular publications dealt with anesthesia fiction are not terribly surprising, what is surprising is that interest in this topic does not seem to wane as people became more accustomed to the use of anesthesia. It appears with persistent regularity until the opening decades of the twentieth century, meaning it took well over fifty years for the public to become comfortable with the practice of anesthesia. Looking at the scientific discoveries and historical events in the early twentieth century, it seems that the anxieties and concerns that inspired anesthesia fiction shifted to new issues; these are perhaps most famously treated in the various comic book action heroes that were developed in the twentieth century like Spiderman, Captain America, and Iron Man, as well as the ubiquitous mad-scientist villains these heroes must face. While writing about our fears of medical and scientific advancements, whether they are of newly introduced anesthetics or of radioactive spiders, may not make our fears go away, such creative exploration of the possible consequences does help us identify what risks we need to guard against.

Notes

1   Edmund Saul Dixon, "My Folly," *Household Words* 9, no. 208 (March 18, 1854): 106–14; Mary Elizabeth Braddon, "Good Lady Ducayne," *The Strand Magazine: An Illustrated Monthly* 11 (February 1896): 185–99; Arabella Kenealy, "A Human Vivisection," *The Ludgate* 2, no. 1 (May 1896): 39–46.

2   Searching for ether produces a lot of false positives because of our use of the phrase "the ether" to refer to the atmosphere. Searching for other anesthetics does not reveal very much because they were not widely known outside of medical circles.

3   *Castle*, Season 4, Episode 14; *King of the Hill*, Season 5, Episode 12.

4   L. T. Meade and Clifford Halifax, "Stories from the Diary of a Doctor: Creating a Mind," *The Strand Magazine: An Illustrated Monthly* 9 (1895): 33–46.

5   Stephanie J. Snow, *The Blessed Days of Anaesthesia: How Anaesthetics Changed the World* (Oxford: Oxford University Press, 2008), 141.

6   Though the Medicines (Chloroform Prohibition) Order of 1979 came into effect in 1980, its aphrodisiac qualities were well known, and both recreational and criminal uses of the drug continued even after it became harder to obtain (J. P. Payne, "Chloroform Abuse," *European Journal of Anaesthesiology* 14, no. 5 (1997): 521, https://journals.lww.com/ejanaesthesiology/Fulltext/1997/09000/Chloroform_abuse__1.8.aspx).

7   Snow, *Blessed Days*, 142.

8   See H. Connor, "The Use of Anaesthesia to Diagnose Malingering in the 19th Century," *Journal of the Royal Society of Medicine* 99, no. 9 (2006): 444–47.

9   Mary Elizabeth Braddon, "Dr. Carrick," *All the Year Round* 20 (July 1, 1878): 1–16.

10 L. T. Meade and Robert Eustace, "Silenced," *The Strand Magazine: An Illustrated Monthly* 14 (1897): 694–703.

11 See L. T. Meade and Robert Eustace's "Stories of the Sanctuary Club," in *The Strand Magazine: An Illustrated Monthly* (III: "The Diana Sapphire," 18 [1899]: 264–77; IV: "East of North," 18 [1899]: 437–48; V: "A Handful of Ashes," 18 [1899]: 549–61; VI: "The Secret of the Prison House," 18 [1899]: 665–78).

12 Charles Dickens, "A Preliminary Word," *Household Words*, March 30, 1850, 1–2, http://www.djo.org.uk/household-words/volume-i/page-1.html.

13 Sir George Newnes, "Editorial," *The Strand Magazine: An Illustrated Monthly* 1 (1891): 1–2.

7

Magic-Portrait Fiction

Diana Bellonby

When Oscar Wilde published *The Picture of Dorian Gray* in 1890, he gave his audience an uncannily familiar reading experience. By the late 1880s, British periodicals abounded with what I call *magic-portrait stories*: tales of male artists who paint dangerously masterful portraits of their muses.[1] Muses in magic-portrait fiction are overwhelmingly female—instruments in dramas of male madness, sexual jealousy, or thwarted marriage. Yet, Dorian Gray greets readers in the opening scene as a *male* beauty beloved by the man who paints his picture. Wilde's novel revises the heterosexual order of a genre that had steadily accrued appeal over the course of the nineteenth century before exploding in popularity during the 1880s and 1890s. Magic-portrait fiction emerged in Germany during the 1790s as a type of *Künstlerroman*, or artist novel. It became a popular story form through Romantic fusions of the artist novel and the haunted portrait in British gothic fiction. Throughout the century, magic-portrait fiction functioned as a vehicle for writers across Europe and the United States, but especially Britain, to articulate ideals and anxieties about gender and sexual identity. In the wake of Wilde's 1895 trials for "gross indecency," in which prosecutors cited passages from *Dorian Gray*, the genre sharply lost favor—and a place in the modern canon.

Magic-portrait fiction is defined by the iconic figures of male artist-hero and tragic female sitter, with the Pygmalion master narrative entangling them in a story about a portrait. In Ovid's myth of Pygmalion, a male sculptor disgusted by living women creates a statue embodying his ideal beauty; he promptly falls in love with his own masterwork, hoping to bring it to life. Conventional magic-portrait stories feature male protagonists who similarly navigate sexual desires, aesthetic ideals, and personal ambitions through the representation of a woman. In a typical tale, a male painter depicts a beautiful woman whose life or marriage depends on his pursuit of an ideal. In Edgar Allan Poe's "The Oval Portrait" (1842), for example, an artist kills his bride in the act of perfecting her portrait. The tragic sitter's image wields the power to ratify or disrupt the painter's self-image, to symbolize his authority over self/other/art or catalyze his degeneration. The genre is defined by the adaptability of its basic formula. The following survey reveals a history of idealistic, gothic, comic, realistic, and aesthetic fiction, patriarchal conservatism and queer-feminist critique, three-decker novels and one-page tales—all structured in some way by a Pygmalion fantasy of aesthetic manhood.

The genre's formal elasticity fosters many types of "magic," or mysterious influence, attributed to the painted portrait. In most works, the portrait operates as a conduit through which a male protagonist names and channels his desires. The muse's image wields power insofar as it fuels desires or effects beyond his control. In some cases, the figure appears to move, but readers discover that its lifelikeness merely reflects the artist's skill or a viewer's psychological unease. In others, the portrait generates supernatural events, such as visitations from the subject come to life. In realistic works, the painting serves as a plot-thickening means of identifying or separating lovers. What unites the various forms of magic in these stories is their interest in the relationship between human and aesthetic influence: a portrait possesses magic when its powers of representation are out of control. This archive encodes a centuries-long debate about representational control, especially men's capacity to control representations of women.

The first magic-portrait stories were borne out of late Enlightenment Germany's culture of *Bildung*, or self-cultivation, an internationally influential movement that generated new theories of education as well as new genres of fiction. The idea driving this movement was that a man could cultivate his greatest self through his appreciation of beauty. Fictions of *Bildung*, such as the *Bildungsroman* (coming-of-age novel) and *Künstlerroman* (artist's coming-of-age novel), chronicle what Friedrich Schiller called the "aesthetic education of man." The movement's founders, Schiller and Johann W. von Goethe, were immersed in neoclassical aesthetics and drawn to the male-creator myths of Prometheus and Pygmalion.[2] Goethe, Schiller, and their circle advanced a vision of freedom-through-art whereby a man's aesthetic judgment of a beautiful woman serves as an indispensable agent of his self-determination. This vision was bolstered by leading gender theories, especially that of gender "complementarity." Wilhelm von Humboldt's *Sexual Difference and Its Influence on Organic Nature* (1795) promoted the ideal of complementarity through a diagnosis of essential differences: men are striving producers, women receptive vessels. In philosophies of art, the gendered phenomena of the aestheticized world echo this binary: women embody beauty; men make, judge, use, and control it—that they may find their place in the world. Nascent genres of developmental fiction, including the magic-portrait story, were fueled by these theories.[3] The result was a Pygmalion ideology of woman-dependent narcissism, not separate-spheres complementarity, fictionalized in Romantic dramas of art-making.

Ludwig von Tieck and Wilhelm Wackenroder begin their foundational *Künstlerroman, Outpourings of an Art-Loving Friar* (1797), with "Raphael's Vision," probably the earliest magic-portrait story. The "art-loving" monk expresses awe upon reading lines recorded in a letter by Raphael: "Since one encounters so few beautiful female figures, I cling to a certain image which dwells within me."[4] This allusion to Pygmalion occasions a reflection on Raphael's tortured process of painting the Madonna. He sought in vain to portray his ideal image of the Holy Virgin until one night when he woke with a start and saw

> a brightness on the wall opposite his couch ... when he looked more closely he perceived that his picture of the Madonna, which had been hanging unfinished on the wall, was now completed and had come to life in the warm radiance. ... The eyes had gazed at him with an expression infinitely touching, and it had seemed as if the figure might move at any moment; indeed he had the impression that it did in fact move. The greatest miracle of all was that it seemed that this was the picture which he had always wanted to paint.[5]

The finished portrait secures Raphael's self-confidence and symbolizes the originality of his vision. Its lifelikeness signals Raphael's genius as a medium of art's divinity. *Outpourings* helped shift attention away from sculpture and drama, the forms privileged by neoclassical aesthetics, and toward visual art, heralding painted portraiture as a vital form for the growing number of Romantics in and beyond Germany. The haunted portrait, then a favorite device in the gothic house of horrors, guaranteed that this shift would endure.

During the 1810s and 1820s, second-generation Romantics like E. T. A. Hoffmann published hybrid literary experiments that mix German aesthetic culture and British trends in gothic fiction inspired by Matthew Lewis and Walter Scott. A painted portrait in Lewis's *The Monk* (1795–96) set an influential precedent. Lewis's titular monk, Ambrosio, idolizes a portrait of the Madonna and (like Pygmalion) distinguishes debased living women from admirable man-made images: "What charms me," Ambrosio reflects, "when ideal and considered as a superior Being, would disgust me, become Woman and tainted with all the failings of Mortality. It is not the Woman's beauty that fills me with such enthusiasm; It is the Painter's skill that I admire, it is the Divinity that I adore!"[6] Later we learn that the pictured figure is a woman named Matilda whose seduction sparks his downfall. Inspired by *The Monk*, Hoffmann wrote *The Devil's Elixirs* (1815), his own horror story of a monk's fall from grace, in which painted portraits play a structural, rather than incidental, role. In the coming years, Hoffmann published a range of magic-portrait stories, including "Der Artushof" (1816), "Die Jesuiterkirche in G." (1816), "Meister Martin der Küfner und seine Gesellen" (1819), and "Die Doppeltgänger" (1822), which variously depict male development and degeneration. The quintessential Hoffmann story revolves around a portrait through which a male hero preserves his ideal image of feminine beauty in place of the inferior woman who inspired it. Other early German magic-portrait stories, such as Tieck's *Die Gemälde* (1821), use a more realistic mode to reimagine the Pygmalion myth.

The next wave of magic-portrait fiction, appearing in France, Britain, and the United States during the 1820s, 1830s, and 1840s, demonstrates a cross-cultural fascination with men whose fates depend on their creation or judgment of pictured women. The genre flourished in gothic tales by Washington Irving, Nathaniel Hawthorne, and Edgar Allan Poe. In Irving's *Tales of a Traveller* (1824), Part I's climactic "Story of the Young Italian" tells of Ottavio, a disillusioned young man who learns how to paint from an old monk, then nurtures his talent by painting, again and again, the face of his beautiful muse, Bianca. Ottavio's hopes of marrying Bianca are thwarted when his friend marries her first, provoking Ottavio to murder his betrayer and live a wretched life of guilt soothed only by portraying the face of his dead friend. Hawthorne's painting master in "The Prophetic Pictures" (1837) captures the seeming, secret flaw in the soul of a new bride, whose enraged husband nearly murders her because of what he thinks he sees in her likeness.

The genre rose in British letters more gradually during the 1830s and 1840s as Germany's aesthetic tradition disseminated across Europe. Magic-portrait fiction may not have thrived beyond Germany were it not for the writings of Germaine de Staël, French critic, novelist, and notorious enemy of Napoleon. Staël challenged the theories of male creative superiority dominant in postrevolutionary Europe, but she also published a treatise, *On Germany* (1813), praising the latest movements in German culture. In this groundbreaking book—so controversial that it was pulped by Napoleon—Staël is credited with coining the term "Romanticism" and spreading German aesthetics across the continent. Just a few years before *On Germany* reached British readers, Staël had published *Corinne, or Italy* (1807), an internationally acclaimed artist novel about a female poet. *Corinne* paved the way for later women writers to resist the patriarchal order of artistic genius in their magic-portrait stories.

Whereas American readers of the early nineteenth century embraced dark, Hoffmannesque tales, idealistic visions of male "self-culture," as Matthew Arnold rephrased the German concept, found no shortage of ambassadors in Britain. Victorian critics Thomas Carlyle, Samuel Coleridge, and John Ruskin, all well-versed in German aesthetics, hailed the power of the male artist-citizen.[7] This optimism about the national-historical potential of men's creative energy characterizes Joseph Hardman's 1829 magic-portrait story, "Colonna the Painter: A Tale of Italy and the Arts," published in *Blackwood's Edinburgh* magazine with the help of Hardman's friend, Coleridge, who selected the story's epigraph from Goethe's *Wilhelm Meister*. Hardman's romance embraces the theme of male sexual jealousy, yet uses the act of portraiture to resolve its hero's troubles. Colonna, a sixteenth-century painter, triumphantly restores his family name, gets his sought-after wife, and murders Barozzo, the man betrothed to the woman he loves, all in the course of painting the affianced couple's marriage portraits. Meanwhile, British and French readers enjoyed plenty of magic-portrait stories about a male artist's vulnerability, such as Honoré de Balzac's "Sarrasine" (1830), *La Maison du chat-qui-pelote* (1830), and "Maître Frenhofer" (1831); Théophile Gautier's "La Cafetière" (1831); and Gérard de Nerval's "Portrait du diable" (1839). These stories traverse a thin line between patriarchal hagiography and psychological horror. From an ideology of male identity formation grounded in woman-dependent yet misogynistic narcissism comes the darkness of fragility, panic, and violence.

In 1850, magic-portrait fiction secured a paradigmatic role in the burgeoning game of high versus low culture. Dante Gabriel Rossetti used the genre to articulate his manifesto, "Hand and Soul" (1850), for the new school of art he and his cofounders called the Pre-Raphaelite Brotherhood, or PRB (see Figure 7.1). "Hand and Soul" tells the framed story of Chiaro dell' Erma, a medieval Italian painter whose portrait of a woman is discovered by a modern male museumgoer enthralled by its "literality."[8] Depressed and alone in his studio, Chiaro receives a visit from an angelic woman: "I am an image, Chiaro," she says, "of thine own soul within thee. See me, and know me as I am."[9] Chiaro's epiphany, voiced by his own soul's female image, reaches a sexually charged climax: she orders him to paint her portrait. After painting a portrait of herself/himself, Chiaro collapses as if in postcoital exhaustion. "Hand and Soul" allegorizes the creative process as a man's auto/heterosexual conquest of his aestheticized self/woman. This process serves his rejection of conventionality in favor of authenticity. The PRB is credited with inventing the avant-garde in Britain and many of the practices associated with it. Famous for polemical manifestoes, elite periodicals, and a cultish devotion to originality, "high" British modernism has its roots in Rossetti's magic-portrait story.

Pre-Raphaelite art contributed to the rise of Britain's Aesthetic Movement, a wave of interest in beauty, art, and design. For the movement's leading voices, publishing an innovative magic-portrait story became a way to assert one's position within the new cultural order—a way to demonstrate the unconventionality of one's style. Whereas Carlyle, Coleridge, and Ruskin

Figure 7.1 Illustrated title page of D. G. Rossetti's "Hand and Soul" (1850; Chicago: Way and Williams, 1895) [Newberry Library, Chicago (Wing ZP 845. K331)].

helped make the terms of Germany's *Bildung* tradition foundational to Victorian debates about the social function of art, the PRB helped brand the scene of portraiture—that of a man painting his female muse—the quintessential scene of male artistic mastery, defined as original genius. Victorian aesthetes from Ouida and Vernon Lee to Walter Pater and Oscar Wilde used the genre repeatedly. Pater, deeply influenced by German aesthetics and Pre-Raphaelite art, devoted most of his oeuvre to male artistic biography. Some of his works take the form of "Imaginary Portraits," biographical reflections that rework the magic-portrait form through homosocial reveries linking the lives of great men. Arguably Pater's most famous piece of writing is his description of the *Mona Lisa*, which he uses to anatomize Leonardo da Vinci's genius: "*La Gioconda* is, in the truest sense, Leonardo's masterpiece, the revealing instance of his mode of thought and work."[10] The lasting fame of the *Mona Lisa* illustrates the wide-ranging impact of the Pygmalion ideology popularized by magic-portrait fiction.

Ever since *Corinne*, women writers used the genre to unsettle the conceptual chain tethering heterosexual masculinity to artistic genius. In "Le Château de Pictordu" (1873), for example, George Sand's narrator tells her granddaughter a fairy tale of matrilineal artistry and self-identification featuring a female artist who paints her mother's portrait. Mary E. Penn's gothic tale for *The Argosy*, "Desmond's Model" (1879), opens with Desmond complaining that if the perfect woman "doesn't turn up soon that great picture, which was to take the public by storm next May, will never be painted."[11] Desmond finds his ideal model in Bianca, but, by story's end, his journey turns into a closer look at her suffering and near-fatal escape from a cruel husband.

As early as 1862 in "Favette and Thargelie; or, My Pastel-Portrait by La Tour," Ouida models the aesthetic prose characteristic of aesthetic fiction while announcing herself as an art critic with the imaginative power to retell the life of a woman pictured by a famous man: "sometimes," she lyricizes, "across the haze of my hookah's smoke, the full laughing lips of my pastel will part, and breathe, and speak to me of the distant past, when Thargélie Dumarsais saw all Paris at her feet, and was not humbled then as now by being only valued and remembered for the sake of the talent of La Tour."[12] Vernon Lee (pseudonym for Violet Paget) began her career as an aesthete by publishing a magic-portrait novel (and ruthlessly satirical *roman à clef*) called *Miss Brown* (1884), which details the misery inflicted on the tragic sitter-wife of an overrated Pre-Raphaelite artist. After the backlash against *Miss Brown*, Lee deployed the genre in subtler, though no less feminist tales, such as "Oke of Okehurst" (1886) and "Amour Dure" (1887). In 1884, Parisian decadent and cross-dressing *salonnière* Rachilde published her explosive *Monsieur Vénus: A Materialist Novel*, which inverts Pygmalion's gendered order. The novel won Rachilde celebrity status, but it was banned as pornographic and she was imprisoned in Brussels.

By the late 1880s, magic-portrait fiction flooded British periodicals. The rise of new visual technology had fueled, not depleted, the appeal of a form defined by the power of a painting. Popular tales, such as Beatrice Harraden's "A Painter's Love" (1887) and Baron Gardiner's "A Story of a Picture" (1888), use the portrait of a beautiful woman to explore matters of male development unrelated to artistic achievement, such as ancestry, money, and, above all, marriage. Henriette Corkran's "My First Sitter" (1885) considers the challenges faced by female portrait painters. Magic-portrait fiction of this period demonstrates the interdependency of mainstream and elite cultures, lived and fictional art histories. George Du Maurier, for example, produced in *Trilby* (1895) a record-breaking success of a magic-portrait novel that satirizes high-art culture, which he based on his own experiences with British aesthetes.

It was during this period that Oscar Wilde wrote *The Picture of Dorian Gray*. As if to ensure the novel's recognizability as a magic-portrait story, Wilde used stock tropes, such as a veiled portrait and a Hawthornian "prophetic picture." The text is a veritable mashup of earlier magic-portrait stories.[13] Works by female and queer writers—above all, Rachilde's *Monsieur Vénus*—emboldened him to reinvent the form in his own way (see Figure 7.2).[14] Paradoxically, *Dorian Gray* is as derivative as it is destructive of the genre's most familiar ingredients. The narrative begins with two men fixated on a portrait, which does exactly what portraits in conventional magic-portrait stories do: it reflects the painter's identity, symbolizes his artistic mastery, and depends for its greatness on the beauty of his muse. Wilde goes further: this sitter has inspired "an entirely new manner in art."[15] But, the muse is a man, and the triangular fixation among Dorian, Basil Hallward, and Lord Henry Wotton on Dorian's likeness leads to his complete loss of control over both his identity and his life—a decadently extreme version of the anxieties portrayed in early magic-portrait fiction. Dorian's only form of mastery is the kind accorded to women: physical beauty. The chronicle of his degeneration relishes in every form of beauty, yet refuses to offer male genius or self-possession or sexual conquest as a salve. In fact,

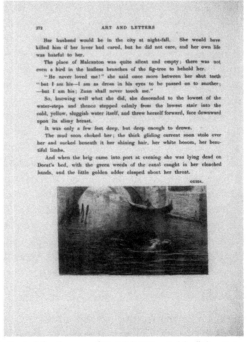

Figure 7.2 Illustrated final page of Ouida's "The Adder" (in *Arts and Letters: An Illustrated Review* (July 1888), 272) [British Periodicals Database (ProQuest)].

Basil warns that mastery is a risk, not a goal. Dorian's fall from grace shows how aestheticizing human beings kills them. His anti-heroism exposes the core of the Pygmalion fantasy—the knot that ties a man's selfhood to his aestheticized other, whether male or female—as fatally violent.

What's more, the story's female muse, Sibyl Vane, becomes a sympathetic victim of Dorian's and Lord Henry's cruelty. The root of anxieties about influence, then, cannot be attributed to that most comfortable of scapegoats: monstrous femininity. Here villainy is caused by the collusions of men and the power of art. The one unquestionably admirable thing in this narrative is Basil's love for Dorian. Nothing in this redrawn picture of male artistic identity sat comfortably with Victorian readers. The backlash was acute. Its ramifications include Wilde's imprisonment after a series of trials in which prosecutors cited passages from the novel. *Dorian Gray* recodified the genre's icons by linking the male artist with what we now call same-sex desire; magic-portrait fiction became associated with Wilde's own life and person. This association triggered the genre's decline, but it also contributed to the cultural construction of male homosexual identity as a perversion of aesthetic masculinity.

In the last decade of the nineteenth century, magic-portrait stories still appeared regularly in British magazines. Significant yet neglected tales from this period include William W. Fenn's "A Painter I Knew" (1892), J. Newton-Robinson's "An Artist's Vision" (1893), J. Fitzgerald Molloy's "The Portrait of Phillis Cromartie" (1893), and Frances Forbes-Robertson's proto-feminist "Jotchie: A Sketch" (1895) (see Figure 7.3), which features an aspiring female artist. Henry James composed at least three in the year 1900 alone ("Hugh Merrow," "The Special Type," and "The Tone of Time"), and Edith Wharton published at least three during this period: "The Portrait" (1899), "The Moving Finger" (1901), and "The Eyes" (1910). Wilhelm Jensen's *Gradiva* (1902), about a man obsessed with a woman portrayed in a Roman bas-relief, can loosely be categorized as a magic-portrait novel—one that inspired Sigmund Freud's essay, "Delusion and Dream in Jensen's *Gradiva*" (1907). Arthur Symons's "The Death of Peter Waydelin" (1905) exemplifies efforts by some modernists to resignify beauty by valorizing ugliness and terror. Excepting these works, the genre fell into obscurity after 1900. High modernists adapted the topos of the portrait and the rhetoric of aesthetic masculinity (think: James Joyce's *A Portrait of the Artist as a Young Man*), but avoided overt identification with the genre.[16] Virginia Woolf obliquely reimagined the form in *To the Lighthouse* (1927). Young artist Lily Briscoe paints a portrait of the story's dead mother, Mrs. Ramsay, but she is plagued by doubt, insecurity, Mr. Ramsay's overbearing presence, and other men's deprecations: "it would never be seen; never be hung even," Lily thinks,

Figure 7.3 Illustrated page from Frances Forbes-Robertson's "Jotchie: A Sketch" (in *The English Illustrated Magazine*, October 1895, 42) [British Periodicals Database (ProQuest)].

"and there was Mr. Tansley whispering in her ear, 'Women can't paint, woman can't write ... '"[17]

Magic-portrait fiction returned fifty years later in Hollywood films such as *Rebecca* (1940), *Laura* (1944), *Portrait of Jennie* (see Figure 7.4), and *Vertigo* (see Figure 7.5).[18] The classic scene of male-mastery-through-portraiture has reappeared in movies such as *Titanic* (see Figure 7.6) and *As Good as It Gets* (1997). In films of the early 2000s, informed by a tsunami of technological advancement, painted portraiture proves too dated a form to command interest as a narrative lynchpin. The Pygmalion premise, however, lives on in films like *Ruby Sparks* (2012, Jonathan Dayton and Valerie Faris) and *Her* (2013, Spike Jonze).[19]

Magic-portrait fiction is easy to neglect because its genealogy stretches across nearly two centuries; its origins demand familiarity with German aesthetic philosophy and a willingness to acknowledge its sexual politics. The form itself entangles many other forms—from classical mythology to coming-of-age novels to gothic devices. On top of these challenges, the genre's

Figure 7.4 Film stills with portrait from *Portrait of Jennie* (Dieterle, 1948).

Figure 7.5 Film still featuring Kim Novak from Alfred Hitchcock's *Vertigo* (1958).

Figure 7.6 Film still featuring Kate Winslet from James Cameron's *Titanic* (1997).

standing as one of the most popular forms of the late nineteenth century was eclipsed with the pernicious spread of homophobia. We neglect the genre at great cost to our understanding of how Pygmalion codes of masculinity still dictate sex and gender norms through visions of men as suffering, human creators and women as the silent, beautiful objects upon whom they depend.

Notes

1   My terminology derives from Kerry Powell's scholarship on late Victorian "magic-picture mania," which he spotted in the early 1980s, though not as a distinct genre. See Powell's "Tom, Dick, and Dorian Gray: Magic-Picture Mania in Late Victorian Fiction," *Philological Quarterly* 62, no. 2 (Spring 1983): 147–70. "Portrait story" is Michal Peled Ginsburg's term for any narrative revolving around a portrait. See his *Portrait Stories* (New York: Fordham University Press, 2015).

2   Ovid's Pygmalion myth represents the most fitting and direct precedent for magic-portrait fiction, but it is not the only one. As Maurizio Bettini argues, stories about a lover, a beloved, and the beloved's image were so common in classical culture as to constitute a "fundamental story" (Bettini, *The Portrait of the Lover*, trans. Laura Gibbs [Los Angeles: University of California Press, 1999], 4).

3   The first *Bildungsroman*, Goethe's *Wilhelm Meister's Apprenticeship* (1795), is structured by a serial courtship plot according to which Wilhelm's maturation progresses through his articulations of desire for a succession of beautiful women (Mariane, Philine, the Countess, Aurelie, Therese, Natalie). Each woman represents a phase in his growth.

4   Wilhelm Heinrich Wackenroder and Ludwig von Tieck, *Outpourings of an Art-Loving Friar*, trans. Edward Mornin (1797; New York: Frederick Ungar Publishing, 1975), 7.

5   Ibid., 8.

6   Matthew Lewis, *The Monk* (1795–96; Oxford: Oxford University Press, 2008), 41.

7   Ruskin burnished the Romantic mythology of male artistic genius in such arguments as these: "Great art is the expression of the mind of a great man, and mean art, that of the want of mind of a weak man" (Ruskin, "The Queen of the Air," in *Works*, ed. Edward Tyas Cook and Alexander Wedderburn [London: George Allen, 1905], 19: 389).

8   Dante Gabriel Rossetti, "Hand and Soul," in *The Collected Works of Dante Gabriel Rossetti*, ed. William M. Rossetti (London: Ellis and Elvey, 1890), 1: 396.

9   Ibid., 392.

10 Walter Pater, *The Renaissance: Studies in Art and Poetry* (1873; New York: Oxford University Press, 1998), 79.

11 Mary E. Penn, "Desmond's Model," *The Argosy: A Magazine of Tales, Travels, Essays, and Poems* 28 (December 1879): 478.

12 Ouida, "Favette and Thargelie; or, My Pastel-Portrait by La Tour," *Bentley's Miscellany* 51 (January 1862): 333.

13 Among the countless earlier texts echoed in *Dorian Gray* are Goethe's *Faust* (1808), Novalis's *Heinrich von Ofterdingen* (1802), Gérard de Nerval's "Portrait du diable" (1839), Hawthorne's "The Prophetic Pictures" (1837),

Savile Clarke's "The Portrait's Warning" (1868), Walter Herries Pollock's *The Picture's Secret* (1883), Rachilde's *Monsieur Vénus* (1884), D. G. Rossetti's "St. Agnes of Intercession" (1886), R. L. Stevenson's "Olalla" (1887), Arlo Bates's "A Problem in Portraiture" (1889), and Ouida's "The Adder" (1888). The subplot of Sibyl Vane reworks "The Adder" in which a peasant woman married to an angry sailor drowns herself when the artist who seduces her while painting her portrait refuses to marry her.

14   Wilde read Rachilde's *Monsieur Vénus* (1884) during his honeymoon and praised it to friends. According to Petra Dierkes-Thrun, private drafts of *Dorian Gray* reference it: Dorian's butler was originally named Jacques (the male muse in *Monsieur Vénus*) and the mysterious book that influences Dorian was initially titled *Le secret de Raoul* (Raoul is the female artist in *Monsieur Vénus*). Both references were dropped before publication.

15   Oscar Wilde, *The Picture of Dorian Gray* (1890; New York: Oxford University Press, 2006), 12.

16   As Jaime Hovey has shown, writers from T. S. Eliot and Marcel Proust to Compton Mackenzie, Djuna Barnes, and Gertrude Stein used the metaphor of portraiture to explore queer identities. See Hovey's *A Thousand Words: Portraiture, Style, and Queer Modernism* (Columbus: Ohio State University Press, 2006).

17   Virginia Woolf, *To the Lighthouse* (1927; New York: Penguin Books, 1992), 54.

18   *Portrait of Jennie* was based on a 1940 novella of the same name by American writer Robert Nathan. The screenplay for *Vertigo*, written by Alec Coppel and Samuel A. Taylor, was based on the French novel *D'entre les morts* (1954) by Boileau-Narcejac (pen name of collaborators Pierre Boileau and Thomas Narcejac).

19   Twentieth-century cinematic adaptations of Pygmalion include *My Fair Lady* (1964), *Blowup* (1966, based on Julio Cortázar's short story "Las Babas del Diablo"), *Mannequin* (1987), and surely others not named here.

8

Topographical Reports of the American Frontier

John Hay

On March 9, 1853, former Secretary of the Navy James Kirke Paulding wrote to Colonel John James Abert, chief of the Corps of Topographical Engineers. Paulding had just finished reading a government document published a few years earlier: the Report of the Examination of New Mexico in the Years 1846–47 by Abert's son, Lieutenant James William Abert. "The style in which this Report is placed before the Public both as to Paper and printing is a disgrace to the Country and to the Congress that permitted such an abortion to be laid before them," Paulding complained. "I ... cannot help sympathising with Lieut. Abert, and his brother officers when they saw their excellent production thus marred in every possible way by misspelling of words, perversions of sense, and mistakes in almost every scientific name Geological, Botanical, and Zoological."[1]

This vitriolic letter ultimately says less about the quality of Abert's text than it does about the serious consideration such government reports on western lands were suddenly receiving as literary publications. Prior to becoming a statesman, Paulding had been an acclaimed author, his titles including the 1818 epic poem *The Backwoodsman* and the 1832 novel *Westward Ho!* His attention to the production values of Abert's report indicates a recognition that state-sponsored topographical surveys were now part of a much larger literary marketplace.

U.S. government reports very rarely reach a popular readership. The few that have become best sellers have tended to address either scandal (the 1998 *Starr Report*) or conspiracy (the 2004 *9/11 Commission Report*). But in the 1840s and 1850s, in the wake of celebrated accounts by John C. Frémont (nicknamed the "Pathfinder"), reports from federally funded frontier expeditions captured the attention of the American public. Frémont's report was "one of novelty, boldness, perseverance, peril and suffering, seldom paralleled in the annals of adventure, and never surpassed by anything that we have read," raved a contemporary review.[2] Many other reports followed, and these topographical texts shared many formal qualities. They are usually presented as daily journal entries that mix narrative description (trials and triumphs, struggles and successes, excursions and encounters) with observational detail (flora and fauna, latitude and longitude, altitude and temperature), and the reports are almost always accompanied by updated maps, charts, and illustrations—perhaps not unlike the material appended to the Tolkienesque world-making fantasies of today.[3] These mid-nineteenth-century state-sponsored reports combined the most compelling features of science and literature to achieve a brief moment of popularity in the years prior to the U.S. Civil War.

Travel narratives generally constituted a major literary genre of that time. Now-forgotten globe-trotters such as Bayard Taylor then enjoyed massive sales and critical praise. "During the first half of the nineteenth century," observes one scholar, "only religious writings exceeded in quantity the number of travel books reviewed and the number of travel narratives published in American journals."[4] Many of these works in the early 1800s were guidebook-style personal impressions of trips to the Old World with titles such as James Fenimore Cooper's *Gleanings in Europe* (1837). But a growing list of prominent publications focused on travels at home rather than abroad—excursions, that is, to America's western frontier.

Accounts of frontier exploration and discovery are arguably among the earliest contributions to American literature. But well-organized, federally funded projects to map territory and collect data seriously got under way following the Louisiana Purchase in 1803. The most famous report published in these early years is the *History of the Expedition under the Command of Captains Lewis and Clark* (1814), a major literary milestone that eventually found devoted readers across the nation. It would later become "a text that explorers and travelers, and even the hacks who didn't get out of the dining car, carried with them."[5] Other accounts of the new territory also appeared at the time—Zebulon Pike's *Account of Expeditions to the Sources of the Mississippi*, for instance, was published in 1810—but such publications were not prolific enough to constitute a new genre. Even the enormous fame of the Lewis and Clark expedition failed to translate into more than modest book sales in the early decades of the century, and many copies of the narrative "languished on the booksellers' shelves."[6]

But then interest in western travel writing waxed considerably in the 1830s. When Washington Irving (considered by many the greatest American writer of the age) returned to the United States in 1832 after spending nearly two decades in Europe (and basing many of his famous tales on his travels), he set his sights to the West, publishing in quick succession *A Tour on the Prairies* (1835), *Astoria* (1836), and *The Adventures of Captain Bonneville* (1837)—the first a personal narrative, the others works of historical nonfiction. Following Irving's lead, other writers scored hits with individual accounts of western travel, including Edmund Flagg's *The Far West* (1838), Richard Henry Dana, Jr.'s *Two Years before the Mast* (1840), Josiah Gregg's *Commerce of the Prairies* (1844), and Francis Parkman's *The Oregon Trail* (1849).[7]

These titles were all accounts by private individuals that largely focused on personal adventure and did not always include the most accurate information. They were far more literary than scientific. Because reliable data was desirable, the U.S. Army established the Corps of Topographical Engineers in 1838 to provide detailed surveys of lands west of the Mississippi River. The topographical reports that began to appear in the 1840s unexpectedly featured intriguing aesthetic qualities. William Goetzmann's 1959 study of these technical documents, which remains the scholarly authority, characterizes them as taking a literary bent: "Incidents were selected, episodes heightened, characters drawn, and exotic background sketched in, so that often the scientific report read like a draft of Walter Scott or Francis Parkman."[8] James Simpson, for example, describes the "towering sublimity" of New Mexico's Cabezon Peak in 1849: "As the morning sun threw its golden light upon its eastern slope, leaving all the other portions in a softened twilight shade, I thought I had never seen anything more beautiful, and at the same time grand."[9] In a different register, Joseph C. Ives relates the "unaffected contempt" and mocking laughter showered on his crew by Paiute Natives unimpressed by the slow progress of the mission's steamboat up the Colorado River in 1858.[10]

In short, these topographical reports constituted a literary microgenre that flourished from the 1840s to the 1870s. Four traits distinguish the texts forming this microgenre: (1) they were funded by the U.S. government; (2) they were written by engineers (rather than professional men of letters); (3) they take the form of dated journal entries; and (4) they reached a popular audience. The microgenre, which remained vibrant for about thirty years, was largely initiated by the immensely influential early work of John C. Frémont, author of one of the first reports commissioned by the Corps of Topographical Engineers.

The results of Frémont's first trip to the Rockies in 1842 were printed by the U.S. Senate the following year in an edition of one thousand copies. Word quickly got around that it was an uncommon document, and Frémont was immediately sent back to the frontier on a second, longer expedition to Oregon. When he returned, his second report was combined with the first and published in 1845 as the *Report of the Exploring Expedition to the Rocky Mountains in the Year 1842, and to Oregon and North California in the Years 1843–'44.* Congress ordered a then-unheard-of print-run of ten thousand copies. As a public document, it was not protected by copyright, and independent publishers such as New York's Daniel Appleton printed their own editions. Sales were strong for several different firms, and over the next dozen years it would become one of the most celebrated books in America. "It is almost impossible to overstate the enthusiasm with which the nation greeted the printed reports of the first two western expeditions," observe Donald Jackson and Mary Lee Spence.[11]

Frémont and his exploits are certainly known to U.S. historians, but the tremendous cultural and literary impact of his *Report* has often been overlooked by literary scholars. Admirers of his writing included Ralph Waldo Emerson, Walt Whitman, and John Greenleaf Whittier. Henry David Thoreau was inspired by the *Report* to measure the depth of Walden Pond while he lived there in 1846.[12] "Frémont has particularly touched my imagination," wrote Henry Wadsworth Longfellow, who borrowed details from the narrative when composing his best-selling epic *Evangeline* (1847)—even adopting the name of one of Frémont's favorite companions, Basil Lajeunesse, for an Acadian character in his poem.[13] Later writers such as Joaquin Miller and Willa Cather also claimed to be influenced by Frémont's *Report*.

What was so groundbreaking about this government document? Frémont's book is a "hybrid text"—a work of topographical engineering, military reconnaissance, scientific study, and personal adventure.[14] The *Report* is flush with data; the reader is hit with a ceaseless barrage of measurements, and the scientific instruments—barometers, thermometers, chronometers, sextants, telescopes—become central characters in the plot. Descriptions of western scenery and wintry conditions are accented with Latin binomials for the vegetation and long digressions on geological strata. Frémont's literary success was due to his ability to take this corpus of scientific observations and transform it into a compelling narrative. He consistently mixes dry scientific facts with juicy accounts of adventure, evincing a "poetic ardor" that, as Allan Nevins observed, had "never before appeared in an official report" (see Figure 8.1).[15] Frémont never hesitates to describe "a view of the utmost magnificence and grandeur" or to praise the "wonderful surefootedness" of his mules. His companions, especially mountain man Kit Carson, become rugged American heroes. They relish the romance of discovery and exult in "standing where never human foot had stood before."[16]

The very form of Frémont's *Report* was both interesting and influential. It appears as a journal, with entries following specific dates, but Frémont did not actually keep a journal on his expeditions; he merely took field notes. When he returned home, his wife, Jessie, helped him to organize and expand these notes into a coherent narrative. "I write more easily by dictation," Frémont later admitted in his *Memoirs*. He thus generated his "journal" after the fact

Figure 8.1 *Col. Fremont Planting the American Standard on the Rocky Mountains*
(New York: Bake & Godwin, 1856) [Library of Congress: LC-DIG-pga-03521].

through discussions with Jessie, who acted as his "amanuensis."[17] So while
the content is factual, the form is something of a fiction. Frémont was not
composing his *Report* in broken snatches by moonlight, even though some
entries appear in the present tense. The sheer weight of these published entries
impressed contemporary readers. As one reviewer remarked, "Seldom has it
happened that any *journal* has been crowded with such masses of material,
and on such numerous and various subjects, or fraught with such respectable
contributions to the general intelligence of the age."[18] "The narrative's journal
format—with its tacit conceit that, at each turn, its author doesn't know what
lies ahead—preserved an in medias res sense of drama," notes biographer
Tom Chaffin, and "it also gave the Frémonts the freedom to structurally shape
the narrative, to give the story the tautness of a good adventure novel."[19]

Frémont's *Report* was so famous as to become a silent stylistic influence
over hundreds of pioneer diarists in the coming years.[20] Most such accounts
were private, but the U.S. annexation of Texas in 1845 and the ensuing
Mexican–American War (1846–48) brought forth several new reports funded
by the U.S. government. Texts such as George Wilkins Kendall's *Narrative of*

the *Texan Santa Fé Expedition* (1844) and James W. Abert's *Reconnaissance of Colorado, New Mexico, Texas, and Oklahoma* (1845) portrayed a new world that, in John O'Sullivan's famous 1845 phrase, had come to seem part of the nation's "manifest destiny." The 1848 Treaty of Guadalupe Hidalgo, which ended the war, resulted in enormous southwestern territorial gains for the United States. And the discovery of gold in California in the same year only added fuel to the fire. Pioneers pouring into the West were eager for information about the terrain, and they favored reliable reports.

William Emory's *Notes of a Military Reconnaissance* (1848), a notable title in this microgenre, was the most significant of these reports stemming from the war. Emory was a topographical engineer who carried Frémont's work with him when he accompanied General Stephen Kearny's "Army of the West" on a campaign to capture California. In detailed journal entries, Emory wonders at his first vision of ancient adobe ruins and weeps at his first mouthful of spicy red chili. He describes the strangeness of the desert environment—petroglyphs, geodes, mirages, tarantulas, cacti. "I was struck most forcibly with the fact that not one object in the whole view, animal, vegetable, or mineral, had any thing in common with the products of any State in the Union," Emory remarks at one point.[21] These exotic qualities fascinated Eastern readers, whose sense of their own country now had to expand to include such features. As they had with Frémont's *Report*, Congress ordered an additional ten thousand copies to be printed, and private publishers also released their own editions.

Following the Mexican–American War, the federal government continued to fund topographical research as part of the United States and Mexican Boundary Survey—research that was heavily influenced by studies for a southern transcontinental railroad route. Discrepancies and inconsistencies on the border, especially in what is now southern Arizona, led to the Gadsden Purchase of 1854, the last large land acquisition for the contiguous United States. William Emory authored the final official report of the Boundary Survey, but ex-commissioner John Russell Bartlett's prodigious 1854 *Personal Narrative of Explorations* is a more powerful literary document to emerge from this postwar project of mapping and exploration, particularly for its poetic emphasis on the antiquity and desolation of the region (especially in its focus on the region's ruins).[22]

Other significant reports, such as Ives's *Report upon the Colorado of the West*, continued up to the outbreak of the Civil War. This interbellum period, from 1848 to 1861, constituted what one historian called a "great reconnaissance" of western lands.[23] But—as with so many genres and categories of American literature—the Civil War disrupted the production and reception of these romantic surveys. The Corps of Topographical Engineers was folded back into the regular Corps of Engineers in 1863. Western exploration did not halt, but the reports more and more took on the character of technical studies for a select readership. In 1879, various extant projects were consolidated into the U.S. Geological Survey, and by then they were no longer perceived as missions of romantic discovery.[24] Daring poetic explorers had been replaced by dutiful professional scientists.

John Wesley Powell's 1869 expedition through the Grand Canyon resulted in what is perhaps the last great work in this microgenre, his *Exploration of the Colorado River of the West and Its Tributaries* (1875) (see Figure 8.2). Powell, who had lost his right arm at Shiloh, experienced thrilling dangers and witnessed sublime beauties, but when he had reported his data to Congress he expressed little interest in publishing a narrative, only doing so years later at the insistence of others. "The exploration was not made for adventure, but purely for scientific purposes, geographic and geologic," he recalled. "I had no intention of writing an account of it, but only of recording the scientific results."[25]

Figure 8.2 From J. W. Powell, "The Cañons of the Colorado" (*Scribner's Monthly* 9.3 (January 1875), 305) [Image courtesy of the University of Arizona Library].

In the early years of the nineteenth century, books about the frontier tended to be literary texts by solitary adventurers. Then, from the 1840s through the 1870s, the fearless explorer and the field researcher were combined in the figure of the topographical engineer narrating a mission of aesthetic discovery. But the scientist ultimately prevailed, and before the end of the century, as Frederick Jackson Turner famously observed, the frontier had come to a close.

Notes

1   Ralph M. Aderman, ed., *The Letters of James Kirke Paulding* (Madison: University of Wisconsin Press, 1962), 536.

2   "Frémont's Expeditions," *U.S. Magazine and Democratic Review* 17 (July 1845): 75.

3   For an excellent account of the illustrated material in these reports, see Ron Tyler, "Illustrated Government Publications Related to the American West, 1843–1863," in *Surveying the Record: North American Scientific Exploration to 1930*, ed. Edward C. Carter II (Philadelphia: American Philosophical Society, 1999), 147–72.

4   Larzer Ziff, *Return Passages: Great American Travel Writing, 1780–1910* (New Haven: Yale University Press, 2000), 59.

5   Kris Fresonke, *West of Emerson: The Design of Manifest Destiny* (Berkeley: University of California Press, 2003), 44.

6   John L. Allen, "'Of This Enterprize': The American Images of the Lewis and Clark Expedition," in *Voyages of Discovery: Essays on the Lewis and Clark Expedition*, ed. James P. Ronda (Helena: Montana Historical Society Press, 1998), 265.

7   Riding this wave, in 1842 Harper and Brothers published a revised and abridged version of the nearly-out-of-print *History of the Expedition* of Lewis and Clark, which went through several editions in the coming years.

8   William H. Goetzmann, *Army Exploration in the American West, 1803–1863* (New Haven: Yale University Press, 1959), 19.

9   James H. Simpson, *Journal of a Military Reconnaissance, from Santa Fé, New Mexico, to the Navajo Country* (Philadelphia: Lippincott, 1852), 29.

10   Joseph C. Ives, *Report upon the Colorado River of the West, Explored in 1857 and 1858* (Washington: Government Printing Office, 1861), 56.

11   Introduction to *The Expeditions of John Charles Frémont, Volume 1: Travels from 1838 to 1844* (Urbana: University of Illinois Press, 1970), xix.

12   Laura Dassow Walls, *Seeing New Worlds: Henry David Thoreau and Nineteenth-Century Natural Science* (Madison: University of Wisconsin Press, 1995), 110.

13 Samuel Longfellow, *Life of Henry Wadsworth Longfellow with Extracts from His Journals and Correspondence*, 3 vols. (Boston: Houghton, Mifflin, 1893), 2:65–66.

14 Michael Bryson describes Frémont's reports as "hybrid texts" in which "the discourses of science and of literature meet and interact creatively—data points are juxtaposed with straight narrative, geological speculation with rhapsodic description of the landscape, botanical observations with buffalo chases" (*Visions of the Land: Science, Literature, and the American Environment from the Era of Exploration to the Age of Ecology* [Charlottesville: University of Virginia Press, 2002], 3).

15 Allan Nevins, *Fremont: Pathmarker of the West* (1939; New York: Longmans, Green, 1955), 121.

16 John C. Frémont, *Frémont's First Impressions: The Original Report of His Exploring Expeditions of 1842–1844*, ed. Anne F. Hyde (Lincoln: University of Nebraska Press, 2012), 74, 85, 87.

17 John Charles Frémont, *Memoirs of My Life* (Chicago: Belford, Clarke, 1887), 163. In *Jessie Benton Fremont: A Biography* (Norman: University of Oklahoma Press, 1988), Pamela Herr argues that Jessie was basically a coauthor of the *Report*. Herr sees "a tension in the narrative between the West of potential settlement—a West Jessie might live in—and the West of poetry and adventure that John preferred" (112).

18 "Frémont's Expeditions," *U.S. Magazine and Democratic Review* 17 (July 1845): 72.

19 Tom Chaffin, *Pathfinder: John Charles Frémont and the Course of American Empire* (New York: Hill and Wang, 2002), 143.

20 According to Andrew Menard, "By the end of the decade [the 1840s] Frémont had become so famous as to be almost invisible as an influence. Hundreds of gold rush diaries would mimic his reports without even bothering to acknowledge them" (*Sight Unseen: How Frémont's First Expedition Changed the American Landscape* [Lincoln: University of Nebraska Press, 2012], xxii).

21 W. H. Emory, *Notes of a Military Reconnaissance, from Fort Leavenworth, in Missouri, to San Diego, in California* (Washington: Wendell and Van Benthuysen, 1848), 77. For more on Emory, see L. David Norris, James C. Milligan, and Odie B. Faulk, *William H. Emory: Soldier-Scientist* (Tucson: University of Arizona Press, 1998).

22 For an excellent account of Bartlett's work, see Robert Lawrence Gunn, *Ethnology and Empire: Languages, Literature, and the Making of the North American Borderlands* (New York: New York University Press, 2015), 145–76.

23 Edward S. Wallace, *The Great Reconnaissance: Soldiers, Artists and Scientists on the Frontier, 1848–1861* (Boston: Little, Brown, 1955). Wallace declared that Ives's *Report* is "the most readable and entertaining narrative of all the official reports by topographical engineers on Western explorations" (175).

24   On the western surveys of the 1860s and 1870s, see Matthew N. Johnston, *Narrating the Landscape: Print Culture and American Expansion in the Nineteenth Century* (Norman: University of Oklahoma Press, 2016), 146–85.

25   J. W. Powell, *The Exploration of the Colorado River and Its Canyons* (New York: Dover, 1961), iii. For a critical examination of Powell's claim, see José Liste Noya, "'Too Vast, Too Complex, Too Grand': Writing Space in John Wesley Powell's *Exploration of the Colorado River and Its Canyons*," *Western American Literature* 51.1 (Spring 2016): 1–38, esp. 5–6.

9

Grangerism

Megan Becker-Leckrone

One of my earliest memories is of working with as much precision a child under five could muster to cut out a printed, colorful illustration—the image was large, had a fold, was made of paper, and *published*—and affixing it to some other paper. I was very proud of my accomplishment: "I have made something very good," I thought. My proud moment then went sideways, and my parents' reaction made it indelibly clear that what I'd done was actually *very bad*. This reception from my most loyal fan base taught me that an act I considered creative was, in fact, destructive to the things that, even then, I loved. I learned, even before I understood the concepts of property and propriety, that there are things we do not do to books. It was not until several decades after my private episode that I realized there was a name for what I'd done: grangerism. It took longer still for me to realize that the rich and serious history associated with the practice has been fraught with the all the social ambivalence and material complexity encapsulated in my own primal scene of bibliographic defilement.

Grangerism, in the simplest definition, is the practice of cutting and pasting illustrations or other material into published books. It draws its name from Reverend James Granger (1723–76), an Oxfordshire Vicar and author of a single, two-volume text, *A Biographical History of England, from Egbert to the Great Revolution* (1769), that combines an inventory of extant historical engravings with brief biographical sketches of the figures depicted. Searching "grangerism" in the online *Oxford English Dictionary* (*OED*) yields first a transitive verb, "grangerize," followed by a cluster of nominal and adjectival variations: grangerism, grangerite, grangerized. Curiously, though the eponymous textual practice sprang up almost immediately following the May 1769 publication of Granger's book, by the mid-nineteenth century it had markedly lost its appeal and prestige. All *OED* usage citations are confined to a single decade (1881–89). This belatedness, this discontinuity between what came to be the common name *for* the practice and the proper name of the author who inspired it, is significant. In the space between James Granger and "grangerism," we can trace a clear transformation.

What started as a respectable, if eccentric, pastime for the elite (part of an actually long-standing and venerable tradition of "extra-illustration") was gradually devalued to a species of textual vandalism, or even madness. With varying degrees of irony, Victorian and Edwardian commentators diagnosed "grangeritis" as a readerly disease, and the "biblioclasts," "book ghouls," and "bibliomaniacs" who succumbed to it figures of pity and revulsion.

This mixed assessment has remained with grangerism ever since. One can read a certain history of ideas about books as such in the consolidation of disapproval around the practice of grangerism, an anxiety about books as commercial products and an often-unacknowledged investment in concepts of originality and singularity. It also marks the locus of basic, yet persistent, misunderstandings, perpetuated by no less than the *OED* itself: "In 1769 James Granger published a 'Biographical History of England,' with blank leaves for the reception of engraved portraits or other pictorial illustrations of the text. The filling up of a 'Granger' became a favourite hobby, and afterwards other books were treated in the same manner."[1]

Though an amateur print collector himself, Granger in fact neither practiced nor encouraged grangerism, at least not wittingly. Envisioning a narrow audience of fellow collectors and fellow bibliophiles, he humbly describes his project, in the book's full title, as "a methodical catalogue of engraved British heads ... interspersed with variety of anecdotes, and memoirs of a great number of persons," aimed at "reducing our biography to a system and help[ing] the knowledge of portraits."[2] The book was a surprise hit. Its reception spurred Granger to publish a large *Supplement of Corrections and Large Additions* in 1774, and, in 1775, a second edition of the *Biographical History* that included all the material of the *Supplement*.[3] None of these volumes contained a single illustration, nor blank leaves for other readers to supply their own.

A historically specific species of an older, more varied practice of "extra-illustration" that has been a source of widespread bibliographic scholarship and a major contribution to the holdings of museums and research libraries, "grangerism" proper has been relegated to the margins of book history, subject to misinformation and misunderstanding. Ironically, the effacement of Granger's *History* from the history of grangerism results from the staying power of the name. "Grangerism" has come to serve "as a byword for extra-illustration" writ large.[4] Book historian Heather Jackson concurs, noting it is "the preferred term in British libraries" for extra-illustration and that "the *OED* treats them as synonyms."[5]

Enthusiasts of Granger's history reanimated a form of "extra-illustration" intense and specific enough for Granger's name, for good or ill, to become indelibly associated with the practice. Among men of sufficient wealth and inclination, *A Biographical History of England* was immediately read as "an organized list of desiderata," inspiring them to acquire and exhibit the illustrations the book described.[6] A letter from Whig member of Parliament Richard Bull to Granger expresses this exuberant, exorbitant interpretation with particular clarity: it was not simply a catalogue or history, but a call to action: "I shall have pleasure in shewing you that I am endeavouring to follow your plan as near as I can." For Bull, that "endeavor" culminated in thirty-six bound folio volumes "enriched," book historian Lucy Peltz tells us, "with upwards of 14,500 rare, historic, contemporary and curious English portraits."[7] Bull's grangerized Granger now resides in the Huntington Library in Pasadena, California. From this reception, Bull's voluminous production, and eventually that of many others, grangerism was born.

Within decades of Granger's *History*, interest in fashioning unique, elaborately embellished versions of his book extended to other histories, inventories, and travelogues—some from earlier works like Edward Hyde, Earl of Clarendon's *History of the Rebellion* (1702–04), others from nearly contemporaneous publications, like Thomas Pennant's *Tour in Wales* (1778) and Henry Bromley's *Catalogue of English Prints* (1793). Authors like Pennant even began, enterprisingly, to publish books expressly intended for grangerizing. The same sense of opportunity seized men like Richard Bull, Mark Noble, and William Richardson, all instrumental in keeping Granger's text in circulation well after its original author's death. Their additions and editions of *A Biographical History* are so woven into its textual history that digital searches of it are as likely to pull up literal spin-offs as they are Granger's original (see Figure 9.1).

Grangerists like Bull sold or published their new creations, thus giving the practice a wider audience, and the mechanical reproduction of the once-rare plates its practitioners brought into greater circulation devalued them in the process. The introduction of republication and trade into what was, "during the 1770s," regarded as a "genteel and rarefied pastime" devalued the practice. Commentators complained that the growing popularity of the practice left a slaughter of "cannibalized" and "mutilated" books in their wake, and blamed "grangerites" for driving up the price of existing "books with engraved portraits to five times their normal value." Others have disputed these charges as unsubstantiated, and even the most widely cited expressions of opprobrium are less scolding and scandalized than they are made to appear.[8] It is often hard to determine if detractors' defense of the book as a sacred, inviolable object was motivated purely by such lofty ideals or mixed with anxieties about disseminating an interest in extra-illustration to another class of book buyers. Peltz points to one entrepreneurial effort to turn "book breaking" into the marketplace as an illustration of the overdetermined

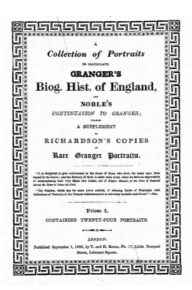

Figure 9.1 *A Collection of Portraits to Illustrate Granger's Biographical History of England, and Noble's Continuation of Granger; Forming a Supplement to Richardson's Copies of Rare Granger Portraits. Volume E, Containing Twenty-Four Portraits* (London: T. and H. Rodd, 1820) [Archive.org].

reactions to an activity that was, by the 1840s, already losing its appeal. An obscure advertisement appears in 1847 for an apparently short-lived business venture called "The Destruction Room"—a kind of "Color Me Mine" *avant la lettre* (see Figure 9.2).[9] The shop supplied surplus magazine and blank folios for "gentleman and ladies" to engage in onsite grangerism. The advertisement shows a large, high-ceilinged "room full of interesting Books, or at least when cut up will be so." It sold what grangerism originally afforded to a privileged few: namely, the chance to transform public materials into a unique, private object. It furnished such materials, "quietly waiting an opportunity to be changed from generals to particulars." Peltz surmises from the "lack of other references" to this venture that it was not a success, and her own reference to the short-lived venture signals a key focus of her study: namely, the precipitous decline of grangerism's cache in the nineteenth and early twentieth centuries. That is the chief conceit of Holbrook Jackson's deliberately odd catalogue of bibliophilic eccentricity, *The Anatomy of Bibliomania* (1930), the most exhaustive compendium of nineteenth-century invective against grangerism. Fashioned in style and method after Robert Burton's famously odd *Anatomy of Melancholy* (1621), Jackson's *Anatomy* describes its subject as "a fair analysis of books and their meaning for all kinds of men and women, with a particular relation of the madness engendered by them and for them in whose extreme cases ... I have explicated."[10] Jackson's penultimate section of the *Anatomy* dwells on a related mania, "grangeritis," which he treats as a disease to be "diagnosed."[11] But without context, one might miss that Jackson's opprobrium is almost entirely tongue in cheek, gently mocking the chorus of disapproving critics he collates encyclopedically. In his antic arrangement, those afflicted with "grangeritis" seem tame when juxtaposed to other of his "extreme cases" of bibliomania. Entire chapters are devoted—again, with a tinge of ironic glee—to those who hoard books, "destroy," "hunt," steal, read or don't read, even "eat" them; to books "bound in human skin," "fragrant volumes," those devoured by the "bookworm"; to using books as medicine, "soporifics," substitutes for human companionship; to the places books are read, "on a journey," "at mealtimes," "in bed," and "on the toilet."

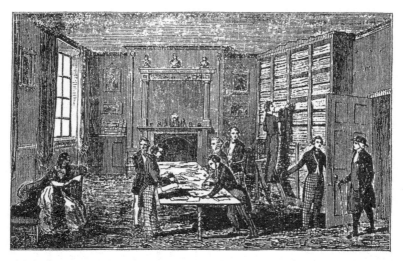

VIEW OF

The Destruction Room, 117, Long Acre.

A room full of interesting Books, or at least when cut up will be so, as far as regards the places they refer to, and quietly waiting an opportunity to be changed from generals to particulars.

117, *Long Acre, August*, 1847.

Figure 9.2 Image/Engraving: *The Destruction Room* advertisement (Peltz, "Facing the Text," 92) [Woodcut vignette from *A Complete Set of Prints, Cuttings, and Pamphlets, from the Gentleman's Magazine, from 1831–1847* (London, c. 1847), 17].

Jackson's chapter "Books as Furniture" has a contemporary feel for anyone who has read home design blogs espousing the decorative pleasure of arranging book spines by color or size, or even creating a snowy minimalist homescape by shelving them with the spines hidden altogether. Jackson disdains the "idle book-hunters" who care nothing for their content, for whom books are "nothing but fashionable furniture."[12] His extreme case, the seventeenth-century Florentine Antonio Magliabechi, whose "library numbered over 50,000 volumes," goes far beyond decoration. Magliabechi, "in his great passion for books," did not merely furnish his home with books, he fashioned a home out of them. "He lived in a cavern of books, slept on them, wallowed in them; they were his bed and board, his only furniture, his chiefest need."[13]

My own primal act of book breaking, in its material specificity, pins me to a moment in time that seems vanishingly old-fashioned: I belong to the last generation for whom the concept of cutting and pasting a block of text or an image would retain a literal meaning and the negative value I was taught to attach to the act. "Cut and paste" has become such a basic function of digital literacy—aural, visual, verbal, textual—that it has lost the status of metaphor. It no longer refers back to an act that breaks up the integrity of some whole, original thing, but now names a fundamental tool for making things as such. In 1996, producer and turntablist DJ Shadow released the first "original" album ("Endtroducing ... ") made entirely of sampled sound, gleaned from a personal collection purported to exceed 50,000 records. It is now widely regarded as a groundbreaking masterpiece. When someone told my young niece, several years ago, "you sound like a broken record," her astute response was, "what's a 'record'?"

There was music before there were records, of course, but all record of musical composition, before the inventions of technology to transmit or reproduce it, was written. Before there were records, there were books, and the functions they served, both officially and unofficially, publicly and privately, belong to a rich and strange history. Those who amassed giant collections did things with them in private, the traces of which exist largely in the margins of book, art, or literary history. In his provocative survey of "Renaissance Books as Furniture," with a nod to Jackson's infamous categorizations, Jeffrey Todd Knight argues that the literary critical tradition of treating "books as information," as neutral vehicles of meaning, overlooks their rich and varied status "as objects or things." Books have always functioned as complex social objects, "with multiple functions, none of which was fully determined by its text."[14] The functions books served in Renaissance households—as places to record family events like births and deaths, debts and lists of property, and much more—draws attention to all of the ways the uses and meaning of books exceed the default assumption that they are mere containers for textual meaning. In his linked studies, *Paratexts* and *Palimpsests*, literary theorist Gérard Genette makes a similar point: we assume that a "literary work consists, entirely or essentially, of a text, defined (very minimally) as a more or less long sequence of verbal statements that are more or less endowed with significance." But how that text is literally *presented* to us, made present to us, matters too. Paratext includes an author's name, title pages, tables of content, prefaces, illustrations, and Genette's book is arranged as a catalogue that accounts for all these and more. These are "what enables a text to become a book and to be offered as such to its readers and, more generally, to the public."[15]

In the rapidly evolving digital age, it is obvious that the myriad ways we juxtapose sound, text, and image have radically redefined our concepts of originality, creativity, art, and information. Indeed, those definitions are in constant flux. Any attempt to account for, much less catalog, all the new modes of expression invented by new ways of organizing sound, text, and image seems impossible, because the possibilities seem infinite and ever new. "Viral" has become the byword for the speed and reach of digital expression, and the ominous, even dangerous, undertone of that descriptor is significant. We marvel at these possibilities, celebrate certain products of them, and fear others; and for every unlikely and previously unimaginable masterpiece, there are far more products whose value is dubious, or worse.

This state of the arts is indisputable. Grangerism, and the art of extra-illustration more generally, reminds us of what we less often realize: that it has always been so. Against definitive assertions that "book lovers are united in condemning this pastime now," there exists voluminous evidence in archives and special collections that an exuberant will to grangerize persisted throughout the nineteenth century and well into the twentieth century. The December 1960 Sotheby's auction of Max Beerbohm's private library and manuscripts included hundreds of "books 'improved' … by the additions of drawings, caricatures or other decorations, notes and parodies, altered illustrations, and mock presentation inscriptions."[16] Beerbohm scratched at frontispiece portraits with a penknife to create subtractive white space, transforming the dignified countenances of Robert Browning and Leo Tolstoy into toothy fops with darting eyes and tapered fingernails (see Figure 9.3). Subtractive layers of black ink turn Stéphane Mallarmé into a pointy-eared, microcephalic ghoul. Other "improvements" were additive: Beerbohm gives the engraved head of Henrik Ibsen a comically yellowed beard, a florid face, set atop a cartoonishly diminutive body. In an antic literalization of Herbert Trench's *Apollo and the Seaman*, Beerbohm merges a newspaper cutout of a shirtless athlete, a crude engraving of a grizzled sailor, and a pencil sketch of a ship at sea.

Figure 9.3 Portrait of Leo Tolstoy, 1897 [Library of Congress]; Colorized frontispiece to Leo Tolstoy, *What Is Art?* (trans. Aylmer Maude (New York: Thomas Crowell, 1899)) [Archive.org]; Beerbohm's "improved" portrait of Leo Tolstoy [Mark Samuels Lasner Collection, University of Delaware].

Beerbohm died in 1956; in the next decade, Terry Gilliam's cut-out animation drove the antic absurdism of *Monty Python's Flying Circus*. Like those inspired by Granger's *Biographical History of England* to cut and paste singular, idiosyncratic national histories, Gilliam's animation draws deeply from familiar signs of Englishness—grangerism for a new century. Both in technique and sensibility, however, Monty Python resembles Beerbohm's most antic and subversive "improvement" projects. Beerbohm's darting eyes and funny teeth are precursors of Conrad Pooh's Dancing Teeth, just as the jointed jaws of Gilliam's talking heads seem like strong precursors of the audaciously crude animation of *South Park*. If grangerism as such remains obscure, its legacy is not. The will to grangerize, like my own, manifests everywhere, from scrapbooking to Pinterest. But it is also the fundamental imperative of social media to generate, in our highly selective and self-conscious curations of experience, through expressive juxtapositions of text and image, *auto*biographical histories. "To the making of" selves, like books, "there is no end."

Notes

1   Heather J. Jackson, who notes the *OED* mistake, also speculates on the source of the error: "Granger himself never published his work with blank spaces for portraits. The misconception reflected in the *OED* may have arisen from later practice and from the fact that some of the few extant copies of the first edition were printed only on one side of the leaf: both British Library copies, for example, appear in this state. But the blank pages were the publisher's substitute for interleaving in copies specifically designed for a group of collectors ... asked to annotate the work, indicating additions that would then be incorporated in later editions" (*Marginalia* [New Haven: Yale University Press, 2001], 187n11).

2   Extended title of *A Biographical History of England*, 2 vols. (London: Printed for T. Davies, 1769), https://archive.org/details/abiographicalhi05grangoog.

3   A largely identical third edition was published posthumously in 1779.

4   Sarah Davison, "Max Beerbohm's Altered Books," *Textual Cultures: Texts, Contexts, Interpretation* 6, no. 1 (2011): 48–75.

5   Jackson, *Marginalia*, 186.

6   Huntington Library, "'Grangerized' Books Take Center Stage at Upcoming Huntington Exhibition, Illuminated Palaces," press release, May 15, 2013, http://www.huntington.org/WebAssets/Templates/content.aspx?id=14386.

7   Lucy Peltz, "Facing the Text: The Amateur and Commercial Histories of Extra-Illustration, 1770–1820," in *Owners, Annotators and the Signs of*

Reading, ed. M. Harris, G. Mandelbrote, and R. Myers (London: British Library, 2005), 102.

8   *Dictionary of Literary Biography*, ed. Leslie Stephen and Sidney Lee (London: Smith Elder and Company, 1903), 8: 373.

9   Peltz, "Facing the Text," 102.

10 Holbrook Jackson, *The Anatomy of Bibliomania* (London: Soncino Press, 1930), 16.

11 Ibid., 576.

12 Ibid., 132.

13 Ibid., 133.

14 Jeffrey Todd Knight, "'Furnished for Action': Renaissance Publications; Books as Furniture," *Book History* 12 (2009): 40.

15 Gérard Genette, *Paratexts: Thresholds of Interpretation*, trans. Jane E. Lewin and Richard Macksey (Cambridge: Cambridge University Press, 1997), 1.

16 *Catalogue of the Library and Literary Manuscripts of the Late Max Beerbohm Removed from Rapallo* [December 12–13] (London: Sotheby's, 1960), title page.

10

Shirley Temple's "Baby Burlesks"

Nora Gilbert

In the spring of 1932, the actress who would go on to become the biggest box office star of the Depression era made her screen debut. She was young at the time—just shy of her fourth birthday—but was still a bit old for the costume she donned through most of the film: a necklace, a diaper, an oversized diaper pin, and nothing more (see Figure 10.1). Nine minutes and fifty-four seconds in length, this microfilm was the first in a series of eight one-reelers produced for Educational Pictures between 1932 and 1933 that featured preschool-aged children performing parodic reenactments of adult classic Hollywood fare. The screwball comedy *The Front Page* (dir. Lewis Milestone, 1931) became *The Runt Page* (dir. Raymond Nazarro, 1932), the war film *What Price Glory* (dir. Raoul Walsh, 1926) became *War Babies* (dir. Charles Lamont, 1932), the Western epic *The Covered Wagon* (dir. James Cruze, 1923) became *The Pie-Covered Wagon* (dir. Charles Lamont, 1932), and so on. Over the course of the series, Shirley Temple and her pint-sized compatriots played soldiers and barmaids, boxers and gangsters, starlets and showgirls, politicians and prostitutes, cowboys and Indians, European missionaries and African cannibals—all while clad in diapers and oversized diaper pins from the waist down. The diapers and pins serve, most obviously, to infantilize the actors who are wearing them, creating a doubled sense of dissonance: preschoolers are both far too young to be shooting guns and performing erotic dances and having babies of their own (Temple plays the mother of three children in some of the films) and also far too old to be parading around in diapers and guzzling milk out of baby bottles.

Collectively referred to as the "Baby Burlesks," this group of films constitutes a microgenre that serves as a key turning point in the history of a larger genre: that of all-child theatrical productions. This genre came into particular vogue in the late Victorian era when, as Marah Gubar has described, "'Miniature' or 'Lilliputian' versions of Gilbert and Sullivan operettas—productions in which every role was played by a child—took the United States and the United Kingdom by storm."[1] The rise of vaudeville came next, with vaudevillian impresario Gus Edwards putting the all-child

Figure 10.1 *The Runt Page* (1932).

model to good (or, at least, lucrative) use in his "Kid Cabarets," the venue through which entertainment icons like Eddie Cantor, Eleanor Powell, and the Marx brothers got their professional starts. And then, of course, came the rise of the Hollywood film industry, which quickly sought to capitalize on audience interest in precocious child actors playing adult roles. At Fox, for example, brothers Chester and Sidney Franklin directed a number of lavish, feature-length films starring a troupe of child actors billed as the "Fox Kiddies," including *Jack and the Beanstalk* (1917), *Aladdin and the Wonderful Lamp* (1917), *Treasure Island* (1918), and an adaptation of *The Mikado* called *Fan Fan* (1918). In the 1920s and early 1930s, child stars Baby Peggy, Baby Rose Marie, Little Mitzi Green, and Jane Withers entertained audiences with their mature and often risqué impersonations of grown-up characters and celebrities. "Thus," as Kristen Hatch (who recently wrote the book on Shirley Temple's influential position in American cultural history) has rightly pointed out, "when Shirley Temple made her debut impersonating sexualized adults in the Baby Burlesks, audiences were already quite familiar with children's erotic imitations, since young actors had been mimicking their elders on stage for over a century."[2]

In trying to understand why theater- and movie-goers were so comfortable with children's "erotic imitations" throughout that century, Gubar and Hatch have come up with a couple of different theories that extend beyond the most obvious, pedophilic one. Borrowing from Marjorie Garber's cultural analysis of cross-dressing, Gubar coins the term "age transvestism" in order to suggest that all-child theatrical productions "may have functioned ... not to buttress a binary opposition like male-female (or in this case, adult-child) but rather to signal a 'category crisis.'" The appeal of watching precocious performers was, in other words, that their "startling competence destabilized the idea that a strict line divided child from adult, innocence from experience."[3] According to Hatch, meanwhile, our modern-day perception of the Baby Burlesks and their kin as "perverse," "untoward" entertainment contrasts sharply with audience perceptions at the time because, back then, "the child was understood to have a purifying effect on even the most scandalous material. When filtered through the body of the sexually innocent child, behavior that would otherwise challenge social mores was transformed into something 'clean' and 'wholesome.'"[4] This all changed abruptly in the mid-1930s, however. The abruptness of the change may be linked in some way to the tightening of the Production Code with the assignment of Joseph Breen to the Hays Office in 1934, though Breen's censoring of children's sensual performances appears to have come only in the wake of growing audience and moral watchdog group complaints. Whatever the cause of the sharp turn in public opinion may have been, as soon as such performances entered the realm of officially "censorable" material, they vanished from the cinematic and theatrical landscapes, more or less for good. (Alan Parker's 1976 musical comedy gangster film *Bugsy Malone* is one memorable exception, though its leads Scott Baio and Jodie Foster were 16 and 14 years old at the time of filming, respectively, which is a far cry from ages 3 to 5.)

On the one hand, then, the Baby Burlesks can be seen as the endpoint of the century-long all-child-production fad. But they also, of course, constitute an important starting point in the annals of American film history: the start of Shirley Temple's astoundingly successful career. Various critics have commented on the sexualizing influence that Temple's background in juvenile burlesque had on her screen persona. Ann duCille's assertion that "the Baby Burlesk shorts deliberately cultivated in the toddler the same erotic savoir faire that made Marlene Dietrich the queen of sex, sin, and song" is a typical remark.[5] In her 1988 autobiography, Temple describes what the Burlesks "cultivated" in her as well, though she does so in a very different tone, from the perspective of the performer rather than the viewer:

> Before long, acting in *Baby Burlesks* demonstrated some fundamental lessons of movie life. It is not easy to be a Hollywood starlet. Starlets have to kiss a lot of people, including some unattractive ones. Often starlets

are knocked down to the floor or pricked by their diaper pins. The hours are long. Some of the positions that must be assumed are downright uncomfortable. Often starlets are required to wear scanty costumes and suffer sexist schemes, such as walking around with a silver arrow stuck through your head.[6] (Figure 10.2)

The "scantiest" costume Temple was required to wear onscreen may have been in her first film, *Runt Page*, but some of her later Burlesk getups were more overtly "sexist," consigning her as they did to such objectifying, stereotypical female roles as the Gold-Digger (Figure 10.3), the Flirt (Figure 10.4), or the Hooker (Figure 10.5). Graham Greene was famously sued for libel in 1937 for the remarks he made in a highbrow, *New Yorker*-style magazine about the titillating wardrobe Temple wore in some of her feature-length films: "In *Captain January*," he quipped, "she wore trousers with the mature suggestiveness of a Dietrich, her neat and well-developed rump twisted in the tap dance ... Now in *Wee Willie Winkie*, wearing short kilts, she is a complete totsy."[7] One wonders (or perhaps one doesn't) what Greene would have said about seeing Temple "twist" and "tap" in nothing but a tarted-up diaper, as she had been made to do a few years earlier.

As quick as critics have been to see the seeds of Temple's eroticized persona being sown in her early one-reelers, less has been made of the relationship between the racial dynamics of the Baby Burlesks and those of her later,

Figure 10.2 *Kid in Hollywood* (1933).

Figure 10.3 *The Kid's Last Fight* (1933).

Figure 10.4 *War Babies* (1932).

Figure 10.5 *Polly Tix in Washington* (1933).

blockbuster films. A good deal has been written about the racial dynamics of the *latter*, to be sure—especially about the cloyingly condescending Little Eva/Uncle Tom dynamic of Temple's repeated pairings with Bill "Bojangles" Robinson. However, her characters' similarly condescending treatment of the non-white grown-ups around her in such films as *Wee Willie Winkie* (dir. John Ford, 1937; Figure 10.6) and *Susannah of the Mounties* (dir. William Seiter, 1939; Figure 10.7) remains undertreated. As is the case with sex, the way that Temple's feature-length films dealt with race is crudely foreshadowed in the Baby Burlesks. For instance, the one African American actor who features prominently in many of the films, Philip Hurlic, is routinely more demeaned and infantilized than the white children surrounding him. In *Pie-Covered Wagon*, to name the most egregious example, while all of the "heroic" white cowboys fend off the advances of the "savage" Indians (all of whom are played by white actors, too), Hurlic is forced to provide "pickaninny" style entertainment as his hapless character is chased by a bear throughout most of the film (Figure 10.8). Besides Hurlic, the only other person of color in the first seven Burlesks is the uncredited black actress who plays the personal maid of several different white characters, two of whom are played by Temple (Figure 10.9).

But then, in the final film of the series, *Kid 'in' Africa* (dir. Jack Hays, 1933), the racial demographics are abruptly reversed. This time Temple is

Figure 10.6 *Wee Willie Winkie* (1937).

Figure 10.7 *Susannah of the Mounties* (1939).

Figure 10.8 *The Pie-Covered Wagon* (1932).

Figure 10.9 *Glad Rags to Riches* (1933).

one of only two white actors in the cast; she plays a "Madam Cradlebait (Missionary)" who is traveling through Africa on a "Cannibal Taming Expedition," as the heavy sign she has two of her black helpers lug along explicitly states (Figure 10.10), while the white actor Danny Boone Jr. plays the Tarzan figure "Diaperzan" who must rescue Madam Cradlebait from the cannibals' culinary machinations (Figure 10.11). And it is in the final, staggeringly offensive moments of *Kid 'in' Africa* that Shirley Temple comes into her own as the patronizing, colonizing presence she will go on to embody in her subsequent work. After Diaperzan easily scares off the cannibals just by staring toughly at them, Madam Cradlebait happily exclaims, "Oh goody! Now you can help me civilize these terrible cannibals! We'll have a civilized city right here in the jungle." Cut to: an urban-jungle set piece that boasts such "humorously"-named businesses as the Hotel Squaldorf, the Weary Nipple Cafe, and the Last Chance Filling Station, to which the natives can now walk up and have what looks like a gas pump (but is really a milk pump) shoved into their mouths for "proper," non-cannibalistic sustenance. After we see Diaperzan and Madam Cradlebait riding high on an elephant through the village they have civilized together, the film (and the Baby Burlesk series) comes to a close with the image of Temple, at last a married, respectable woman, knitting contentedly on the front porch of her treehouse as her husband tends to the baby crying inside with a fresh diaper—to be fastened, of course, with an exaggeratedly large diaper pin.

Figure 10.10 *Kid 'in' Africa* (1933).

Figure 10.11 *Kid 'in' Africa* (1933).

Indeed, the always-prominent sight of the oversized diaper pin almost *has* to be there, throughout the series, to remind us that we are in the land of parody. For really the only thing separating the casual racism and sexism of the Baby Burlesks from that of the classic Hollywood films they are supposed to be spoofing is the age of the actors who are, cringe-worthily, being made to reenact them. And even though Shirley Temple officially shed her diaper pins when she made her feature-film debut in 1934, she never quite shed them in spirit. During the years in which she was the reigning box office queen of the world—a world that was experiencing an enormous amount of social and political unrest, including in its many colonized regions—Temple continued, with her perpetually chubby cheeks, ringlet curls, and babydoll dresses, to combine a delayed sense of babyhood with a jarring sense of premature sexuality and condescension toward non-white characters and cultures. Taken together, the eight constituents of the Baby Burlesks microgenre can be seen to gesture, in historically important ways, to the kinds of deeply discomfiting racial and sexual relations that would go on to pervade and characterize the career of the most globally influential child star of all time.

Notes

1   Marah Gubar, "Who Watched *The Children's Pinafore*?: Age Transvestism on the Nineteenth-Century Stage," *Victorian Studies* 54, no. 3 (2012): 410.

2   Kristen Hatch, *Shirley Temple and the Performance of Girlhood* (New Brunswick: Rutgers University Press, 2015), 118.

3   Gubar, "Who Watched," 411.

4   Hatch, *Shirley Temple*, 109.

5   Ann duCille, "The Shirley Temple of My Familiar," *Transition* 73 (1997): 15.

6   Shirley Temple Black, *Child Star: An Autobiography* (New York: McGraw-Hill, 1988), 21.

7   Graham Greene, *The Graham Greene Film Reader: Reviews, Essays, Interviews and Film Stories*, ed. David Parkinson (New York: Applause Theatre Book Publishers, 1995), 233.

11

Nudie-Cuties

Cynthia J. Miller and Thomas M. Shaker

Bold, daring, tantalizing, and playful, nudie-cuties are a microgenre of exploitation films that use thin, amusing, and often implausible story lines to create a context for nudity and titillation. The films, predominantly produced in the 1960s, feature nubile young women in varying states of undress, but portray no physical contact between these women and male actors. The males, in fact, are generally shy, awkward, eccentric, or ineffective, and the objects of their attention are generally framed as unattainable or "out of their league." Producer Russ Meyer, known for his work in exploitation and cult films, explains that in nudie-cuties "women are always in charge—the men are the klutzes."[1]

Shocking and forbidden in their day, and condemned as evidence of moral decline, these films are now considered to be naïve and exhibit a certain nostalgic charm—as products of a time of generalized innocence—appealing more to voyeuristic impulses than those that are directly sexual in nature. Nudie-cuties never feature full frontal nudity or explicit sex that, at the time, was prohibited by the Motion Picture Production Code (MPPC). Instead, they focus on the display of the breasts and buttocks of young women with ideal body types for their era. With several nudie-cuties to his credit, Meyer affirmed that the films' main features are "big bosoms and square jaws (big bosoms on the women, and square jaws on the men)."[2]

Independently produced, nudie-cuties were feature films produced quickly and on an extremely low budget. Meyer and his contemporaries had little concern for production values, but rather relied on the "tease"— the promise of sights never before seen, beauty never before exposed. Films were frequently made "on location" in parks and nudist camps to avoid incurring studio production fees. In his autobiography, exploitation producer Dave Friedman describes writing the script for *The Adventures of Lucky Pierre* (1961) in six hours, joking to Barbara Lewis, wife of his partner, filmmaker Herschell Gordon Lewis: "This isn't *Gone with the Wind*, dear."[3] Trailers, lobby cards, and taglines for these low-budget teasers all beckoned to prospective male viewers with promises of the forbidden. They would, of course, be disappointed in the end, but most clung to the unspoken hope that maybe "next time" their chosen film would deliver, and box office receipts seldom suffered. Friedman confided, "You sell the sizzle, not the steak ... It worked for Barnum, it worked for Bailey, it worked for [filmmaker Kroger] Babb, and it works for me!"[4]

Nudie-cuties, along with their predecessors, sex hygiene films (which promised to educate viewers on a range of topics from venereal disease to the birth of a baby), were shown largely in "grindhouse" theaters, as were the "roughies"—brutal, misogynistic films depicting rape and torture—that would follow them. Generally found in urban areas and seedy neighborhoods, the grindhouses were predecessors of adult movie theaters, which would not come into their own until the Motion Picture Association of America (MPAA) rating system instituted the "X" rating for adult films.

No other microgenre of film is so aptly and cheerfully named as the "nudie-cuties" (see Figure 11.1). The films mark a shift from on-screen nudity that was deemed "educational" to displays of the body (generally female) that were openly intended to titillate, making these films a significant, if brief, contribution to motion picture history. The regulation of narrative and visual content was uneven and ineffective in early cinematic history. Prior to 1935, when the Motion Picture Production Code, or Hays Code, was established, suggestive situations and brief nudity were allowed. The Hays Code (1935–54) regulated cinematic content and explicitly prohibited both full nudity and overt portrayals of sexual behavior, even between consenting adults, on screen. The Code was a set of directives that were voluntarily adopted by major Hollywood studios, designed to head off governmental content censorship and the banning of motion pictures. Sex in films has been around as long as film has, but while available, films with explicit sexual content were often informally distributed and usually screened in back rooms and at bachelor parties. Truly "pornographic" commercial films were not produced and distributed by established film companies until after the Hays Code was replaced by the MPAA rating system in 1968.

"Educational films," however, were exempt from prevailing regulations, and independent filmmakers frequently circumvented censorship rules by laying claim to the "educational" designation. Offering significant commentary on social attitudes, values, and fears of the day, these films depicted how horror, shame, and despair met characters who defied conventional morality, serving as a caution to all who might consider a journey down the "wrong" path. Alcohol, drugs, gambling, and sex result in pregnancy out of wedlock, ostracism, prison, disease, and even death for the unfortunate characters (generally naïve young women who venture from rural areas to the "big city") who become their victims. With taglines like

Figure 11.1 Film poster for *Mr. Peters' Pets* (1963).

"Weed with Roots in Hell!" "Shocks that Rock the Town," "A Tragic Lesson in Love," and "One Night of Bliss for 1000 Nights in Hell!" these films, which saw their golden age in the 1930s – 1950s, promised to educate "Adults Only" in the evils that threatened both their personal lives and social worlds.

The most popular among these early exploitation films were the "sex hygiene" films and nudist camp movies that showed nudity as part of their "public service." Nudie-cuties took their initial cue from these nudist camp films of the 1950s, after Judge Charles Desmond issued a landmark ruling that nudity, per se, on screen was not indecent. Desmond ruled in favor of Walter Bibo's film *Garden of Eden* (1954), which depicted nudism. Bibo wrote:

> There is nothing sexy or suggestive about it … nudists are shown as wholesome, happy people in family groups practicing their sincere but misguided theory that clothing, when climate does not require it, is deleterious to mental health by promoting an attitude of shame with regard to natural attributes and functions of the body.[5]

Following the Supreme Court ruling that films set in nudist camps were exempt from the ban on nudity on screen, and deemed "educational," grindhouses were flooded with films set in nudist camps with actors "wearing nothing but the wind."[6] These nudist camp films served as the predecessors of nudie-cuties, which expanded upon the "naked in nature" scenario to include nudity in a wide range of settings.

Film companies eager to take advantage of these changes in social morals went from simply depicting nudist lifestyle activities (doing laundry, having conversations, eating meals) to developing nudist lifestyles in the plots for their films. These often outrageous plots include bank robbers who hide out in a nudist colony to escape the law and astronauts who travel to the moon and discover a race of topless moon people (see Figure 11.2). Filmmaker John Waters is quoted in *The Other Hollywood* as saying, "I saw them all. Not just the exploitation movies, but the nudie movies, which had to be the most ludicrously unsexual films ever made, like a girl on a pogo stick or a nude volleyball game. You just saw their backs—asses and tits, but never dicks."[7] After a court ruling in the mid-1950s relaxed restrictions on nudity in mainstream movies, film studios were allowed to incorporate nudity into their plot, rather than just use the camera to "observe" lifestyles or medical procedures.

With titles like *The Immoral Mr. Teas* (see Figure 11.3), *Diary of a Nudist, The Adventures of Lucky Pierre, Nude on the Moon,* and *Thar She Blows!,* nudie-cuties routinely promised more than they would ever deliver, but it was all achieved with a wink and a smile. Given the rapidly changing social norms of the 1960s, however, the nudie-cutie period did not last long. It is generally recognized as running from 1959, with the release of *The Immoral*

Figure 11.2 Film poster for *Nude on the Moon* (1961).

Mr. Teas, to its last gasps in 1970, as the X-rated film industry took hold. Friedman contends that "the heyday of the nudie cuties was 1967, 1968, 1969 and 1970. Those were the days I was turning out *Brand of Shame, The Head Mistress, Lustful Turk, Trader Horny, Thar She Blows … The Erotic Adventures of Zorro*—some of the greatest films of the genre. Classics that still live today. Ha ha ha ha."[8] Friedman and his longtime partner Dan Sonney exited the industry shortly after the sea change created the MPAA rating system. "It was like opening a show with the third act," Friedman lamented, "they left nothing to the imagination."[9]

Nudie-cuties, however, played a significant role in motion picture trends in mid-century America, introducing filmgoers to on-screen nudity as lighthearted entertainment. With the help of changing social values, shifts in gender roles, and the groundbreaking magazine *Playboy*, unabashed nudity and sexuality in women rapidly came to be seen as fashionable, chic, and more acceptable in society. Sadly, once truly pornographic films became mainstream and videocassettes achieved mass-market success, the innocence, suggestiveness, and naivete of the nudie-cutie seemed mild and dated, and soon disappeared from the screen. The sexploitation subgenre that followed, the "roughies," was marked by social tension, gender antagonism,

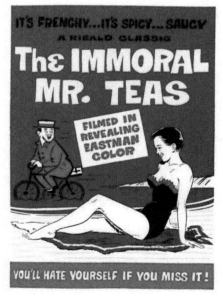

Figure 11.3 Film poster for *The Immoral Mr. Teas* (1959).

and graphic violence toward female characters. While sex still was not portrayed on screen, the roughies held none of the innocence and good-natured comedy that made nudie-cuties successful at the box office.

Since the era of the nudie-cutie was so brief, the players involved were few and were often associated in various combinations on film projects. But during the decade in which these films were produced, there was a plethora of output. Nudie-cutie filmmakers Meyer, Doris Wishman, and Herschell Gordon Lewis led the pack. Meyer was "something of a one-man studio," he "produced, directed, financed, wrote, edited and shot 23 tantalizing but teasing films that pioneered a genre of skin flicks with much violence and large-busted women but little sex."[10] Jimmy McDonough relates that Meyer claimed to be "truly a genre unto himself."[11] Meyer is credited with making the first nudie-cutie, 1959's *The Immoral Mr. Teas*. Known for employing large-breasted actresses as his trademark in his films, Meyer became the self-proclaimed king of the nudies. Gary Johnson writes:

> Because of movies such as *The Immoral Mr. Teas*, the era of the nudie-cuties was born. These movies were part comedies and part cheesecake exhibitions. A typical story would focus on a simple working man as he made his daily rounds and encountered a variety of naked and nearly-naked women. No sex, mind you, takes place in these movies. Just lots of wide-eyed gawking.[12]

If Meyer was king, then Wishman was queen. Wishman, in fact, claims that she, rather than Meyer, made the first nudie-cutie with *Nude on the Moon*—a film that has also achieved cult status over the years. Wishman's foray into film began as a hobby in 1958, after her 31-year-old husband died of a heart attack. Her first film *Hideout in the Sun* (1958) was reportedly made for $10,000 borrowed from her sister. One of her films starred burlesque queen Blaze Starr (*Blaze Starr Goes Nudist*). She went on to make a few pornographic films in the 1970s and joined the slasher genre craze with *A Night to Dismember* in 1989.

Another nudie-cutie auteur, Lewis, and his partner Friedman, made the now-classic *The Adventures of Lucky Pierre*. They also released *Boin-n-g!!* (1963), a film that was marketed to exhibitors as "a positive plethora of pulchritude," with "prized and prime princesses pleasingly, provocatively and prismatically presented for your pleasure and profit."[13] Once the nudie-cuties' heyday had passed, Lewis, in association with Friedman, went on to make the films for which he is best remembered: *Blood Feast* (1963) and *Two Thousand Maniacs!* (1964). The extremes to which these films shocked the senses gave Lewis notoriety as the pioneer of on-screen gore.

Joining Wishman, Meyer, Lewis, and Friedman in the nudie-cutie game were well-known figures such as celebrated photographer Bunny Yeager, who was acclaimed for her photo shoots with pinup model Bettie Page, and filmmaker Barry Mahon, who would go on to produce children's films in the 1970s. It can be difficult to pin down key female actors in this microgenre, as many used stage names, and several starred in only a single film. Often, the female characters did not have names, and were listed in the credits simply as "woman with fish" or "woman with kitten," making the characters as anonymous and interchangeable as the women who portrayed them. Notable among these are actress/screenwriter Allison Louise Downe (who is also credited with the screenplay for *Blood Feast*), Stacey Walker, Virginia Bell, Maria Lease, and Connie Mason (who later appeared in television's *Marcus Welby, M.D.*). Mason's spouse, actor William Kerwin, frequently appeared in male roles in nudie-cuties such as *The Adventures of Lucky Pierre, Boin-n-g!!, Bell, Bare, and Beautiful,* and *Goldilocks and the Three Bares,* all while working in television series such as *Wagon Train, Wide Country,* and *Slattery's People.*

For these films, continuity and quality were not major concerns. They were cheap to make—*Mr. Teas* cost $24,000—and, for the most part, were shot without synchronized sound. The audio was all added and dubbed later in the editing room. All of the microgenre's films had one theme in common: attractive young women with large breasts, who were featured naked from the waist up. Most of these films incorporated shy and ineffective male characters and comedy into their "scripts," which were often written by multiple authors in a single session. Those sessions, according to Lewis, typically involved a significant consumption of alcohol.[14]

While considered by their filmmakers, as well as contemporary critics and scholars, as part of the sexploitation subgenre of exploitation films, nudie-cuties, however, featured no negative consequences in their sexualized romps. They were simple, blatantly flirtatious, and (for their era) all in good fun. Co-ed naked volleyball or bumbling eccentrics sneaking peeks at beautiful women in their undergarments were difficult to take seriously. Their gimmicks, such as x-ray glasses or magic potions, served a dual purpose—as a means of introducing both nudity and comedy. Sex, in this microgenre, was, in fact, a laughing matter.

These films seem tame by present-day standards, with their contrived plots and utter absence of sex. As part of an early wave of adult films, however, they were scandalous in their day, creating scenarios for putting women's idealized bodies on display. However, these films also reflect a playfulness and innocence about nudity, voyeurism, sex, etc., that was lost as motion picture content became more explicit, second-wave feminism altered gender relations, and political concerns shifted throughout the 1960s. Screened today, these films would be considered highly problematic for their objectification of women and promotion of voyeurism, but in the context of the mid-twentieth century, they formed part of a constellation of entertainment forms, from burlesque to the follies to film that began at the turn of the century and both glorified and objectified particular idealized female types and roles.

Nudie-cuties, in fact, had significant ties to classic burlesque as well as to pinup. Meyer frequently used burlesque footage in his early films, and later, Rose LaRose, owner of a burlesque house in Ohio, commissioned Lewis and Friedman to create a series of short films that would appeal to her audiences: "little self-contained short subjects, each having some pretty, naked girls."[15] Instead, Friedman promised her a feature made of ten-minute segments, each self-contained, and the result was a nudie-cutie roll that would reinforce the link between film and burlesque. Both shared a "celebration" of male fantasies of women, as well as the narrative device of creating scenes that created reasons for nudity, or partial nudity— bathing, changing clothes, swimming, house-cleaning, nudist camps, etc. These early sexploitation filmmakers routinely filmed burlesque acts by stars such as Lili St. Cyr and Tempest Storm as they were being performed, and then edited them into reels known as "roadshow shorts." Pinup icon Page also appeared in similar reels with titles like *Teaserama* created by sexploiteer Irving Klaw. Exploitation filmmakers generally agreed that, unlike conventional actresses (or raw recruits) who might be willing to do nude scenes but had to overcome a certain shyness, burlesque performers were used to taking off their clothes in front of audiences, making them more "natural" and less self-conscious in front of a camera during a single take.

With such easy access to "talent" and low production costs, nudie-cuties featured prominently in mid-century American filmmakers' attempts to make money at the box office by venturing into territory where mainstream studios feared to tread. Independent directors and producers such as Meyer, Friedman, Lewis, Wishman, and others whose work resided outside the studio system pushed at the boundaries of what the Hays Code would permit in order to carve out their own box office niche. Many would also later lay claim to serving as the vanguard of filmmakers fighting for freedom of expression on the screen: "We were on the front lines," Friedman contended.[16] In large part, for a short time, that was true.

Notes

1 *Something Weird*, S2, Ep. 10, September 23, 2015, https://www.youtube.com/watch?v=Td1h31HguUU.

2 Ibid.

3 David F. Friedman, *Youth in Babylon: Confessions of a Trash-Film King* (New York: Prometheus, 1990), 264.

4 *Mau Mau Sex Sex*, directed by Ted Bonnitt (2001).

5 Eddie Muller, *Grindhouse: The Forbidden World of Adults Only Cinema* (New York: St. Martins, 1996), 62.

6 *Mau Mau*.

7 Legs McNeil and Jennifer Osborne, *The Other Hollywood* (New York: Regan, 2006), 1.

8 Ibid., 11.

9 *Mau Mau*.

10 Myrna Oliver, "Russ Meyer, 82; Iconic Sexploitation Filmmaker," *Los Angeles Times*, September 22, 2004, http://articles.latimes.com/2004/sep/22/local/me-meyer22.

11 Jimmy McDonough, *Big Bosoms and Square Jaws: The Biography of Russ Meyer, King of the Sex Film* (New York: Three Rivers Press, 2006), 122.

12 Gary Johnson, "Russ Meyer: *The Immoral Mr. Teas* and *Mondo Topless*," *Images: A Journal of Film and Popular Culture*, July 28, 1999, http://www.imagesjournal.com/issue08/reviews/mrteas.

13 William Grimes, "Herschell Gordon Lewis, a Pioneer of Gore Cinema, Dies at 90," September 28, 2016, https://www.nytimes.com/2016/09/28/movies/herschell-gordon-lewis-a-pioneer-of-gore-cinema-dies-at-90.html.

14 Friedman, *Youth in Babylon*, 264.

15 Mike Quarles, *Down and Dirty: Hollywood's Exploitation Filmmakers and Their Movies* (Jefferson: McFarland, 2001), 30.

16 *Mau Mau*.

Giallo

Gavin F. Hurley

"Giallo" is a microgenre of predominantly Italian film, although its influence has been felt internationally. Throughout the 1960s and 1970s, giallo films (or gialli) helped popularize the type of psychological horror film established by Alfred Hitchcock and also influenced the first wave of slasher horror films in the late 1970s and early 1980s. Moreover, gialli blend European artistic film with American horror film in a way that augments each tradition. Although often overlooked by the academic community as grindhouse or exploitation cinema, 1960s and 1970s gialli acted as a crucial segue in the history of genre film.

The name "giallo" developed out of the pulp tradition of murder mystery books. "Giallo," or "yellow" in Italian, refers to the yellow covers of American and British pulp detective novels printed by Italian publishers beginning in the late 1920s.[1] After the Second World War, these detective novels transformed into "anti-detective" novels where the detective, as the central authority within the story, becomes destabilized.[2] Whereas detective novels by Arthur Conan Doyle and Agatha Christie have plots that revolve around the expertise of highly competent detectives, anti-detective novels resist this tendency.

Influenced by the postmodernity of the era, anti-detective novels embrace a chaotic type of mystery that delays resolution and suspends closure.[3] The earliest gialli, such as Mario Bava's *The Girl Who Knew Too Much* (1963) and *Blood and Black Lace* (1964), emerged from this postwar literary trend and became even more prevalent in the 1970s. Giuliano Carnimeo's 1972 giallo film *The Case of the Bloody Iris* adapts this anti-detective trend by undercutting the competency of the detectives themselves. In the film, the police commissioner seems more interested in collecting rare postage stamps from crime scenes than solving murders. Unsurprisingly, the police pursue the wrong suspect for most of the film. Jennifer (Edwige Fenech), one of the women pursued by the killer, has to investigate the suspects herself and ultimately solves the mystery.

As adaptation of a literary anti-detective microgenre into cinema, gialli like *The Case of the Bloody Iris* were propagated by the already established success of Italian *polizieco* cinema (police dramas). Remixing both anti-detective stories and police dramas, gialli advantageously used each of the respective popularities to emerge as a dominant, albeit marginalized, cinematic microgenre in Europe and America beginning in the early 1960s. Unlike Italian police dramas, however, giallo cinema offers a highly stylized mixture of horror and murder mystery. The destabilized detective narrative, which features unsettling elements such as mentally delusional characters and explicit displays of violence, integrates horror tropes while never abandoning its strong roots in mystery fiction. Generally, gialli can be considered greater than the sum of their parts. Although they use elements of mystery and horror genres, gialli offer a distinct type of cinema that can be both stylish and gritty. The violence is often depicted using artistic approaches such as unique camerawork, colorful lighting, and lush settings. Due to this balance of style and grittiness, gialli offer a visually appealing experience, one that approaches occasionally graphic material like nudity and violence with artistry.

Because giallo strays from pure horror and mystery categorizations, some scholars have posited that giallo is not a conventional genre at all; rather, they propose giallo as a *filone*, which gestures to a type of "tradition," "vein," or "series of interconnected streamlets branching from the main genre river."[4] In *La Dolce Morte*, a scholarly examination of giallo film, Mikel Koven explains that, as a *filone*, giallo revolves around vernacular culture, one that resists high art or art-for-art's-sake culture. As vernacular films in the 1960s and 1970s, gialli were not merely popular or commercially successful; rather, they were genuinely the "people's cinema." Gialli relied on familiar ideals, conventions, and references. These expected elements range from wealthy attractive characters and well-known city settings to everyday product placement such as J+B Scotch Whiskey (see Figure 12.1). Familiar patterns and references can comfort everyday audiences and help manage expectations.

Gialli, however, also resist mere repetition of the familiar. Gialli directors and writers offset the predictability of the films—as well as the boredom that can accompany the predictability—by using unique characters, constructing creative suspense scenes, and, of course, suspending the mystery of the killer's identity. *The Case of the Bloody Iris* offers an array of unique characters: a model who was a member of a sex cult, a jealous sex cult leader, a dashing rich architect, a successful stripper, a police commissioner who collects postage stamps, a retired professor who incessantly plays the violin, an elderly Catholic woman who buys murder mystery magazines, and the woman's burn-victim son who lives in the closet of her apartment. Moreover, the film includes several creative settings, including a steam-filled boiler room and a junkyard at night. Because of these unique elements, gialli demand an audience's close attention.

Figure 12.1 In *Bloodstained Shadow* (1978), Count Pedrazzi (Massimo Serato) hears a killer in his house as he drinks several glasses of prominently displayed J+B Scotch.

The vernacular approach contrasts with art-house cinema, which demands a more patient audience because of the complexity and indirectness of art-house abstraction. By contrast, gialli offer rhetorical dimensions meant to engage everyday audiences: whodunit plot constructions peppered with red herrings. In Luciano Ercoli's *Death Walks on High Heels* (1971) (see Figure 12.2), for example, an unknown masked "blue-eyed" killer stalks Nicole Rochard (Susan Scott) throughout the film in order to steal her father's unethically acquired diamonds. Viewers of the film meet an array of characters who serve as red herrings: Nicole's ex-boyfriend who owns a set of blue contact lenses, a blind man receiving experimental eye surgery, and several other suspicious blue-eyed characters. These red herring-filled whodunit plots—inherited from the detective and anti-detective pulp fiction traditions—contribute a key rhetorical dimension to the giallo film. Whodunit plot constructions make the identity of the killer the central plot concern, presenting puzzles for audiences to solve as they watch the films. This participatory approach immerses viewers in the films as active, amateur investigators. Consequently, many giallo filmmakers deliberately use amateur investigators as their protagonists. Such characters serve as viewer surrogates. The protagonist and the viewer both commune as amateur detectives: the surrogate character attempts to solve the mystery from inside the fiction and the viewer attempts to solve it from outside.

Horror genre components supplement these mystery plots. An unknown dangerous killer pervades giallo plots and subsequently kindles anxiety in the audience. However, gialli never kindle anxiety through unknown *supernatural* elements: the plots and characters are all grounded in material reality. Audiences of gialli, much like audiences of Hitchcock films, anticipate moments of violence. This anticipation of violence, which is prolonged by suspenseful scenes, offers a dimension of horror that cooperates with the whodunit mystery structure. For instance, Sergio Martino's *The Strange Vice of Mrs. Wardh* (1971) offers several suspenseful scenes that cooperate with

Figure 12.2 A killer stalks Vanessa Matthews (Claudie Lange) in *Death Walks on High Heels* (1971).

its mystery elements. In one scene, as Julie Wardh (Edwige Fenech) quietly walks through a parking garage at night, a black car associated with the killer suddenly speeds by her, evoking a jump-scare from the audience. Flustered, Julie opens the elevator door to escape the garage only to be attacked by a disguised killer with a straight razor who then stalks her around the parking garage for several suspenseful minutes. This scene demonstrates a typical stalk-and-slash scene from a horror film; however, the car attacker and the elevator stalker are clearly two different people, implying that not one but two killers pursue Julie. In a later scene, Julie and her husband visit the house of Ivan, Julie's ex-boyfriend who they presume to be her stalker. This scene closely resembles a classic gothic horror sequence. Unfolding over a span of almost five minutes, the couple cautiously walks through an empty old mansion using only a lighter to light the way. In generic gothic manner, the dark scene is interspersed with creaky doors and false-scares (also known as "cat-scares"). It ends with the couple finding Ivan dead in his own bathtub. Like the parking garage scene, the mansion scene provides information about the killer(s') identity/identities via a fear-based horror approach rather than a tamer approach fit for mysteries or police procedural dramas.

The cooperation of horror and mystery makes gialli unique, especially in the 1960s and 1970s; still, the films exhibit specific stylistic elements that are particular to the giallo microgenre. One important element concerns camerawork. To facilitate affective anxiety within gialli in a way that differentiates them from generic whodunit mysteries and mainstream horror films, giallo directors often innovatively use first-person point-of-view camera shots throughout their films. Directors integrate first person, so that viewers can experience the fictional world through the eyes of the killer, often wearing black gloves to conceal their identity from the viewer. Dario Argento, a pioneer of the giallo, often used this "killercam" approach in his films, but he also experimented with other points-of-view (see Figure 12.3). For instance, Argento presents a murder witness's point-of-view in *The Bird with the Crystal Plumage* (1970) and *Deep Red* (1975) and an unorthodox ghost-like point-of-view in *Tenebrae* (1982). Other giallo directors emulated Argento's unique first-person point-of-view approach, and like Argento they also creatively experimented with point-of-view. For example, in *The Girl Who Knew Too Much* (1963), Mario Bava offers a fuzzy point-of-view to signal the hazy subjective state of a concussed victim, and in *The Fifth Cord* (1971), Luigi Bazzoni offers a pin-hole camera view that restricts the subjectivity of the shot to presumably increase the suspense.[5]

These directors' experimental uses of point-of-view reveal important strategies employed in gialli. Principally, the first-person point-of-view serves an active rhetorical role. As a vernacular type of film, the first-

Figure 12.3 First-person "killer cam" angle in *Seven Blood-Stained Orchids* (1972); Elena Marchi (Rossella Falk) stares into the camera as she is pursued by her killer.

person point-of-view immerses the viewer into the giallo film. It unites the subjectivity of the viewer with the subjectivity of a character in the film. Therefore, it attempts to increase a viewer's adherence to the fiction. First-person point-of-view sequences force viewers from a third-person spectator point-of-view into the heads of the films' characters so that they must see and hear fictional events through the eyes and ears of the characters. These shifts to first-person point-of-view can make the danger—and by extension, the fear—seem more real. Additionally, first-person and experimental points-of-view disrupt the conventional passive point-of-view adopted in traditional filmmaking. This disruption can help giallo films destabilize the viewer's narrative experience. A cinematographic shift can upset the comfortable film-viewing experience to which viewers are accustomed. By plunging the viewer into the fiction itself or an experimental point-of-view, viewers are jolted from the third-person objective point-of-view into a new, often more immersive, way of experiencing a fictional world. Overall, these new and strange approaches to camerawork are consistent with the unsettling horror elements of gialli.

Finally, giallo films utilize a variety of aesthetic props and environments, such as art, architecture, art deco, music, dance, and fashion (see Figure 12.4). Many times these elements act as stylistic garnishes, but in the case of

Figure 12.4 Surrounded by fashion magazines, music, artistic décor, and bottles of alcohol, Minou (Dagmar Lassander) washes down some pills with whiskey in *The Forbidden Photos of a Lady Above Suspicion* (1970).

Argento's gialli, paintings and music can be read as crucial aspects of the plot. For example, *Deep Red* involves a childish wall painting and a curious piece of music and *Tenebrae* revolves around a novelist character's literary work. However, as stylistic garnishes, more general aesthetics pervade all gialli. Naturally, they exemplify important dimensions of European cosmopolitan culture that gialli generally depict. Yet, a focus on aesthetics provides a means of positively offsetting any unsettling aspects of the films (such as the violence) to sustain audience interest. After all, beautiful art, catchy music, regal settings, and attractive people satiate an audience's desire for sensory pleasure.

The films' deliberate attention to captivating art, music, fashion, and home décor serve a deeper purpose as well. As a vernacular type of film shown in grindhouses rather than art-houses, gialli defend the importance of aesthetics, revealing that popular culture can also value art. Contrasting with much of American Hollywood entertainment, gialli offer a "both/and" artistic sensibility: an entertaining film that is also grounded in aesthetic appreciation. Argento's gialli illustrate this inclusive "both/and" relationship with more overtly artistic versions of the giallo film that also entertain everyday audiences.

As a bridge extending into postmodern horror cinema, gialli have influenced 1980s, 1990s, and twenty-first-century horror by establishing the foundation for popular slasher horror movies of the 1980s and early 1990s. Generally, gialli became less popular in the early 1980s partly because of the insurgence of late 1970s/early 1980s American slasher films. These movies—such as John Carpenter's *Halloween* (1978) and Sean Cunningham's *Friday the 13th* (1980)—enjoyed more financial success than European gialli. In addition, slasher movies, widely distributed through the American home video rental culture of the 1980s (rather than via grindhouse theaters), ultimately replaced giallo.

Slasher films certainly borrowed tropes from the giallo tradition, including stalk-and-slash suspense, a killer's concealed identity, and the hedonism of its characters. In fact, arguably the first slasher film was Bava's *A Bay of Blood* (1971). Bava was also considered the first giallo director, directing early influential gialli like *The Girl Who Knew Too Much* (1963) and *Blood and Black Lace* (1964). Slasher films can, therefore, be seen as close cousins of giallo films. To the undiscriminating viewer, gialli and slasher films are comparable. Gialli such as Sergio Martino's *Torso* (1973) and Argento's *Tenebrae*, for instance, are often mistaken for slasher films since they offer a more horror-centered, violent approach; still, both *Torso* and *Tenebrae* are unmistakably gialli.

Categorically, slasher films are undoubtedly horror films that abandon much of the detective/anti-detective narrative approach that emerged from the pulp murder mystery tradition. However, as critics point out, this distinction still does not account for early slasher films like *Happy Birthday to Me* (1981) and *My Bloody Valentine* (1981) and later ones like *Scream* (1996), which involve anti-detective murder mysteries but are not considered giallo. The more nuanced traits of gialli can clarify this distinction. First, gialli "whodunit?" plotlines extend across several days, even weeks, whereas slasher films often take place in a single night.[6] Additionally, gialli are necessarily set in city environments, whereas slasher films are almost always set in confined suburban or rural settings.[7] In fact, some slasher films limit the setting to one night at a single house. Gialli, on the other hand, almost always distribute crimes throughout an entire city or over multiple cities. Although both slasher and giallo films favor explicit hedonism (partying, sex, alcohol), giallo, as discussed, emphasizes aesthetics and beauty more than its less elegant counterpart. The characteristics of slasher films—that is, condensed timelines, close spaces, and a lack of aesthetic introspection—naturally allow for quicker action, more explicit violence, and denser suspense. Consequently, slasher films offer more adrenaline-inducing sensory experiences rather than the mental stimulation of the slower-paced whodunit style of giallo.

Slasher films supplanted gialli in the early 1980s. This shift is a part of a larger trend in horror cinema. Over the decades, audiences of horror have favored more action and extreme violence in their films. This trend can be evidenced by the mainstream torture-porn cinematic trend in the 2000s (e.g., *Saw* [2004], *Hostel* [2005], *Captivity* [2007], *The Human Centipede* [2009]) or Rob Zombie's violent 2007 remake of John Carpenter's fairly conservative *Halloween* (1978). Across the decades, audiences seem to crave faster and more extreme action. More exciting slasher films seem to have replaced gialli because the latter require more patient attention from audiences.

Despite the cultural shift away from the giallo film, its influence has not completely disappeared. Italian directors like Lamberto Bava (son of Mario Bava) and Michele Soavi continued the giallo tradition in the late 1980s with giallo-inspired films like Bava's *Delirium* (1987) and Soavi's *Stagefright* (1987). Similarly, mainstream thrillers like *Basic Instinct* (1992) as well as films by Brian DePalma and Quentin Tarantino can be seen as inspired by the giallo microgenre. European directors such as Helene Cattet and Bruno Forzani have also provided newer iterations of giallo (or neo-giallo) with films like *Amer* (2010) and *The Strange Color of Your Body's Tears* (2014). Gialli are still actively reissued by companies such as Blue Underground and Arrow Films, and contemporary remakes, for example, of Argento's *Suspiria*, attest to continued interest in giallo cinema.

Notes

1   Ian Olney, *Eurohorror: Classic European Horror Cinema in Contemporary American Culture* (Bloomington: Indiana University Press, 2013), 106.
2   Ibid.
3   Ibid.
4   Mikel Koven, *La Dolce Morte* (Lanham, MD: Scarecrow Press, 2006), 5–6.
5   Ibid., 147.
6   Ibid., 164.
7   Ibid.

13

Nuclear Realism

John Carl Baker

In the early 1980s, a series of made-for-television films addressed the prospect of nuclear war in a self-consciously realistic style. Although speculative in the sense that they dealt with an event that had yet to occur, these telefilms treated their subject matter in a deadly serious manner, stressing to audiences that nuclear war was a very real—and absolutely terrifying—possibility. *The Day After* (1983), which was watched by more than 100 million people, is easily the most famous of these films, but others include *Testament* (1983), *Threads* (1984), and *Countdown to Looking Glass* (1984). Collectively, this microgenre can be accurately dubbed "nuclear realism." At a time of heightened Cold War anxiety, as millions of activists took to the streets to protest the arms race, this microgenre tapped into popular fears about nuclear war and helped publicize the disarmament cause. In this chapter, I describe the historical and cultural context of nuclear realism, outline its major characteristics, and briefly situate its decline in terms of the overall fate of the disarmament movement.

The early 1980s was a moment of profound existential tension in the United States and around the world. The fear of nuclear war permeated public life. After the detente of the early and mid-1970s, relations between the United States and USSR went rapidly downhill—eventually reaching a nadir not seen since the Cuban Missile Crisis. Heightened tensions had an adverse impact on nuclear arms control negotiations. President Jimmy Carter withdrew the second Strategic Arms Limitation Treaty (SALT II) from congressional consideration after the Soviet invasion of Afghanistan and embarked on an arms buildup that Ronald Reagan inherited and expanded. A larger nuclear arsenal, including the production of systems like the neutron bomb and the MX missile, became a key element in this abrupt rightward turn.

Reagan had been a right-wing dissenter from detente, and his election to the presidency was met with alarm both domestically and abroad. Reagan oversaw massive increases in military spending and staffed his administration with anticommunist ideologues known for hawkishness toward the Soviets. In the first two years of his administration, several officials were quoted saying extremely provocative statements about nuclear war. The most notorious comment was made by Deputy Under Secretary of Defense T. K. Jones, who seemed oddly optimistic about the prospects for national survival after a nuclear conflict, declaring, "If there are enough shovels to go around, everybody's going to make it."[1] Statements like Jones's were being made at a time when spending on nuclear weapons was increasing and the world seemed to be hurtling toward disaster.

Tensions worsened during Reagan's first term. The United States and the North Atlantic Treaty Organization deployed nuclear missiles to Western Europe, provoking huge protests in numerous cities. Administration officials continued to speak intemperately, with Reagan himself infamously calling the Soviet Union an "evil empire" in a speech before the National Association of Evangelicals in March of 1983. Later that month, Reagan publicly announced the Strategic Defense Initiative (SDI), a clear challenge to the Anti-Ballistic Missile Treaty of 1972. Although framed as a purely defensive measure, SDI threatened the second-strike capability of the USSR and seemed to confirm Soviet fears that the United States was planning a massive first strike. 1983 became a particularly inflammatory year for U.S.-Soviet relations. The USSR shot down a Korean airliner in September after mistaking it for a U.S. spy plane. And in November, the United States participated in Able Archer 83, a war game so realistic and provocative that the USSR put its forces on alert.

A homegrown movement against the arms race grew in response to these tensions. In particular, the push for a bilateral U.S.-Soviet "freeze" on the production, deployment, and testing of nuclear weapons gained popularity with the American public. Organized around the simple idea of halting the arms race as a first step toward rolling it back, this "nuclear freeze movement" soon became the largest U.S. mass movement since the Vietnam War. The term "freeze movement" was widely used as a catch-all term for disarmament activism writ large, but at the granular level opposition to nuclear weapons was politically quite diverse, made up of professional organizations like Physicians for Social Responsibility (PSR), "awareness raising" advocates like Ground Zero, direct action proponents such as the Livermore Action Group, and many other ideological formations.

These groups disagreed about tactics and aims, but they tended to share what anthropologist Hugh Gusterson calls a "culture of terror."[2] By encouraging the public to "think the unthinkable," activists hoped to force a personal confrontation with the effects and purpose of nuclear weapons, a stark contrast with the euphemistic language employed by elected officials and the defense establishment. The movement emphasized that nuclear war was a real possibility, with potentially catastrophic outcomes for human civilization. Activists wore radiation suits at protests, held "die-ins," showed horrific images from Hiroshima and Nagasaki, and generally tried to shake the public out of its complacency about the Cold War. PSR, for instance, was known for organizing events called "bombing runs," in which a medical professional would describe the impact of a nuclear weapon on a local city before a rapt audience. Presenters employed maps with concentric circles to methodically illustrate the effects of a nuclear blast as they extended outward from ground zero. Local landmarks were included in these descriptions to further concretize the typically abstract discussion of nuclear war. Speakers emphasized the impossibility of a medical response to such an attack: the point was that preventing nuclear war was the only real option.[3]

PSR's contribution to the culture of terror became highly influential. Jonathan Schell cited a 1980 PSR symposium in New York as an influence on the article series that became *The Fate of the Earth,* and a Los Angeles event was attended by several people who later contributed to iconic nuclear realist film *The Day After.*[4] The connection between movement culture and nuclear realism was not always this direct, but the microgenre clearly borrowed from and contributed to the movement's wider culture of terror. Just as the antinuclear movement sought to pierce through the abstractions employed by politicians and defense intellectuals, nuclear realism mobilized visceral images and intense verisimilitude to terrify audiences and hopefully spur them into action against the arms race.

Reviewers' responses to the four films varied, but a discussion of their realism was a common theme. *Time's* Jay Cocks complimented *The Day After's* "spookily accurate scenario for Armageddon."[5] *The Globe and Mail* praised the "sheer, engrossing credibility" of *Countdown to Looking Glass.*[6] Janet Maslin, writing for *The New York Times,* described *Testament* as "very realistic."[7] In the *Washington Post,* Colman McCarthy even dismissed the notion that *Testament* was science fiction, declaring it instead to be "science reality."[8] Clearly the films were experienced as believable, with this sense of authenticity a key part of their appeal and salience.

All "realist" texts, however, must construct their sense of verisimilitude through a series of aesthetic choices. In the case of nuclear realism, this construction occurs through several elements, three of which are most prominent: "everyman" characters in ordinary settings, extreme viscerality (including both bodily gore and emotional intensity), and a peculiar form of reflexivity, in which diegetic mass media are employed to deliver in-world "news" and the consumptive form (television) mirrors the way apocalyptic news would likely be delivered. In what follows, I briefly outline these three characteristics by citing examples from the films. *Countdown to Looking Glass,* it should be noted, clearly lacks the other films' ordinariness of setting and cast. That said, I would argue that its general sensibility and surfeit of the other qualities justifies its inclusion in the microgenre. Also worth noting here is the influence of Peter Watkins's banned 1965 telefilm *The War Game*, whose subject matter, faux documentary style, and unrelenting bleakness prefigured nuclear realism in many respects.

Nuclear realism utilizes locations that are remarkably unglamorous to remove a sense of a spectacle and ensure the films' content seems familiar and down-to-earth. These aren't the blockbuster disaster films of the 1970s, in other words: the destruction of coastal metropolises like Los Angeles (as in *Earthquake*) or stunning fictional settings (like *The Towering Inferno*'s "Glass Tower") is nowhere to be found. *Threads* is set in industrial Sheffield, UK; *The Day After* in Lawrence, Kansas, and Kansas City, Missouri. *Testament* takes place in the San Francisco Bay area, but the action occurs in a suburban community indistinguishable from similar locations across the United States. *The Day After* also heavily emphasizes rural locales, depicting salt-of-the-earth victims in flyover country. Several small Missouri towns are referenced in character dialog, and a quaint country farmhouse serves as one of the film's main settings. The opening montage of the film includes literal amber waves of grain.

The characters of nuclear realism mirror the ordinariness and familiarity of the film's settings. *Threads* follows the lives of two working-class families who are about to be joined by a marriage. *Testament* depicts the impact of nuclear war on a middle-class suburban family and their tight-knit local community. *The Day After* features an extensive cast of everyday archetypes: a doctor and his wife, a farmer and his family (including a soon-to-be-married daughter), a serviceman called into duty, a pregnant mother, a hospital nurse, professors, university students, and others. The class dimension is notable: Jason Robards's doctor is one of the few truly affluent characters featured in the films. The characters are meant to be recognizable and relatable, in the hope that their real-world counterparts—the mass audience of television—will feel compelled to take action against the arms race.

The second major characteristic of the microgenre is extreme viscerality, which contains both physical and psychological dimensions. Most of the films have elements of both, although *Threads* and *The Day After* tend to stress gore and bodily failure, while *Testament* and *Countdown to Looking Glass* place a stronger emphasis on psychic trauma and affective intensity. In the *The Day After* and *Threads*, viscerality is displayed and evoked through stomach-turning special effects: horrific burns, open wounds, and the symptoms of radiation sickness—including uncontrollable vomiting, incontinence, and bleeding from atypical orifices. For example, a postattack sequence in *The Day After* depicts young widow Denise (Lori Lethin) bleeding from between her legs during a church service, the blood spreading slowly over her light-colored dress. Similarly, *Threads* portrays an elderly character soiling herself and infamously concludes with the birth of a hideously deformed child: the bestial product of an irradiated British countryside.

Testament does not contain much gore, although the threat of radiation sickness lingers throughout the film as a quiet doom that slowly decimates the local population. It is the psychological trauma of this mass death, however, that receives the most attention, as Carol (Jane Alexander) and other parents face the impending deaths of their children with denial and despair. Carol—widowed by the nuclear attack—sews her children's burial shrouds, angrily interrupts a minister to ensure her youngest is entombed with his beloved teddy bear, and struggles to carry on amid a catastrophe committed by invisible figures who will never be brought to justice. A pivotal scene finds Carol cautiously explaining sex to her adolescent daughter. She struggles to describe sex's emotional dimensions, knowing her child will never grow up to experience it. *Testament*'s mood is more than somber: it is despondent. Little can be done to alleviate suffering after the fact. The time for action is now, the film implies, before the senseless deaths of your loved ones and the collapse of human society.

Countdown to Looking Glass contains an emotional intensity more akin to a traditional thriller, but its "live news" conceit and well-plotted "reporting" on a growing international crisis combine to create a gripping narrative. A fictionalized broadcast in the style of *War of the Worlds*, viewers are dropped into the crisis in medias res and immersed in on-location "live" journalism, this-just-in alerts, and running commentary by media pundits. Eric Sevareid, an actual broadcaster and winner of several Peabody awards, hosts the proceedings. Two members of Congress, Eugene McCarthy and Newt Gingrich, even play themselves. Global tensions rise over the course of the newscast and culminate in the live broadcast of a nuclear exchange between the United States and USSR in the Gulf of Oman. The film concludes with the president's airborne command plane taking flight and the initiation of the Emergency Broadcast System: the implication being that full-scale nuclear war is about to begin. Far more scenario-driven than the other films, the events that lead to nuclear confrontation in *Countdown to Looking Glass*—a global banking crisis, a coup in the Middle East, a maritime confrontation between world superpowers—are hardly far-fetched. Their similarity to actual historical events grants the scenario an eerie degree of plausibility and was apparently effective. During a 1988 rebroadcast on WTTG, frightened viewers in the Washington DC area, unable to get through to the station's switchboard, contacted the *Washington Post* to ensure an attack was not underway.[9]

Although most apparent in *Countdown to Looking Glass*, fictionalized mass media is a fixture of the microgenre. In the films, diegetic televisions and radios babble a backstory to the impending attack. In *The Day After* and *Threads*, several protagonists ignore news reports of an international crisis and only recognize the gravity of the situation once a nuclear attack is viewed as imminent. (In both films, a young couple's upcoming wedding distracts from the increasingly unsettling news.) In *Threads*, the BBC incessantly broadcasts the real-life *Protect and Survive* series of civil defense shorts. These crudely animated films were designed to calmly explain to the public how to build fallout shelters, preserve water, prevent exposure to radiation, and—ominously—dispose of corpses. In *Testament*, the news of a nuclear blast comes from an emergency bulletin that breaks into a regularly scheduled program. Cut off mid-broadcast, the television signal abruptly ceases—presumably, never to return.

The emphasis on mass media as the means of delivering apocalyptic news is notable because all four films were themselves products of television, rather than traditional Hollywood cinema. *The Day After* was broadcast to 100 million people on ABC. *Threads* was a BBC production that was later broadcast in the United States by Ted Turner's cable channel TBS. *Countdown to Looking Glass* was an early production of HBO that also aired on Canada's CTV. And although *Testament* received a theatrical release (and garnered an Academy Award nomination), it was filmed as part of PBS's *American Playhouse* series and later broadcast by the channel. This shared connection to television is important because it is bound up with the politics driving the microgenre. Nuclear realist films were not constructed to be subcultural phenomena. They embraced the mass viewership of television to communicate the dangers of nuclear weapons to as large an audience as possible. But this choice of media form also added weight to the media content. In the real world, disconcerting news of a nuclear crisis would be consumed via mass media, and the reflexivity of "watching television on television" imparts a further degree of verisimilitude to the microgenre. Nuclear realism employs the mass media of the present to portray the mass media of a possible near future. As in other examples of the "culture of terror," the message is to act now to prevent this disturbing future from ever coming to pass.

Nuclear realism was over by 1985. Its decline paralleled that of the nuclear freeze movement, which fractured after the 1984 presidential election. But the freeze and wider disarmament movements had succeeded at their most basic aim: preventing nuclear conflict. They brought the Reagan administration back from the brink and forced the United States to pursue arms control talks with the Soviet Union, negotiations that would lead to landmark agreements like the Intermediate-Range Nuclear Forces Treaty and, ultimately, the end of the Cold War. To lament the loss of nuclear realism is to miss its openly instrumental purpose: bolstering public fear of nuclear war and channeling it into political action. Nuclear disarmament remains an aspirational goal, but the overall trajectory is positive. In 1986, there were more than 70,000 nuclear warheads on earth. Today, there are fewer than 14,000.[10]

Nuclear realism is a compelling example of a productive relationship between social movements and mass media. It serves as a reminder that mass media texts can have significant real-world implications, especially when connected to a discrete political project. Drawing a direct causal line between nuclear realism and the end of the arms race would be overstating the case, but the films certainly acted in concert with the wider disarmament mobilization to raise public concern about nuclear weapons and force governments to take action. Few film genres—micro or otherwise—can claim a tie to such an existential accomplishment and, if only for that, nuclear realism should be recognized and praised.

Notes

1   Robert Scheer, *With Enough Shovels: Reagan, Bush, and Nuclear War* (New York: Random House, 1982), 18.

2   Hugh Gusterson, *Nuclear Rites: A Weapons Laboratory at the End of the Cold War* (Berkeley: University of California Press, 1998), 197.

3   Mary Neal, "Rhetorical Styles of the Physicians for Social Responsibility," in *Peace Action in the Eighties: Social Science Perspectives*, ed. Sam Marullo and John Lofland (New Brunswick: Rutgers University Press, 1990), 167–74.

4   David Cortright, *Peace Works: The Citizen's Role in Ending the Cold War* (Boulder: Westview, 1993), 32.

5   Jay Cocks, "The Nightmare Comes Home," *Time*, October 24, 1983, http://content.time.com/time/magazine/article/0,9171,926302,00.html.

6   Rick Groen, "Countdown to Looking Glass: Chilling and Superb," *Globe and Mail*, January 7, 1985, M9.

7   Janet Maslin, "Screen: Testament, After a Nuclear Blast," *The New York Times*, November 4, 1983, C8.

8   Colman McCarthy, "Testament of Commitment," *Washington Post*, March 24, 1983, A19.

9   John Carmody, "The TV Column," *Washington Post*, October 4, 1988, D8.

10 Hans M. Kristensen and Robert S. Norris, "Status of World Nuclear Forces," May 2019, https://fas.org/issues/nuclear-weapons/status-world-nuclear-forces.

14

Anti-Sitcom Video Art

Susanna Newbury

In the 1960s and 1970s, artists in the United States, Japan, and Western Europe began to make use of a technology newly debuted on the consumer electronics market: the portable video camera. First offered by the Japanese company Sony in 1965, the portable camera wasn't cheap. (Initial costs ranged from $1,000 to $1,500 per unit.) But in countries whose rapid postwar economic growth converged with burgeoning media markets, the equipment quickly made its way into public hands. Television studios, art schools, and media collectives all acquired recording equipment for experimentation before the medium's potential became clear. Artists were among the first to digest their product as a new phenomenon, observed but unclassified. Training their PortaPaks on themselves, their colleagues and lovers, outlandish spectacle and private fiction, they began to map (and skewer) what had become known as "middlebrow" culture, providing sadistic twists for emerging audiovisual norms of the broadcast public. In other words, they began to inhabit television to leverage it to their own imaginative ends, as video art (see Figure 14.1).

For art historians, the concept of video art is somewhat divided. We see it most often as a documentary supplement to live performances, produced both for archival and exhibition purposes, as subsets of broader conceptual, performance, or feminist art practices emerging since the 1960s. Or we see it as the experiments of a more recent generation of practitioners, those who grew up under the watchful eye of cable television, video games, or the blue-lit world of screens. Today, the instant replay of basic human life is everywhere. Forty years ago, however, video art charted this new media reality before its technological capacity.

Many artists experimented with TV from its earliest days as a medium. Nam June Paik played with the TV set as apparatus and the signal as agent of abstract distortion in a career that lasted from 1960 to 2006, coining the phrase "the electronic superhighway" along the way. Nancy Holt, Richard Serra, and Chris Burden experimented with TV as a distribution network, appearing live on local broadcasts to perform nonsensical acts. In art schools

Figure 14.1 Still from Michael Smith, *It Starts at Home* (1982) [Courtesy of Electronic Arts Intermix (EAI), New York].

and on college campuses, students turned increasingly to the medium as a means of documentation and personal expression. Even museums and art galleries attempted to get in on the action, with the Metropolitan Museum of Art and Museum of Modern Art in New York testing their own broadcast programs, and Berlin gallerist Gerry Schum debuting his *Fernsehgalerie* with a program of artists' videos on Land Art.[1]

But for others, adapting TV as a tool of fine art production wasn't the goal. Reprogramming mainstream forms of narrative by highlighting and subverting the formal codes of television as a popular medium became a way to undermine the normative power of media messaging. Attention by artists to TV and video not only as medium but as subject and form was different—a narrower tranche of the genre. For many video artists in the 1970s and 1980s, TV's influence merged perfectly with the artist's role as conceptual prankster. Through satirical occupation of TV genres such as the variety show, the infomercial, the family sitcom, the talk show, and proto-reality, disparate artists such as Paul McCarthy, Michael Smith, and Jaime Davidovich embraced kitsch for its cultural persuasion, humor, and emotional repression. They acquired, assembled, and archived what one prescient woman-on-the-mall-court interviewee called (in 1980, mind you) "basic, instant life." Thirty-odd years before the founding of Vine, twenty-five before the debut of *Keeping Up with the Kardashians*, and fifteen years before Peter Weir's *The Truman Show* (1998), such artists pioneered a microgenre that has since gone viral in our social media world: video art's role as anti-sitcom. Absorbed from the id of commercial TV on the verge of cultural hegemony, such artists sketched a nascent distributed media consciousness, outlining how TV's forms reprogram our brains.

For the kind of microgenre we're considering here, the major catalytic factors were the advent of cable TV (CATV) and the creation of nonprofit production and distribution centers around the nation. Cable began in the 1940s as a patchy fleet of small, independent service providers set up to improve long-range broadcast for rural communities.[2] That mission changed across two decades, and 1960s cable companies pivoted increasingly to the provision of for-pay programming offerings outside of the three major (free) broadcast networks. Wary of this turn of events at a time when academics, cultural critics, and government officials had turned their attention to the power of the television medium to shape sociopolitical events, in 1969 the Federal Communications Commission (FCC) enacted regulatory measures to try to even out accessibility, mandating each cable company make at least one public access channel in its network.[3] Such policy, the FCC argued, would allow the community "a practical opportunity to participate in community dialogue through a mass medium," causing others to argue cable would continue to "serve as a community information reservoir, transmitting a broad spectrum of cultural programming, educational material, and local governmental activities to the communities it services" by allowing the public free access not only to its distribution platform but also to equipped production studios.[4]

Nonprofit institutions also stepped into the gap between artists and cable broadcasting. The Long Beach Museum of Art (LBMA) began collecting videos in 1974 and outfitted its building with an editing room known as the Artists' Post-Production Studio (APPS).[5] The California Institute of the Arts (CalArts)—the region's premier art school, founded by Walt Disney and a hotbed of experimental and conceptual practices in the 1970s—also served as an early-adapter of video technology, encouraging its student-artists to experiment with video as a tool of composition, documentation, and as a new medium of art production. In upstate New York, artists began Videofreex, a video/television content collective that took over a low-power TV station in the Catskills. In Chicago, the School of the Art Institute of Chicago founded the Video Data Bank as a distribution and archiving organization for artists' videos before the work found a secure place in museum collections or art markets. In Minneapolis, Syracuse, Boston, and New Orleans such community-organized spaces sought to provide access to and feedback between broadcast television and ordinary people as counterpoint to consolidation and privatization.[6]

While there was certainly a robust feedback loop between the film and television industry and artists' communities in the LA of the 1970s, independent, nonprofit entities like LBMA were the ones actively promoting the development and distribution of video art in the public sphere. One of the most famous videos produced with LBMA support is Paul McCarthy's 1987 *Family Tyranny/Cultural Soup*. McCarthy is known for making art that subverts commercial television in order to explore the repressed violence enacted by popular media.[7] Primarily using performance and video, he mixes pop and trauma into a roiling stew of kitschy tropes. With the artist or a stand-in appearing as a garish clown-figure as host, the viewer is subjected to the normative expectations of TV programs with fantastical and nightmarish distortions: a children's program run aground on sexuality, a sitcom where chaos reigns over narrative resolution. Familiar, everyday objects—consumer goods like mayonnaise, ketchup, Vaseline, and dog food that typically pop up in commercial breaks—become Janus figures, with McCarthy redirecting consumerism to express the repressed psychological underbelly of advertising desire.[8] Featuring puppets, actors, and tableaux of found objects—dolls, mannequins, masks, condiments, cooking equipment, and beyond—McCarthy's videos recycle pop culture as surreal and terrorizing, placing thoughts at the edge of propriety front and center in recognizable, formulaic scenarios.[9]

Among the most familiar convergences of consumerism and desire in resolved narrative format is the 1950s American sitcom. McCarthy's *Family Tyranny* is, in these terms, an eight-minute nightmare reversal of the themes of *Father Knows Best*. It is set in a wood-veneer paneled cabin interior, carpeted in bright green, and set with a folding table, chair, and a variety of objects that, at first glance, look as though they belong in an artist's studio, garage, or rec room. On closer inspection, the objects' logical cohesion fails. We see a paint-spackled plastic jug, plastic shape models, reused pantry jars filled with a white liquid that looks like paint, and, creepily, the ripped-off head of a plastic baby doll, eyes toward the camera and yellow hair painted on its squeezable noggin. In the video a son, played by artist Mike Kelley, tries to escape the abuse of his rampaging, gargling father, played by McCarthy (whose face is never shown), interspersed with vignettes featuring the set props.[10] Instead of offering sound advice and comfort, the father alternately berates and beats the son, pantomimes raping him, and performs acts of torture on his surrogate, a volleyball-sized Styrofoam sphere, all the while muttering,

He's been a very bad boy. Very bad boy. Gonna make him eat what he doesn't want to eat. Gonna make him do what he doesn't want to do. Just take him back like that. My daddy made me eat this, and he's gonna eat this. We take this and shove it into his face; he's been a very bad boy.

Sequences of explicit violence appear in real time, then quickly merge into the playtime fantasies of an overgrown child. In *Family Tyranny* it's unclear from the video image what is physically present and what is superimposed on the still life of objects. Shots fade into and out of each other, hovering like creepy premonitions over the scene. The scenarios continue until the video fades to black. Credits roll under a sweetly synthetic musical track that suggests a return to the family sitcom, peacefully resolved against our better judgment.

The relationship to television isn't just formal. *Family Tyranny/Cultural Soup* was produced via LBMA's grant production program Open Channels, which commissioned video art intended for distribution on its broadcast series. Nor is the set-staginess of its production value incidental. Shot over two days in suburban Alhambra Cable's three-camera studio, McCarthy designed and built the sets as rough approximations of those of sitcoms. The convergence of video, violence, and the uncanny nature of TV sets was nothing new to McCarthy, who spent his time at the University of Southern California's film program working in the media office of the dental school and, in grad school at CalArts, working in video patient documentation at a psychiatric hospital.[11] Later he worked as an assistant on film sets, operating the camera and handling props. He recalled in a 2007 interview:

The soundstage can be disorienting ... You're on a set and there's a house, and you go through the door—which is supposed to go into the living room—but you enter a partial room facing another set of the outside of a grocery store. You're standing inside but you're outside, all of which is inside a soundstage. These are dreamscapes.[12]

The disorientating about-face of soundstages—the thin separation between the world of fiction and the real world of emotion—is one McCarthy plies particularly well, unmasking the story lines TV shows often gloss over. Maggie Nelson has written that *Family Tyranny*'s physical and pantomimed sexual abuse scenes become unwatchable toward its conclusion, even displaced as they are into a critique of mainstream television entertainment. McCarthy's point, she writes, is that "things do and do not remain 'only what they are:' that is the slippery space from which work like McCarthy's derives so much of its power."[13] The psychological haunting she identifies in much of the artist's work may be a familiar dynamic to those of us who consume a lot of television these days. Its power comes from a narrowing separation between the narrative on the screen and its audiences' remarkable ability to convert outrage into simple entertainment.[14] Although never broadcast through "Open Channels," *Family Tyranny/Cultural Soup* remains one of video art's most psychologically probing examinations into the repressed underbelly of mainstream, family-oriented sitcoms.

Even if it had made it to air, *Family Tyranny*, like most video art, would have been difficult to catch. Absent museum exhibitions or screenings at brick-and-mortar art institutions, opportunities to see independently produced video art were quite rare, and even then, tended to be one-off "events." Understanding this, many artists combined video art with the appropriation of television genres as an attempt to break through with broadcast content, merging making with the creation of artist-owned distribution networks. Such networks served as the broadcast bulletin boards of artist communities, playing its residents back to each other in batty late-night episodes. In New York, Davidovich helped found New York's Cable SoHo in the early 1970s as a collaboration between local collectives and arts nonprofits.[15] As the organization's first program director, he established the Artists' Television Network, a consortium of artist-public access production organizations based at the Manhattan Community TV (MCTV) cable access station, in 1977 and went on to produce such cult shows as *Portrait of the Best Artist*, *Soho Television Presents*, "*Composite TV*" *Views of SoHo*, and collective MICA-TV's interview series with emerging artists.[16]

Davidovich's own production *The Live! Show* provides a good example. Conceived as a "variety show for the avant-garde," it ran in 1979 and later aired weekly 1982–84. Recorded at artist-run facilities around the city, production was bare bones: "You didn't have a script or a whole staff of floor managers," Davidovich remembered. "The rest was anything goes."[17] Each *Live! Show* episode was hosted by Davidovich in his alter-ego, Dr. Videovich, a patient mélange of artist, psychiatrist, and showman specializing in "curing television addiction."[18] Individual segments utilized different TV formats (the call-in, the talking head interview, the public television cultural program, the home-shopping show, the bandstand showcase) popularized commercially as early as the 1950s. These original segments, which often involved the unknown cable audience calling in pranks, were interspersed with both live and taped presentations of video and performance art by figures such as Laurie Anderson and John Cage. It even offered at-cost advertising for community businesses.

Like *Family Tyranny*, *The Live! Show* was an absurdist take on medium conventions. One recurring segment, "Video Shop," featured Davidovich live-casting home shopping sales of bric-a-brac from his home and studio, including a *Dukes of Hazzard* TV tray ($4.00), a commercially produced doodle adhesive film and erasable markers to color over your TV set (Mr. Winky Dink, $3.95), and business-sized stationery sets featuring black-and-white gloves, hands, and female bodies ($3.95 each). On the January 21, 1983, episode, artist and songwriter Paul McMahon appeared as the "Rock and Roll Psychiatrist," standing in a suit and with a guitar before a childlike backdrop rendering of a living room, improvising advice, set to song, in response to each audience member's call-in query.

> Caller: "Doctor, doctor, I don't have many problems, but maybe you could help me with my few problems ... Like, well, I'm an alcoholic."
> McMahon: "I think I can help you, I think I hear what you're talking about [begins strumming and singing]. I lost my job, and a feel like a slob. All I do is sit around my house thinking, there's nothing that I can do to stop myself from drinkin'. My wife hates me, my kids think I'm a jerk. And I hate president Reagan because I'm out of work, and I'm depressed, this is not the best year for me."
> Caller [fake-crying]: "Doctor, thank you!"

And the point was, all TV is wacko. Programs like *The Live! Show* merely foregrounded its confected status. Like an art party led by an out of place safari guide, *The Live! Show* posed a provocative question: not how to see art on TV but how to see TV, through art, as a constructed medium. As William Hohauser, studio manager for Metro Access and a frequent *Live! Show* director, remembered of the experiential dimension of cable access at the time:

> You turned to [channels] C and D, and we were like, "What is this? Who are these people? Everything's black-and-white, and it's blurry and oddball. The channels never explained, "This is public access. Why don't you come down and do something?" It was just title cards. Maybe somebody announced the next program, but usually not. The shows just came on and off. There were no listings, and you couldn't find out what was going to happen next. Just these sparks of wackiness that you would come across when you turned the dial on the cable box.[19]

Fittingly, that spark of wackiness *The Live! Show* ended each episode with a 1979 Ilene Segalove video produced at LBMA's production studio, showing a California license reading "TV IS" with the righthand portion of the plate covered in dirt or shit, then washed off to reveal the word "OK" rolling after the credits. The car's horn toots and its engine revs, leaving the camera in its dust as it peels off. Manhattan, we bid you good night!

Francesco Casetti has remarked of the effect of contemporary network and digital technology that media, while changing a spectator's relation to the world, is itself constantly evolving. Functioning previously as "instruments for exploring the world and for facilitating dialogue between people," media has morphed into way stations for intercepting information from our social and virtual worlds. Screens, upon which such information plays, are "no longer surfaces on which reality is relived" but now "transit hubs for the images that circulate in our social space."[20] Rather than providing a window onto a world unified by its ubiquitous transmission, media serves as an everchanging platform for self-presentation, whether witting or not. It temporarily suspends the merging scenes of our everyday lives in fixed images, available to both private and unknown audiences.

This is yet another way to think about the microgenre of video art that plays with TV norms. Its practitioners appropriate and recirculate, perform and gather, and make present the culturally invisible forms of messaging naturalized in the overwhelming world of the screen. Even as it tickles the viewer with admissions of its fictionalized facsimile of basic, instant life, these artists feed TV back to viewers in satirical, alternative forms, daring them to connect the dots.

Like McCarthy and Davidovich, Michael Smith's work experiments with appropriated entertainment forms through a structure of vaguely nonsensical character performances.[21] In 1979, he began writing a series of intermittent television episodes featuring himself as "Mike," a somewhat isolated, slightly misfit every-guy whose daily routines are captured on television and whose saturation with media drives him to hallucinogenic neurosis.[22] "Mike" is a blank platform, a go-between for the spectator and the story, a constant presence against which the viewer can see or understand contextual change.

Like his maker, Mike is a baby boomer whose recorded activities demonstrate an increasing symptom of our time: that representation only exists in circulation. In one episode, a music video called "Go for It Mike" shot in a variety of earnest settings on the Texas set of a Western town, the character romps through a satirical version of Ronald Reagan's 1984 "Morning in America" ad, miraculously succeeding at everything he does. Smith's 1987 short "Mike" shows the character wandering through his daily life as if in a sequence of lowbrow advertisements. "Hm, I think I'll have a cup of coffee," Mike says to the screen as he rolls over in bed, every bit the Folgers spokes-husband. As Mike, now in a bathrobe, looks into the camera, he cocks his mug, and a suave voiceover narrates, *Coffee. A Meal in a Cup.* In the bathroom, Mike tosses disposable razor after disposable razor and finds visible release in rubbing a Q-tip into his ear, being sure to give each product its own framed still on screen. In his bedroom, searching for something clean to wear, Mike pulls out a crisp button-down and shows it to the camera. Where we expect to see a brand insignia, the word "Mike" appears instead—on his lapel, his tie clip, the label of his jeans. A sultry female voice ends the commercial: "Mike. Make the Ordinary Extraordinary."

Smith's videos point at the ways in which media projectively structures personal life through a routinized parade of products and pleasurable associations—success, self-recognition—and, in turn, repackage everyday life as aspirational narcissism. In each, the subject of media attention functions itself as a platform, a surface upon which associations land to be acquired, assembled, and archived into a profile of identity. Before the advent of social media, in Smith's 1980s world the platform isn't technological. Instead, it is the human psyche's increasing conditioning by media. In *It Starts at Home* (1982), the viewer falls further into the swirling mind of Mike in a musical medley shot in a Manhattan apartment interior set, which is revealed to be a recursive and dizzying saturation of cable TV media. We see that, following an on-screen visit from the Cable Guy, ensconced in his home, Mike becomes the subject of a real-time television show playing at smoky bars and in the homes of his friends, who call him to ask when he got a show. As the episode unfurls, we see the backstory of how Mike was discovered. The Cable Guy was an emissary of a fast-talking producer, played by a disembodied toupee. The toupee encourages Mike, stuck in his home, to audition different conventional gambits, from a vaudeville performance to neighbor-comedy featuring a friend who happens to stop by, only to get sucked into the production. In the toupee's ultimate resolution, "Mike's Show" is simply a continuous shot of two guys, sitting next to each other in armchairs, looking befuddled at the TV, which, they now realize, records them live and beams them out to the neighborhood cable network, that protean version of our network of affinity: the internet.

It is astonishing in 2019 to watch these early video works by Smith, Davidovich, and McCarthy precisely because of the ways they dissect and anticipate the insurgent influence of TV's narrative structure on our lives—by presenting them against the grain of professional production value and formal convention as shapers and shifters of attention. Such artists, in addition to generating their own content, present and perform what art historian Jonathan Crary termed in the late 1980s "techniques of the observer." Written, as Crary himself acknowledges, at the dawn of digital and virtual imaging systems, his book examined nineteenth-century transformations in the role of the observer—a process the author described as engaged "fundamentally [with] questions about the body and the operation of social power"—in a moment of profound technological change.[23] Observing the nascent medium of television and technology of platform broadcasting in the late 1970s and into the 1980s, these anti-sitcom video artists diagnosed its operations of social power as precisely such a technique, a rooted way of seeing that has since transcended apparatus, network, and form to shape the ways we relate to one another in the present as the human products of observation.

Notes

1   The curator Barbara London has chronicled these and other milestones in video art in "Video: A Selected Chronology, 1963–1983," *Art Journal* 45, no. 3 (Autumn 1985): 249–62.

2   See Patrick R. Parsons, *Blue Skies: A History of Cable Television* (Philadelphia: Temple University Press, 2008).

3   As Parsons notes, the FCC mandated systems with more than 3,500 subscribers to offer at least one channel and systems in the top 100 markets to offer four (ibid., 256).

4   Cited in "Toward Community Ownership of Cable Television," *The Yale Law Journal* 83, no. 8 (July 1974): 1709.

5   These included plans to form the museum's own cable television channel (sadly never fully realized). Kathy Rae Huffman, "Exchange and Evolution: Worldwide Video Long Beach, 1974–1999," in *Exchange and Evolution: Worldwide Video Long Beach, 1974–1999* (Long Beach: Long Beach Museum of Art, 2011), 13.

6   For more, see London, "Video," and David Joselit, *Feedback: Television against Democracy* (Cambridge: MIT Press, 2007).

7   Ralph Rugoff, "Mr. McCarthy's Neighborhood," in *Paul McCarthy* (New York: Phaidon, 1996), 32.

8   Ibid., 35.

9   Ibid., 54.

10 *Cultural Soup*, the seven-minute video that follows, extends this story with McCarthy the father playacting a Julia Child-type cooking show, making soup out of dolls and mayonnaise in a rec room.

11 Paul McCarthy, interview by Glenn Phillips, May 8, 2007. Published in *California Video: Artists and Histories* (Los Angeles: Getty Research Institute, 2008), 170, 171.

12 Ibid., 173.

13 Maggie Nelson, *The Art of Cruelty: A Reckoning* (New York: Norton, 2011), 162.

14 Paul McCarthy, interview by Kristine Stiles, in *Paul McCarthy*, 22, 26.

15 Maeve Connolly, *TV Museum: Contemporary Art and the Age of Television* (Chicago: Intellect, 2014), 204.

16 London, "Video," 258.

17 Leah Churner, "Un-TV: Public Access Cable Television in Manhattan: An Oral History," February 10, 2011, http://www.movingimagesource.us/ articles/un-tv-20110210.

18 Ibid.

19 Ibid.

20 Francesco Casetti, "What Is a Screen Nowadays?" in *Public Space, Media Space*, ed. Chris Berry et al. (London: Palgrave, 2013), 17.

21 "Mike Kelley—Michael Smith, MOCA U—MOCAtv," YouTube, June 27, 2014, https://www.youtube.com/watch?v=Y-lmuiK4Ado.

22 "Michael Smith—In Focus—The Artist's Studio—MOCAtv," YouTube, April 15, 2013, https://www.youtube.com/watch?v=neB8NPXfRGk.

23 Jonathan Crary, *Techniques of the Observer: On Vision and Modernity in the Nineteenth Century* (Cambridge: MIT Press, 1990), 3.

15

Home Depot Art

Danielle Kelly

Imagine a construction site: red or brown earth punctuated by towering configurations of rebar, two-by-fours, and scaffolding, with the occasional lonely digger or two. It is an arrangement of recognizable things that gains meaning through proximity, whether by association to the site or between the objects themselves. The very nature of a construction site is such that it is in progress, latent, approximate. It also hints at a very human foible: to build, to expand, on the brink of something. Raw construction supplies and hardware store materials are naturally imbued with this quality of *potential*, teetering between almost-ness and almost nothing-ness, reaching toward assembly while maintaining an airless state of disassembly.

Now imagine similar materials in an art gallery. Like a construction site, innocuous objects are arranged in proximity and activate one another. Fencing, wood, buckets, and safety cones mix with Budweiser cans, rubber chickens, and handcuffs, aggregating into large-scale constructions that are formally rigorous even as they spasmodically dissolve into chaos or uncertainty.[1] Artist Cady Noland uses these building supplies in her sculptural installations, sometimes sparingly, and always in combination with other objects. As ritualized objects of American life, hardware store supplies can be utilized to arrange, intimate, or suggest, hovering at the notion of process. Each object almost aggressively retains its individuality all while somehow coalescing into an uneasy whole, intentionally made palliative by the inclusion of easily identifiable cultural elements like a stray American flag.[2] The combined effect results in magnetic works like *The American Trip* (1988) or *Untitled* (1989), artworks in which the spectacles of violence and public humiliation, paranoia, and media manipulation capture acute afflictions of American life (see Figures 15.1).[3]

Like kids in a candy shop, artists love hardware stores. Supplies are affordable, accessible, and available in abundance. They are also potent and receptive, easily persuaded to adapt to an artist's formal or conceptual concerns. Artists may delight in the retinal qualities of a material, its color or surface quality, or they might luxuriate in how something smells or feels. For

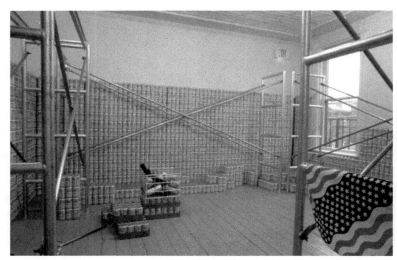

Figure 15.1 Cady Noland, *Untitled* (Exhibition: Mattress Factory, October 14–December 22, 1989) [Courtesy of the Mattress Factory Museum, Pittsburgh, PA].

some artists, deep engagement with a substance and its physical qualities is at the heart of the creative process. The application of formal strategies can provide a direct aesthetic means of visually accessing a notion or unifying a seemingly discordant collection of objects or ideas. A sculpture constructed from a seemingly unrelated variety of textures and materials is instantly unified if the artist paints the whole thing red, to offer a simplified example. These same formal qualities are also a huge part of the allure of building supplies, and nonartists are no less susceptible to the temptation. The big-box hardware store can be an earthly sensorial delight: the smell of freshly cut pine, the disco glitterati of light as it reflects off the long rows of nuts and screws, the silky-smooth porcelain of a brand-new toilet. The tactile pleasures of Home Depot are undeniably beguiling.

Hardware stores are also like giant idea factories, alluring to those artists more inclined toward intellectual stimuli rather than sensorial ones. Walk the aisles of the average big-box hardware store and the urge to renovate, build, or repair is inevitable. Who wouldn't want to make something new or fix something broken? Each shelf is flush with potential, promising the path to a new project or the solution to an old one. Home repair supplies can be useful and anonymous (a bucket, a hammer) and quite capable of independent function. Some building materials, on the other hand, incline toward operating conditionally, functioning exclusively in relationship to a place, object, or position, without which they become useless, absurd, or abstract (a drill bit, a pipe elbow). Some might suggest order or organization, psychologically reinforcing an existing boundary or the potential to create new ones (caution tape, safety cones). Others possess physical weight or monumentality that intimates architecture, suggesting a formidable or home-like structure (drywall, bricks, concrete, crown molding). Each possesses conceptual potential and a mutable singularity: a self-contained "thingness" that also continually points at that which is other/new/better/ worse. A solitary hammer resting on a table is just a tool at rest, but it also contains all of the things a hammer can do, make, or destroy. "I like using objects in the original sense," Noland has stated, "letting them be what they are."[4]

But hardware store love does not an artistic genre make. Is there such a thing as "Home Depot Art"? Certainly not one that any contemporary working artist or art critic seems interested in claiming. For any person who loves hardware stores *and* contemporary art, though, it has enjoyed a decades-long vitality. It is doubtful that the hardware store impulse has gone unnoticed, especially given the art world's tendency toward obsessive self-analysis. Maybe it's just not cool to talk about. But the signs, or rather the objects, are all there: everything from house paint and buckets to plastic sheets and cement mixers are fair game as artistic materials. As boundaries continue to dissolve and artists work across genres beyond the confines of monolithic categories such as "painter" or "sculptor," more artists continue to pillage hardware stores for plain old useful *stuff*.

Historically, the artistic appeal of hardware or construction supplies is far more complex than simply providing a formal or conceptual playground. As compared to traditional art supplies, modest building materials have a history of radical activism within the art world. The incendiary potential of blue-collar construction supplies cannot be overstated. Internationally, the 1950s, 1960s, and 1970s saw varying emergent artistic movements that embraced simple, humble, industrial, and/or found materials. Neo-Dada in America, Nouveau Realisme or Arte Povera in Europe, and Mono-ha in Japan were each in their own way a reaction to a skyrocketing art market, political forces, or oppressive institutions. While distinct in motivation and appearance, each embraced a defiant aesthetic philosophy realized by some combination of assemblage, collage, performance, or conceptual art. The use of nontraditional art materials or strategies was an attempt to free the artists from the societal confines, or economic barriers, of that rarefied world. Instead of expensive marble, steel, or oil paint, these artists used construction supplies, everyday items, or found objects. The use of humble and accessible materials was outrageous at the time, an affront to tradition that allowed for a critique of the establishment, a relatable point of entry for rigorous inquiry into the image/idea/object itself, and a serious appraisal of the creative process as a whole.

These days, the use of utilitarian materials in contemporary art is no longer very radical, although it can be radically subversive. Pop into any graduate program in the visual arts and you will likely find a student lovingly arranging construction cones or determinedly shaping industrially fabricated wire mesh, with a little quick-mix concrete thrown in for raw visual, or literal, stabilizing effect. Perusing the local big-box store for art supplies has become a time-honored, if maligned, art school tradition. The cheap, abundant materials arrive with built-in meaning, adding instant depth to a student project struggling to find its conceptual footing. Although an artist will likely move on from such theoretical exercises as their work matures, most artists continue to use big-box hardware stores for straightforward, affordable building supplies. But some dig in: buckets and house paint and bricks and wood become core media.

The resulting artworks come in all tantalizing shapes and sizes. The universe of artists using hardware store supplies is an incongruent, overlapping ecosystem. Jessica Stockholder and Rachel Harrison combine an excess of everyday, pop cultural objects with hardware store finds. Stockholder joyfully expands the notion of painting through sculpture and installation, deftly constructing works that tilt endlessly between the two and three dimensional. Works like the *Assist* series (ongoing) and *Lay of the Land* (2016) are just two recent examples from a career spanning thirty years (see Figures 15.2 and 15.3). *Alexander the Great* (2007) and *The Spoonbender* (2011) evidence Harrison digging into cultural associations with humor and formal intellect, compiling awkward monuments to crap and chaos (see Figures 15.4 and 15.5). Phoebe Washburn (*Nothing's Cutie*, 2004; *True, False Slightly Better*, 2003) accumulates worn or weathered construction materials to create literal giant waves of aggregate refuse (see Figures 15.6 and 15.7). Her chosen materials translate into work both modest and monumental. And Kate Gilmore (*Beat It*, 2014; *Between a Hard Place*, 2008) builds structures that confine, limit, or contain her physically in drywall and plaster, which she then relentlessly claws, tears, kicks, and punches her way through in a process documented via strenuously claustrophobic videos (see Figures 15.8 and 15.9).[5] Andra Ursata, Maya Lin, Cameron Rowland, Jesse Robinson, Kate Gilmore, Seth Price, Mark Bradford, Tom Sachs, los carpinteros, Shirley Tse, Jesse Darling, Judy Pfaff, Gedi Sibony, and Chelsea Pegram are a small sampling of the countless established and emerging artists orbiting this genre.

Figure 15.2 Jessica Stockholder, *Assist #1: A Cyst* (2015) (© Jessica Stockholder) [Courtesy of the artist; Kavi Gupta, Chicago and Mitchell-Innes & Nash, New York].

Figure 15.3 Jessica Stockholder, *Lay of the Land* (2014) (© Jessica Stockholder) [Courtesy of the artist; Mitchell-Innes & Nash, New York, and Galerie nächst St. Stephan, Vienna].

Figure 15.4 Rachel Harrison, *Alexander the Great* (2007) (Photograph: Jean Vong) [Courtesy of the artist and Greene Naftali, New York].

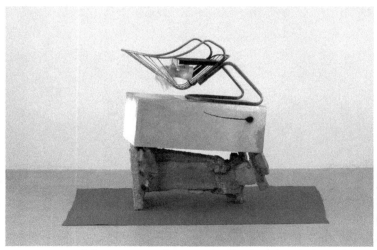

Figure 15.5 Rachel Harrison, *The Spoonbender* (2011) (Photograph: John Berens) [Courtesy of the artist and Greene Naftali, New York].

Figure 15.6 Phoebe Washburn, *Nothing's Cutie* (Exhibition: LFL Gallery, September 2–October 2, 2004) [Courtesy of the artist].

Figure 15.7 Phoebe Washburn, *True, False, and Slightly Better* (Exhibition: Rice University Gallery, January 24–March 24, 2003) [Courtesy of the artist].

Figure 15.8 Kate Gilmore, *Beat It* (2014) (Commissioned by H&R Block Space at Kansas City Art Institute) [Courtesy of the artist].

Figure 15.9 Kate Gilmore, *Between a Hard Place* (2008 video stills) (Commissioned by ICA Philadelphia) [Courtesy of the artist].

Most of the artists who parlay in Home Depot supplies are masters of proximity. Cady Noland, Jessica Stockholder, and Rachel Harrison, for example, have a keen sense of studied arrangements, of placing seemingly unrelated crude, banal, or pop cultural objects together to serve a greater purpose or idea. Each object is dynamic, deftly activating one another in readily identifiable ways. The materials an artist chooses are potent formally or culturally, carrying with them experiences and implications that transform as they entangle with our own. In America, construction supplies are widely available to almost anyone with access to a hardware store and the resources to make a purchase. Whether assembling furniture or renovating a bathroom, lots of people have experienced holding a hammer or arranging sheets of plywood. The average person likely knows from personal experience the sensation of running a hand across a silky-smooth sheet of drywall or the vibrational hum of sandpaper in motion. All of these seemingly anonymous objects or experiences have cultural meaning, personal or shared. The value of such associative potential is not lost on artists.

This democratic spirit of Home Depot as art supply store means that anyone has access to scalable materials. The hardware store is full of row upon row of industrially fabricated items, each made to a specification that allows for it to interlock or connect with some other item or object to function. And on a mass scale, these items are all the same. As artists use these materials, they begin to understand the intention behind how or why something is made a certain way and how they all fit together. But the artists' endgame is to bend that purpose to match the needs of the artwork.

There exists, however, a real and uncomfortable tension in some of the artworks mentioned here. For all the democratic spirit of modest hardware store stuff, the effect of the gallery context, along with the art-world financial and critical mega-machine, is disjunctive. These artists are not laborers, and the work they make will end up in elite spaces far removed from the realm of Home Depot, in stark contrast to the spirit of their source. Also, trends have a cycle that hyper-refines meaning and value. From its first breath to its last whimper as a waning fad, a once popular style or theoretical approach invariably loses steam and becomes passé. If it resonates, a mode of art-making may become part of the vernacular, as it evolves into something stylized or historical—an aesthetic reference point that can be quickly summoned with a few smart visual clues. Sincerity is easily rendered self-conscious or even sardonic.

In 2015, writer and visual artist Seth Price published a piece of dystopic art-world auto-fiction entitled "Fuck Seth Price," followed subsequently by a conceptually adjacent exhibition. In the novel, the antihero "Seth Price" is a disillusioned contemporary artist who has a very astute, if cynical, tried and true recipe for creating successful artwork: "Any number of methods or styles would do, so long as the result looked 'cool,' ensuring that the painting would seem classic and minimal while emanating a vague awareness of rich historical struggle."[6] According to fictional Price, a "lack of concern for traditional skill," a "cynical irreverence," and a punk-like "dismissal of history" are all the boxes you need to check if you want to make fashionable contemporary art.[7] And of what did real-life artist Seth Price's nonfiction exhibition *Wrok Fmaily Freidns* (2016) consist? (See Figure 15.10.) Sculptural installations of plywood, plastic netting, PVC pipes, and other raw building supplies, a minimal and arguably historical collection of signifiers pirouetting between banal self-loathing, satire, and sincerity.[8]

At its best, Art (with a capital A) is magnanimous. Unfortunately, Art can also operate from a very unwelcoming, rarified place, with artistic media greasing the wheel. Aside from the implied exclusivity of institutions and galleries, throughout most of its existence, the primary materials of an artist were very, very expensive. Pigment, oil paint, marble, and stone would all be well out of reach of most artists, requiring the financial support or leverage of a sponsor. This shifted over time with increased availability and lower costs, but until quite recently art had to be made out of the *correct* stuff in the *correct* manner to be taken seriously. Ideas of monumentality, quality, and value are still to some extent limited by tired notions of material, scale, class, or intention.

Figure 15.10 Seth Price, *Wrok Fmaily Freidns* (2016) (Exhibition view at 356 S. Mission) [Courtesy of the artist].

Cue Mark Bradford, a master of monumental detritus, whose work exemplifies some of the best of what the hypothetical genre of Home Depot Art can be. Bradford skewers American culture and history but is not necessarily interested in the singularity of a specific material. Instead, he works in accumulation, the messy gunk and stuff of culture. Bradford has a predilection for local advertising and material media culture: the modestly produced posters, hand-painted signs, and paste-up advertisements of his LA neighborhood.[9] The artist pulls from this ephemeral urban wallpaper as both media and inspiration, and combines it fluidly with affordable construction supplies, rather than art supplies, in his creative process.

Bradford's recent large-scale installation *Pickett's Charge* (2017) is a 400-foot circular collection of abstract paintings that physically embody the violent heart of American history (see Figures 15.11–15.13). The source imagery, an 1883 cyclorama by artist Philip Philippoteau depicting the Battle of Gettysburg, is almost imperceptible. Layer upon layer of paper thickly accumulates into unwieldy paintings, whose surfaces have been relentlessly mined in a ferocious process of sanding, tearing, and scarring. Bits of cord or rope hang from sections and extend in great loops on the sides of the paintings, as swaths of paper hide or reveal information in tandem. Where representation has been almost entirely obliterated, a maelstrom of anger, frustration, and fear emerge, articulated in paper, glue, house paint, and bungee cord: simple, relatable stuff transformed.

Figure 15.11 Mark Bradford, *Pickett's Charge* (2017) (© Mark Bradford) (Exhibition: Hirshhorn Museum and Sculpture Garden, Washington D.C.; photographer: Cathy Carver) [Courtesy of the artist and Hauser & Wirth].

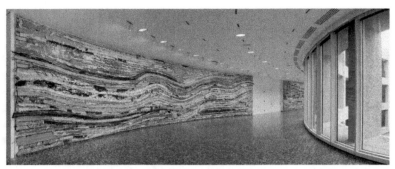

Figure 15.12 Mark Bradford, *Pickett's Charge* (2017) (© Mark Bradford) (Exhibition: Hirshhorn Museum and Sculpture Garden, Washington D.C.; photographer: Cathy Carver) [Courtesy of the artist and Hauser & Wirth].

Figure 15.13 Mark Bradford, *Pickett's Charge* (2017) (© Mark Bradford) (Exhibition: Hirshhorn Museum and Sculpture Garden, Washington D.C.; photographer: Cathy Carver) [Courtesy of the artist and Hauser & Wirth].

Pickett's Charge materially decimates one moment in U.S. history to create a new ground upon which to assemble an-*other* horrifying and disjointed, if openly marginalized, history of the United States. As an artist who is also black and queer, Mark Bradford faces a multivalent web of obstacles and assumptions, rooted not only in the structural racial and social prejudices of American society but also that of the art world. Bradford navigates these obstructions in a deeply discerning way that finds the artist critiquing, challenging, and manipulating these conditions by being, unequivocally, himself.[10] Bradford's chosen materials are essential to this process. He maximizes the materials' unassuming status while pushing through its perceived high-art limits, into an abstraction that precisely pinpoints this moment in time.

The layers of material culture and unassuming hardware store supplies that make up Bradford's complex abstract paintings can be a jarring revelation, particularly in concert with the breathless process of destruction and metamorphosis embodied in the work. Mark Bradford is vocally committed to using modest or easily accessible materials, coming full circle to his activist-artist forebears of decades ago. His art supply store of choice? Home Depot. "If Home Depot doesn't have it," he has said, "Mark Bradford doesn't need it."[11] Long live Home Depot Art and its democratizing and subversive effect.

Notes

1   Mark Kremer and Camiel van Winkel, "'Metal Is a Major Thing and a Major Thing to Waste': Interview with Cady Noland," in *Witness to Her Art*, ed. Rhea Anastasia and Michael Branson (Annandale on Hudson: Center for Curatorial Studies Bard College, 2010), 156.

2   Ibid.

3   Michele Cone, "Cady Noland," in *Witness to Her Art*, 155.

4   Ibid.

5   Anna Watkins Fisher, "Like a Girl's Name: The Adolescent Drag of Amber Hawk Benson, Kate Gilmore, and Liv Young," *The Drama Review* 56, no. 1 (Spring 2012): 58.

6   Ross Simonini, "Less Like Art: Seth Price as Author," *Art in America*, April 29, 2016, https://www.artinamericamagazine.com/news-features/news/less-like-art-seth-price-as-author.

7   Ibid.

8   Ibid.

9   Katy Siegel, "Somebody and Nobody," in *Mark Bradford*, ed. Christopher Bedford (Columbus: The Ohio State University, 2010), 106.

10 Ibid., 105.

11 Calvin Tomkins, "What Else Can Art Do?" *The New Yorker*, June 22, 2015, https://www.newyorker.com/magazine/2015/06/22/what-else-can-art-do.

16

The Mommy Memoir

Mary Thompson

The mommy memoir is a type of life-writing that gained popularity in the 1990s and early 2000s. The texts that comprise this microgenre are narrated from the perspective of a mother, usually addressing an audience of primarily (new) mothers. Mommy memoirs recount stories of motherhood—including struggles to conceive and unexpected pregnancies—childbirth, breastfeeding, and the early months of child-raising. Not to be confused with memoirs by daughters writing about their mothers, the mommy memoir gives a narrative voice to the maternal perspective, which has been culturally silenced by experts. Some mommy memoirs were culled from writings that began as web logs (mommy blogs), whose diary format and ambivalent tone chronicled the daily and mundane experiences of motherhood.[1]

Mommy memoirs are keenly aware of the surveillance of mothers that gained renewed intensity in the late twentieth century.[2] In response, the narratives adopt an ambivalent tone that balances the authors' love for their children with a rejection of normative motherhood. One of the first chronicles of maternal ambivalence in book-form was Anne Lamott's *Operating Instructions: A Journal of My Son's First Year* (1993).[3] Lamott recounts how, after previously having an abortion during her lowest moment of drug and alcohol addiction, she gains sobriety and again becomes pregnant—this time with her son. In recovery, she embraces the challenge of motherhood as a spiritual act, redemption, and motivation for being one's best self. On the one hand, Lamott's narrative captivates with its breathless, wonder-filled tone: "Sam [her son] looks up into my face like maybe my freckles are forming themselves into familiar letters."[4] On the other hand, it adopts the same honesty for relating tales of maternal doubt and frustration:

> One of the worst things about being a parent, for me, is the self-discovery, the being face to face with one's secret insanity and brokenness and rage. Someone without children, who thinks of me as being deeply spiritual, said the other day that motherhood gave me the opportunity to dance with my feelings of inadequacy and anger, and my automatic response

was to think, Oh go fuck yourself, you New-Age Cosmica Rama dingdong head—go dance with *that* one.[5]

Ayelet Waldman also writes critically of external expectations on mothers, observing that women have been enlisted in the surveillance of each other, a betrayal that only adds to maternal self-doubt. Waldman, who is married to the writer Michael Chabon, created an internet firestorm when she stated in *The New York Times* style section that she loved her husband more than her children.[6] The disparaging backlash—primarily from mothers—was immediate and voluminous and contributed to her writing *Bad Mother*, in which she responds: "One of the darkest, deepest shames so many of us mothers feel nowadays is our fear that we are Bad Mothers, that we are failing our children."[7]

For many writers, the ambivalent tone is adopted in response to the proliferation of normative advice in popular media. The editors of *Breeder*, a volume of first-person narratives about alternative motherhood styles, rebelliously proclaim, "We aren't the neo-June Cleaver corporate beauties you see in the mainstream parenting magazines, and we aren't the purer than thou organic earth mamas you see in the alternative glossies."[8] A direct contrast to the tone of parenting magazines and in open defiance of experts and advertisers in those publications, mommy memoirs seemingly fulfill a need for books on motherhood that resist normative prescriptions for bodies and behaviors. In the mommy memoir, authority and expertise arise from experience in the trenches and take the form of raw confessions about failures, ambivalence, mishaps, and guilt.

Mommy memoirs do not stop with subverting righteous busybodies and media ideals. Most mommy memoirs rely on the plot device of rebellion against traditional authority—especially Western doctors and one's own mother—and an assertion of the self. In *Baby Love*, Rebecca Walker struggles for self-definition against the medical establishment and in the shadow of her famous and formidable mother, Alice Walker. In her opening chapter, Walker accuses her mother's generation of not realizing "that they had to *give* adulthood to their daughters by stepping down, stepping back, stepping away, and letting the daughter take center stage."[9] When told by her doctor that homebirths are "more for the mother" and giving birth in hospitals prioritizes the baby's needs (appropriately), Walker flares, "How dare she pit me against my baby!"[10] In a similar rejection of medical expertise, Angela Morrill depicts her struggle to have her desire for a homebirth respected. Morrill tells her midwife that she is five feet tall and weighs 220 pounds, and "I didn't want to be treated as high risk because of my weight."[11] Skeptical of hospital births, vaccines, and c-sections, mommy memoirs often reflect—for better or for worse—a mosaic of messages from the 1970s women's health movement and the twenty-first-century internet, which the authors leverage against traditional forms of authority.

Mommy memoirs also rebel against the authors' feminist foremothers. Many authors of mommy memoirs identify as feminists but are at odds with what they thought feminism told them about motherhood. Mommy memoirs often repeat the line of reasoning expounded in the notorious 2003 *The New York Times Magazine* article by Lisa Belkin titled "The Opt-Out Revolution," in which she reported that women were dropping out of fast-track professional careers by choice to stay at home and raise children. Fed up with feminist messages to "have it all," these women were finding pleasure in identifying as the stay-at-home moms their feminist mothers warned them against becoming.[12] An early mommy memoir that anticipated this message is Anne Roiphe's *Fruitful* (1996). Roiphe's narrative—written retrospectively after her daughters are adults—challenges what she claims is feminism's neglect of mothers and families. Cautioning that feminist movement could end on the "rock pile of tarnished visions," Roiphe announces:

> I want my daughters to understand that their easy, natural, assumed feminism, the careers that they are launched on, will be impinged on by their emotional lives. I want them to find better ways of being both mothers and working women. I'm frightened they might sacrifice one for the other. I want to warn them that the feminism I preached needs to be tempered with connection and love, for partner and child. I want them to understand that life is not a gaggle of political slogans, however stylish, smart, politically correct they might be.[13]

Her memoir defends motherhood by claiming—falsely, many would argue— that feminists have devalued its worth in favor of careers. Similarly, Waldman started a career as a lawyer (her mother's expectation) but abandons it to become a full-time mother and part-time writer: "Our mothers and the professors of our women's studies courses had told us that it was our job to do it all, without warning us how impossible that task would be."[14] Walker, probably the mommy memoirist with the biggest feminist shoes to fill, warns ominously, "I didn't know that the showdown between the ideas of my mother's generation and my own was inescapable."[15] While many mommy memoir authors—such as Walker—claim feminist identities,[16] their texts often argue against a feminism that, frankly, many feminists would not recognize. Mommy memoirs usually neglect to critique how patriarchy structures the workspace and caregiving arrangements; instead, feminism and feminists are cast as antagonists to the narrator.

While professional careers outside the home are eschewed by most mommy memoirists, the occupation they embrace—presumably for its assimilation into the domestic space—is the career of writer. An implied conflict between motherhood and writing career characterizes most plots, as in *Fruitful* when Roiphe sketches the contours of the old debate over whether or not woman lacks the focus to create art because she "cannot close herself off" to the needs of others.[17] Without taking a side, Roiphe concedes to the binary terms of this debate, concluding, "I would rather have a child than a book."[18] However, most mommy memoirists—who are college graduates of a later generation than Roiphe and who took a women's studies course where they read Virginia Woolf, Tillie Olsen, and Alice Walker—are aware of the trope of the woman writer, who—lacking a room of her own—has her voice interrupted by the heteropatriarchal demands placed on wives and mothers. These writers deconstruct the old debate with gusto. Mommy blogs productively lend themselves to interrupted writing *and* reading—for, as Woolf famously said about women's domestic lives, "interruptions there will always be."[19] Furthermore, mommy memoir books assert themselves as conclusive proof that twenty-first-century women can be both mothers and published writers—in fact, they become writers because of motherhood. Walker, afraid that she would lose her professional identity, set herself an annual goal after having her son: "I am now closer than ever to writing a book a year, and I owe it all to Tenzin."[20] Similarly, the poet Sherry Thompson remarks, "I am an artist *because* I have children."[21] Waldman, after deciding to quit her job as a lawyer to stay home with her children, confesses that "worst of all, I was bored"; however, she "found something else to do" and "began writing."[22]

A final theme that is common to mommy memoirs is the intersection of motherhood with twenty-first-century technologies. These narratives simultaneously revel in and fret over assisted reproductive technologies, prenatal testing, and hospital childbirths—aspects of the medicalization of pregnancy. This paradox is laid bare by accounts of prenatal testing. As Rayna Rapp predicted, women are reluctant "pioneers" on the frontier of this emerging technology.[23] The memoirs by Beck and Waldman both poignantly capture the distress produced by a diagnosis of genetic anomaly. During her very-wanted third pregnancy and following an amniocentesis, Waldman learned that her baby had a trisomy—a triple chromosome where there should be only two—and would likely be born with Down syndrome. After agonizing over the decision with her husband, she had an abortion and began a long process of grieving. Martha Beck also learns that the child she is carrying will likely be born with Down syndrome. In *Expecting Adam* she narrates her decision to take her pregnancy to term and the near-universal opposition with which she is met.[24] In both memoirs by Beck and Waldman, amniocentesis presents difficult choices, of which abortion is only one.[25]

Other mommy memoirs present technologies that support less difficult choices. In "Real Moms" Sara Manns recounts the experience of seeking in vitro fertilization with her lesbian partner (they ultimately adopt a child). In "The Pump and I," Alisa Gordaneer muses on the technology of the breast pump. With her "four-month-old baby, on [her] right breast and his mechanical brother—a space-age contraption of bottle and trumpet and aquarium tubing hooked up to a black box—on [her] left," Gordaneer provides readers with an ironic perspective on the technology that frees women to work at jobs outside the home.[26] Expanding the definition of technology to include the internet offers yet another example of how motherhood is entering a cyborg age. In a chapter titled "Tech Support," Waldman remarks on her reliance on internet support groups for her insights into motherhood: "When I realized I was pregnant with Zeke, the first thing I did—even before making a doctor's appointment to verify the accuracy of the two pink lines— was join an online support group for pregnant women due in June."[27] Indeed some scholars have argued that the supportive and politicizing communities that are fostered by mommy narratives hold radical potential for mothers.[28] However, other scholars contend that, by 2018, many texts merely reflect curated lifestyles, pitchwomen, and influencers.[29]

Although mommy memoirs have been popular (internet searches will turn up hundreds of titles)—or perhaps due to their commercial success— the genre has been dismissed by critics. The chosen narrative form—mostly diaries, chronicles, or epistolary narratives that address fellow mother-readers or a future child ("Dear Baby…")—marks them as chick lit. Marketing and critical reception of the mommy memoir reflect prevailing gender politics: the labels of *momoir* and *mommy memoir* stigmatize these woman-authored texts as distinct from memoirs about fatherhood, which are judged on literary merits and seldom demeaned by cutesy titles.[30] Michael Bérubé's memoir about his son with Down syndrome, for example, is not considered *daddy-lit*.[31]

From another perspective, "Ain't I a Mommy" by Deesha Philyaw rightfully asks about the absence of mommy memoirs by women of color (Walker's memoir is a notable exception).[32] Different cultural histories and relationships to the labor force have made black motherhood and the writing about it different from white motherhood. White women's empowerment through the Cult of True Womanhood has produced the pressure and privilege to opt out of careers, an option that has not historically been available to black women. The commercial success of mommy memoirs by white women who are preoccupied by this theme reflects the cultural recognition of some (white, middle class) women's legitimacy and authority to write about motherhood, while nonwhite women's experience and authority remain underrecognized. In this sense, the genre reinforces the normalization of middle class, white motherhood in the global North and obscures the struggle that poor and nonwhite women engage in to be seen as legitimate mothers. The lack of demand for and publication of texts by women of color reveals the ideological and political work performed by the mommy memoir. These questions about the mommy memoir combined with the genre's challenges, both self-imposed and external, make this short-lived phenomenon and its legacy a complex one.

Notes

1   See, for example, Alice Bradley's *Finslippy*, published as *Let's Panic about Babies!* (New York: St. Martin's, 2011), and Rebecca Woolf's *Girl's Gone Child*, which she started in 2004 and published as *Rockabye: From Wild to Child* (New York: Seal Press, 2008).

2   See, for example, Susan Douglas and Meredith Michaels's discussion of the larger cultural phenomenon they call "the new momism" in *The Mommy Myth: The Idealization of Motherhood and How It Has Undermined All Women* (New York: Free Press, 2004).

3   Anne Lamott, *Operating Instructions: A Journal of My Son's First Year* (New York: Ballantine Books, 1993).

4   Ibid., 38.

5   Ibid., 39.

6   Ayelet Waldman, "Truly, Madly, Guiltily," *The New York Times*, March 27, 2005, https://www.nytimes.com/2005/03/27/fashion/truly-madly-guiltily.html.

7   Ayelet Waldman, *Bad Mother: A Chronicle of Maternal Crimes, Minor Calamities, and Occasional Moments of Grace* (New York: Anchor, 2009), 3.

8   Ariel Gore and Bee Lavender, eds., *Breeder: Real-Life Stories from the New Generation of Mothers* (New York: Seal Press, 2001), xiii.

9   Rebecca Walker, *Baby Love: Choosing Motherhood after a Lifetime of Ambivalence* (New York: Riverhead, 2007), 6.

10 Ibid., 90.

11 Angela Morrill, "Birth," in *Breeder*, 45.

12 Lisa Belkin, "The Opt-Out Revolution," *The New York Times*, October 26, 2003, https://www.nytimes.com/2003/10/26/magazine/the-opt-out-revolution.html?mtrref=www.google.com&gwh=E70068DAAB9DF7E2562A06540529229A&gwt=pay.

13 Anne Roiphe, *Fruitful: A Real Mother in the Modern World* (Boston: Houghton Mifflin, 1996), x–xi.

14 Waldman, *Bad Mother*, 39–40.

15 Walker, *Baby Love*, 8.

16 See also Naomi Wolf's *Misconceptions: Truth, Lies, and the Unexpected on the Journey to Motherhood* (New York: Anchor, 2001).

17 Roiphe, *Fruitful*, 207.

18 Ibid.

19 Virginia Woolf, *A Room of One's Own* (1929; New York: Harcourt, 2005).

20 Walker, *Baby Love*, 204.

21 Sherry Thompson, "Mother Tongue," in *Breeder*, 75.

22 Waldman, *Bad Mother*, 40.

23 Rayna Rapp, *Testing Women, Testing the Fetus: The Social Impact of Amniocentesis in America* (New York: Routledge, 2000).

24 Martha Beck, *Expecting Adam: A True Story of Birth, Rebirth, and Everyday Magic* (New York: Three Rivers, 1999).

25 Irene Vilar's *Impossible Motherhood: Testimony of an Abortion Addict* (New York: Other Press, 2009) presents a different story of abortion and motherhood. Vilar, who had fifteen abortions in as many years, describes herself as an abortion "addict," who is only "cured" when she embraces motherhood.

26 Alisa Gordaneer, "The Pump and I," in *Breeder*, 55.

27 Waldman, *Bad Mother*, 70.

28 See Lisa Hammond, "'Mommyblogging Is a Radical Act': Weblog Communities and the Construction of Maternal Identities," in *Mothers Who Deliver: Feminist Interventions in Public and Interpersonal Discourse*, ed. Jocelyn Fenton Stitt and Pegeen Reichert Powell (Albany: SUNY Press, 2010), 77–98; Emily January Peterson, "Mommy Bloggers as Rebels and Community Builders," *Journal of the Motherhood Initiative for Research and Community Involvement* 6, no. 1 (Spring/Summer 2015): 9–30; Andrea Buchanan, "The Secret Life of Mothers: Maternal Narrative, Momoirs, and the Rise of the Blog," *The Mothers Movement Online*, 2006, http://www.mothersmovement.org/features/06/02/a_buchanan_1.html; and Jaqueline McLeod Rogers and Fiona Joy Green, "Mommy Blogging and Deliberative Dialogical Ethics," *Journal of the Motherhood Initiative for Research and Community Involvement* 6, no. 1 (Spring/Summer 2015): 31–49.

29 Sarah Pullium Bailey, "What Ever Happened to the Mommy Blog?" *The Chicago Tribune Online*, January 29, 2018, http://www.chicagotribune.com/lifestyles/parenting/ct-mommy-blog-disappear-20180129-story.html.

30 Ibid.

31 Michael Bérubé, *Life as Jamie Knows It: An Exceptional Child Grows Up* (Boston: Beacon, 1996).

32 Deesha Philyaw, "Ain't I a Mommy?" *Bitch Magazine* 40 (Summer 2008): 47–52, https://www.bitchmedia.org/article/aint-i-a-mommy-0. See also Nicole Willey, "In Search of Our Mothers' Memoirs: Redefining Mothering through African Feminist Principles," in *Motherhood Memoirs: Mothers Creating/Writing Lives*, ed. Justine Dymond and Nicole Willey (Bradford: Demeter, 2013), 233–60.

17

Minecraft Fiction

Michael T. Wilson

While shopping for e-books, adult readers may have browsed past a list of titles like *Diary of a Noob, Diary of Steve the Noob, The Quest for the Diamond Sword*, and *Diary of a Power-Hungry Sheep* without any clear sense of just what the books were and quite possibly without paying any closer attention. Younger readers are much more likely to recognize titles like these as speaking directly to one of their most common generational experiences: playing the video game *Minecraft*, officially launched by Mojang in 2011 and then purchased in 2014 by Microsoft for 2.5 billion dollars.[1] A sizable range of *Minecraft* books, including fiction, quickly sprang up alongside the game that *The New York Times* called in 2016 "a global sensation, captivating a generation of children," with "over 100 million registered players": Amazon's Kindle section lists over 3,000 *Minecraft* titles, including fiction.[2] Public libraries have embraced *Minecraft* books as yet another avenue to entice "reluctant readers" into greater literacy,[3] and often make the game itself available to young patrons as a way to bring them into library spaces in pursuit of those broader educational goals.[4] As part of the massive *Minecraft* mediasphere, *Minecraft* fiction both draws from the game itself and expands upon it in ways that create a unique literary experience and also seem to express the generational concerns and assumptions of its often youthful authors and almost entirely youthful readers.

Minecraft fiction shares common traits because it derives at least some of its elements from the game, first released for computer platforms and then ported to almost every video game console, tablet, and cell phone platform over the next few years. Crucially for its incorporation in fiction, the game itself is a "sandbox," which is to say a "procedurally generated" game more-or-less randomly generates the world for each new play, and does so without a strongly imposed narrative line that guides the player from point to point in order to complete that narrative, unlike, for instance, popular video games like the *Assassin's Creed* series. Instead, the game allows the player to work with what is often described as a "virtual Lego set," the basic element of the block, cubes of various substances and qualities that comprise literally everything that the player can see, touch, manipulate, and build in the game world (see Figure 17.1).

Equally important for the open-ended purpose of the fiction it inspires, there is no dialogue whatsoever in the game until the very end credits, although most "living" creatures and other elements make some sort of noise. At the same time, and in the same way as other fanfiction narratives, the game offers authors working within the *Minecraft* microgenre a common range of the settings, objects, natural resources, monsters, and "non-player characters" that appear in the game itself. *Minecraft* fiction authors are thus free to incorporate those elements in a way that might act as writing prompts or "plot generators."

The game, in other words, hands the player a world of blocks with set properties, and the player explores that world and creates their own narrative, learning and surviving the world's dangers, and crafting from those blocks useful items and structures; each player's experience is thus unique in one sense, but also alike in being created through a similar set of experiences due to the unvarying set of components. The game itself is strikingly accessible to children while at the same time remaining useful to higher educational and creative goals. One public librarian's blog notes that the University of Texas at Dallas created and launched "Polycraft World," "a comprehensive mod for *Minecraft* that features petrochemical refining, harvesting of new ore types and the construction of polymers, plastics and specialty items," and London's Tate Museum offered Tate Worlds, "in which works of art from their collection are reimagined as *Minecraft* worlds that users can download and explore."[5]

Figure 17.1 Sample *Minecraft* scene (Mojang © 2009–19. © 2019 Microsoft) ["Minecraft" is a trademark of Mojang Synergies AB].

For those not belonging to its distinct demographic of child and "tween" readers, *Minecraft* fiction is most interesting not for its literary and aesthetic appeal, although individual books and authors rise to entertaining levels even for adult readers, but for the way it encompasses a truly remarkable range of cultural and historical elements. At its most fundamental level, for instance, both the game and its fiction may be interpreted as "robinsonades" or castaway narratives in the vein of Daniel Defoe's *Robinson Crusoe* (1719). *Minecraft* titles also often adopt epistolary or diary techniques of other early English novels such as Samuel Richardson's *Pamela* (1740). Others recount journeys into unfamiliar territory in the style of James Cook's 1784 travel memoirs, such as the *Diary of Steve the Noob* series (a new player is a "noob"), following the first-person avatar's adventures and travel across "Minecraftia." The first "authorized" *Minecraft* novel was *World War Z* author Max Brooks's *Minecraft: The Island: An Official Minecraft Novel* (2017), with the protagonist described as a "cuboid": "a hero stranded in an unfamiliar land, with unfamiliar rules, learning to survive against tremendous odds."[6]

Much, perhaps most, *Minecraft* fiction follows the robinsonade template, emphasizing the day-to-day life of a character, including nonhuman characters, striving to survive and thrive in a recognizably Minecraftian world by utilizing its resources. Just as *Robinson Crusoe* dwells in considerable depth on Crusoe's attempt to create a home, books like *Diary of Steve the Noob* (Book 3) offer a procedural look at the protagonist's "crafting" of survival tools from the various cubes that make up the *Minecraft* landscape and its creatures: "Suddenly Steve had an idea! Diamonds could be found in a Nether fortress. If Steve obtained diamonds, he could craft a powerful diamond sword to attack the armored zombie."[7] This process of finding components and creating new objects from them seems deeply satisfying for young players and readers alike. As Clive Thompson notes in *The New York Times*, "'Children,' the social critic Walter Benjamin wrote in 1924, 'are particularly fond of haunting any site where things are being visibly worked on. They are irresistibly drawn by the detritus generated by building, gardening, housework, tailoring or carpentry.'"[8] The robinsonade template continues through narratives that follow the presumed lives of other *Minecraft* creatures and monsters as well, like *Diary of a Power-Hungry Sheep*, *Diary of a Blaze*, and *Diary of a Minecraft Zombie*.

While *Minecraft* fiction thus evokes the very roots of the Western novel, the books themselves often speak directly to the experiences of their young readers and relatively young authors. The language itself is often informally conversational: "I got super excited at that point because that book was the answer to my problem."[9] During a fight with the "Skeleton King" in *Diary of Steve the Noob*, Steve asks for a "time-out."[10] The stories frequently reflect the school-and-media saturated lives of modern children: young zombies have to go to school to learn how to frighten villagers, and then speculate that zombies themselves may have come from "a plague that originated from some secret military experiment," although, as the young zombie narrator notes skeptically, that theory comes from "Creepy," who "watches too much television," and that really the Endermen monsters are "probably a secret club, and only the coolest kids can be a part of it."[11] The dangers of adventuring reflect not just fantasy monsters but the nature of school life: when protagonist Steve is praised by the village girls ("Oh, he is cute"), his embarrassed response is "I just stuffed my face full of cookies. It was so delicious."[12] The age-old confusing impulses of preadolescence are thus neatly encapsulated in a single sentence of a book that exists in a purely electronic form.

At the same time, *Minecraft* fiction has been deeply shaped by the nature of new media and publishing, to the extent that it is difficult to imagine it outside that context. *Minecraft* fiction overlaps significantly with the internet explosion of fanfiction, with almost 7,000 narratives of various lengths at fanfiction.net. Many *Minecraft* fiction authors and series are published through Kindle Unlimited, Amazon's subscription service that makes it painless for young readers to work their way through multiple books without repeated parental authorizations and involvement. *Minecraft* video streamers like Youtuber Captain Sparklez, a 26-year-old who, as of 2015, had 9 million subscribers and netted an estimated 13.7 million dollars from streaming and narrating his adventures largely in *Minecraft*, reinforce the *Minecraft* mediasphere that supports its fiction.[13] Likewise, in *Herobrine: The Anti-Hero*, Herobrine expresses the precise values of new media's streamers in his desire to "prove to the world that I am *Minecraft*'s strongest warrior .... I'll be in commercials and magazine ads and stuff. Sounds like the good life, alright."[14] Many of the narratives comprising *Minecraft* fiction itself frequently break the fourth wall by commenting directly on the game's mechanics ("the target hit box is too small or something," the protagonist complains in *Diary of Steve the Noob*) and the meta-nature of their own narration (Zack Zombie's mother explains that "'zombies are mobs created by computer programmers at Mojang to make the game of *Minecraft* a more challenging and enjoyable experience.' Whenever my Mom uses big words, I know she's hiding something").[15]

The thematic elements of the narratives, or at least those aimed at children and tweens, are firmly anchored in the traditional themes of books for those ages, with a "Generation Z" postmillennial emphasis. Characters are concerned about nutrition ("The rush of sugar and carbs kicked in"), acknowledgments of their efforts ("The chief met me later in the day and gave me a medal for my service"), difficulties with social circles ("Some of the villager kids are real jerks"), a sense of "information wants to be free" justice ("I figured since he wouldn't help me get unlimited arrows from the enchanted book, I'd just use his house to craft some arrows instead; seems fair enough"), school safety issues (*Why didn't they put in a rear exit? That's fire safety 101!*"), a skeptical contemporary view of postmodern life (the Mayor is "quick to act and is already working on damage control"), anticipation or experience of teenaged parties ("Unfortunately, we partied way into the night, and we got louder and louder"), age-centric fears ("I thought about peeing on the building, but I didn't want to risk a ticket for public urination"), and resisting parental pressure ("I don't want to be a blacksmith or a butcher").[16] There is also a strong emphasis on community service and self-sacrifice. Although there is no intrinsic game mechanic requiring such actions, protagonists frequently emerge as defenders and leaders of their respective groups: "Steve knew he had to help them. If he didn't do something heroic soon, he would be a no-good coward who let the village get destroyed."[17]

Protagonists are often strongly grounded not only in the details of *Minecraft* the game but in the day-to-day family jokes and experiences of the game's young players: "I'm not saying Dads don't mean well. It's just that they don't have a great track record when it comes to preparing for these trips. Moms on the other hand, prepare for everything."[18] Occasional characters pop up to voice the sorts of advice children always hear from parents and authority figures ("you just … need to make a plan, do some studying, I dunno, you can't just wander about and hope for the best"), or a zombie's parents ("'Don't go out during the day because you'll burn yourself! Blah, blah, blah,' they say").[19] In another clear link to both the game's mechanics and the youth of many authors and readers, characters are repeatedly concerned about getting, "taming," and caring for pets like wolves, ocelots, and other animals.

Antagonists are defined as those who make trouble for others needlessly. A recurring villain and antagonist in much of the fiction, for instance, is the shared-server, multiplayer video game concept of the "griefer," defined by *Oxford Living Dictionary* as "(in an online game or community) a person who harasses or deliberately provokes other players or members in order to spoil their enjoyment."[20] In Winter Morgan's *Quest for the Diamond Sword*, the protagonist "liked villagers better than other explorers like him, because they couldn't be griefers and couldn't harm him" and later "Steve had encountered his first griefer and had walked away alive."[21] The definition of "griefer," however, seems expandable in a strikingly post-9/11 fashion that enforces community norms in a way that emphasizes the security of the group over other concerns. The mayor of the new village in the second book of *Diary of Steve the Noob* tells him that "as long as you are not a trouble maker, you may stay in our village," and when an angry villager from Steve's first village shows up in *Diary* 9, blaming Steve for its destruction at the end of the first *Diary*, the mayor first expels and then arrests him "as a troublemaker" without stopping to consider the possible validity of his complaint. A related theme appears in 16-year-old author Sean Kay Wolfe's *The Elementia Chronicles*, where three new players, or "noobs," find themselves fighting more experienced players, led by the king, who are trying to drive them out.[22] In both instances, a welcoming and relatively secure community of players is the underlying value under threat.

While many of the books follow the iterative nature of the game itself (explore, craft, fight, repeat), more uniquely interesting works, whether defined in literary or cultural terms, have emerged from the *Minecraft* fiction microgenre. "Steve the Noob's" *Diary of Chester the Sheep* offers up an animal-rights quest for safety and community, with Chester fleeing the farm where animals are killed and eaten, and finding a pastoral utopia with "tons of farm escapees here."[23] Other books aim squarely at comedic takes on the *Minecraft* universe: "Crafty Nichole's" *Diary of an Angry Alex* casts the female version of the player's character as a disgruntled coworker with Steve (the male version of the player's character), who is angry because Steve takes all the glamorous and enjoyable jobs and leaves Alex to do the rest.[24] The book uses the diary format to clever effect—"1:30pm": Steve has "now enchanted his diamond sword. Good for him," followed by "2:00pm: He is now showing off his new sword to the farm animals," and then "9:30pm: Steve needs to fall in a hole." In the tradition of classical farce, Alex decides to chat with skeletons to enlist them in her quest to kill Steve: "[skeletons] hang out under trees. This could be a possible conversation topic." In the new media tradition of crowd-sourcing, "Crafty Nichole" also solicits reader suggestions for other book topics, and her *Diary of a Power-Hungry Sheep* lists two such contributing readers in its tale of Lenny, a sheep that rebels against its role as a harvestable *Minecraft* resource: "I have broken the chains of my oppressors. No more will I labor in their lush green fields, munching the sweet pixelated grasses. Mmm … so crunchy. Perhaps just a nibble more. No! The cost of collaboration is too high."[25]

Other books create nuanced psychological portraits of even the secondary creatures in the game: "Steve the Noob's" *The Librarian* explores the life of a common village character (a non-player character or "npc" in gaming terms, who cannot be played or controlled by the player) on a very specific quest: Jacob the librarian goes in search of an overdue book, checked out by Mr. Baggs, a disguised wither skeleton.[26] Jacob's quest requires him to understand his own psychological nature and manage it: "I was Jacob the Librarian, who never did anything out of the ordinary. I always followed a schedule.

I always followed my schedule exactly. I turned my eyes so they wouldn't look at anyone. I felt everyone judging me." Jacob's daily life presents repeated challenges:

> 8:00 pm: I had been practicing what to say for a few hours now. Dinner had been small and simple, so I had plenty of time to practice. Maybe I should've gotten one of my friends to help me. I didn't know if I was being my usual Jacob self or if I was actually being charming .... Sometimes it was extremely hard for me to tell the difference.

Within the context of a literary character composed entirely of cubes and pixels, this *Minecraft* book has credibly mapped the broad contours of a life's challenges and rewards in a genuinely moving way.

Yoked as it is to the popularity of a video game, *Minecraft* fiction may seem unlikely to maintain its own niche, but like the *Harry Potter* novels, the game continues to draw in enthusiasts as they age into the demographic that finds it most appealing, children and young tweens. Freed from traditional publishing constraints, the books themselves will remain available in e-book venues, never going out of print as so many children's books have in the past. The *Minecraft* microgenre thus seems likely to survive into the future, and as new authors emerge, to continue to reflect key elements of cultural and demographic change.

Notes

1   Kevin Roose, "Things That Make Me Feel Old: What Is Minecraft, and Why Did Microsoft Just Pay $2.5 Billion for It?" *New York Magazine*, September 15, 2014, http://nymag.com/daily/intelligencer/2014/09/why-microsoft-paid-25-billion-for-minecraft.html.

2   Clive Thompson, "The Minecraft Generation," *The New York Times*, April 14, 2016, https://www.nytimes.com/2016/04/17/magazine/the-Minecraft-generation.html.

3   Wade Gegan, "13 of the Best Minecraft Books for Kids Who Are Reluctant to Read," *Fractus Learning*, March 24, 2017, https://www.fractuslearning.com/best-Minecraft-books-for-kids.

4   Brian Vander Veen, "The Educational Merits of *Minecraft*," *Spokane County Library District*, January 8, 2015, https://www.scld.org/the-educational-merits-of-Minecraft.

5   Ibid.

6   Marsh Davies, "Max Brooks Is Writing a Minecraft Novel! Oh Yes!" *Mojang*,
    September 24, 2016, https://www.mojang.com/2016/09/max-brooks-is-
    writing-a-Minecraft-novel-oh-yes.

7   "Steve the Noob," *Diary of Steve the Noob (An Unofficial Minecraft Book)*
    (Seattle: Amazon Digital Services, 2015–18).

8   Thompson, "Minecraft Generation."

9   "Steve the Noob," *Diary of Steve the Noob*, Book 1.

10 "Steve the Noob," *Diary of Steve the Noob*, Book 8.

11 "Zack Zombie," *Diary of a Minecraft Zombie: A Scare of a Dare
    (An Unofficial Minecraft Book)*, Book 1 (n.p., Zack Zombie Publishing,
    2015).

12 "Steve the Noob," *Diary of Steve the Noob*, Book 9.

13 Tom Gerencer, "Captain Sparklez Net Worth and Earnings," *Money Nation*,
    December 5, 2015, http://moneynation.com/captainsparklez-net-worth-
    and-earnings.

14 "Steve the Noob," *Herobrine: The Anti-Hero (An Unofficial Minecraft Book)*
    (Seattle: Amazon Digital Services, 2015).

15 "Steve the Noob," *Diary of Steve the Noob*, Book 6; "Zombie," *Diary of a
    Minecraft Zombie: A Scare of a Dare (An Unofficial Minecraft Book)*, Book 1
    (n.p., Zack Zombie Publishing, 2015).

16 "Steve the Noob," *Diary of Steve the Noob*, Book 1; Erik Gunnar Taylor
    ("Cube Kid"), *Diary of an 8-Bit Warrior: An Unofficial Minecraft Adventure*,
    Book 1 (Kansas City: Andrews McMeel, 2016); "Steve the Noob," *Diary of
    Steve the Noob*, Book 1; "Steve the Noob," *Diary of Steve the Noob*, Book 13;
    "Steve the Noob," *Diary of Steve the Noob*, Book 1; Taylor, *8-Bit Warrior*.

17 Winter Morgan, *An Unofficial Gamer's Adventure: The Quest for the
    Diamond Sword: A Unofficial Minecrafter's Novel*, Book 1 (New York: Sky
    Pony, 2014).

18 "Zach Zombie," *Diary of a Minecraft Zombie*.

19 "Steve the Noob," *Diary of a Bad Blaze (An Unofficial Minecraft Series)*
    (Seattle: Amazon Digital Services, LLC, 2015); Zombie, *Diary of a Minecraft
    Zombie*.

20 "Griefer," *English: Oxford Living Dictionaries*, accessed August 20, 2018,
    https://en.oxforddictionaries.com/definition/griefer.

21 Morgan, *Quest for the Diamond Sword*, Book 1.

22 Sean Kay Wolfe, *The Elementia Chronicles: Quest for Justice: An Unofficial
    Minecraft-Fan Adventure*, Book 1 (New York: HarperCollins, 2015).

23 "Steve the Noob," *Diary of Chester the Sheep (An Unofficial Minecraft Book)*
    (Seattle: Amazon Digital Services, 2017).

24 "Crafty Nichole," *Diary of an Angry Alex: [An Unofficial Minecraft Book]*,
    Book 1 (Seattle: Amazon Digital Services, 2015).

25 "Crafty Nichole," *Diary of a Power-Hungry Sheep: Book 1 [An Unofficial
    Minecraft Book]* (Seattle: Amazon Digital Services, 2015).

26 "Steve the Noob," *The Librarian (An Unofficial Minecraft Book) (Librarian
    Diary Book 1)* (Seattle: Amazon Digital Services, 2015).

18

Heavy Metal Microgenres

Heather Lusty

Traditional heavy metal is not a microgenre—it is the wellspring from which all heavy metal bands draw. Black Sabbath, formed in 1968, is usually identified as the first "real" heavy metal band, although they had good company, including Blue Cheer, Accept, and dozens of other bands across the globe experimenting with heavy rock sounds. Yet Sabbath's influence is undeniable, and in their shadow, metal developed in the 1970s. Some bands identify with a particular metal microgenre that captures their spirit or thematic focus; others eschew labels. Bands are also categorized by fans and record companies. Many bands easily fit into multiple microgenres of heavy metal, both generally and by era or album(s). Occasionally microgenres come out of cities or regions; at other times, microgenres develop organically on an international level. Heavy metal musicians harness a wide variety of musical, vocal, temporal, and thematic approaches, all of which influence the still popular microgenres discussed briefly here. A quick look at some of the more significant heavy metal microgenres reveals the range of varied and distinct forms of heavy metal expression, which continues to evolve.

In the early 1970s, heavy metal offshoots began to appear, many highly technical and experimental. Avant-garde/avant-metal, or experimental metal, is characterized by experimentation and innovative, large-scale elements of sound, style, and vocal techniques. Elements of progressive rock, jazz-fusion, and heavier sounds from death and extreme metal make this style notable. Avant-garde metal thrives in local scenes, such as the San Francisco Bay Area, Oslo, and Tokyo, but some of the best avant-metal bands like Gojira (Bayonne, France) emerge from more unexpected locales. Progressive metal, drawing from the progressive-rock tradition, uses unusual and dynamic time signatures, lengthy compositions, complex song structures, and extended instrumental solos exhibiting instrumental mastery. From Rush to Queensrÿche to Dream Theater and Opeth, progressive metal continues to be one of the more innovative microgenres. Djent, an offshoot of progressive metal, makes use of palm-muted, distorted guitar chords and rhythmic complexity (TesseracT and Meshuggah). Space metal is an offshoot known for loose, lengthy song structures based around instrumentals, often otherworldly and hypnotic. Orange Goblin is one of the best in this microgenre.

One of the most important microgenres, heavily influential across the board, is the New Wave of British Heavy Metal (NWOBHM) (1979–83), which had a brief but influential heyday during the decline of mainstream punk and the rise of New Wave. The subgenre incorporated diverse influences from mainstream and underground styles, with fast, aggressive tempos and raw, self-produced recording. Lyrics explored mythology, fantasy, horror, the "rock life," and other escapist themes. Iron Maiden, Motörhead, and Saxon influenced legions to follow them into power chords and hard drinking. Speed metal, the earliest form of thrash, emerged from the NWOBHM. It retained the melodic approaches and fast tempos used by early heavy metal bands but sped up the tempos and technical complexity. In response to heavy metal's predominantly dark themes, Christian metal materialized in the late 1970s as an organized expansion of evangelism into mainstream U.S. culture. Christian metal bands view their music as a peaceful counterbalance to dark, negative, aggressive secular metal. And while heavy metal was initially an Anglo-American movement, it is a global scene today, with the Spanish-speaking world now one of the most prolific metal-producing areas. Latin metal infused heavy metal riffs with Latin influences and instrumentation, including Spanish-language vocals and Latin percussion and rhythms (like salsa). South American Latin metal bands often incorporate elements of traditional music—the most successful in this microgenre to date are Sepultura and Soulfly—but the popularity of heavy metal in Latin America today is driving a whole new movement in this vein.

The technical skill involved in heavy metal is often overlooked. Power metal, a hybrid of speed metal and heavy metal, driven by double-bass drumming, fast pacing, melodic guitar, power-chord progressions, and high-pitched vocals, is one of the more enduring microgenres from the 1970s that is still widely popular. Thematically, fantasy is a popular focus; lyrics embolden individual courage and empowerment. The North American style, which sounds similar to speed metal, took on a harder edge in the 1980s; the second style, emerging in Europe, Japan, and Latin America, has a lighter, melodic sound often incorporating keyboards. Helloween (Germany), Loudness (Japan), and Stratovarius (Finland) are stalwarts of power metal. Another highly technical microgenre is neoclassical or shred metal, heavily influenced by classical composition, using instruments, scales, and melodies typical of classical music. Shred guitar is a technical style of guitar soloing; rapid scales and arpeggios are the norm. Guitarists use cross picking, sweep picking, and economy picking (each of which produces a different sound). Yngwie Malmsteen is probably the most renowned guitarist in this microgenre.

Strongly influenced by early metal acts like Black Sabbath, doom metal is characterized by slower tempos, low-tuned guitars, and a heavier, dramatically epic sound. From Pentagram and Blue Cheer in the 1970s, Paradise Lost and Cathedral in the 1990s, to Beastmaker and Draconian today, doom bands are dexterous and long-lived. Splinter subgenres of doom include death/doom, which largely dwells on fear and anticipation of death; drone metal, defined by its droning notes/chords that are repeated and sustained throughout a song/movement, and guitars drenched in reverb and feedback; funeral doom, a crossbreed of death-doom with funeral dirge, evoking emptiness and despair; and sludge metal, derived from doom, with elements of hardcore punk/Southern rock. Horror metal is doom metal gone sideways; incorporating imagery from horror films and early shock-rock acts, Alice Cooper and W.A.S.P. pioneered this microgenre, making names for themselves by focusing on sinister or morbid themes, playing heavy, slower, melodic songs, and occasionally using corpse paint and other elements of theater. Danzig, Cradle of Filth, Carach Angren, and Necrophagia carry the torch today. Another splinter of doom is stoner metal—a slower, low-tuned, bass-heavy version of metal, which incorporates elements of psychedelic rock, doom metal, and blues-rock, with retro production values and melodic vocals. Kyuss, Sleep, Electric Wizard, and Black Label Society exemplify this hard-toking genre.

In a rejection of the threatening, gritty overtones of most late 1970s metal, glam or hair metal oozed onto the scene. The most visible and flamboyant microgenre to come out of the 1970s, glam metal was primarily a visual style. Its musicians are remembered for their big hair, heavy makeup, and feminine clothing (spandex, scarves, and bangles). KISS and the New York Dolls influenced later 1980s icons Mötley Crüe, Poison, and Hanoi Rocks. Glam is only mostly dead; Black Veil Brides are a contemporary prefabricated music-industry shot at the big-looks, big-money "goth" rock style, but their music is as terrible as their fashion, and they have little in common with their forefathers. Most American self-styled "metal" bands today fall into this rather cringeworthy legacy.

Another important offshoot of early heavy metal is the "extreme" style. "Extreme metal" is an umbrella term that encompasses numerous microgenres generally recognized by sonic excess. Major subgenres include black, death, doom, speed, and thrash metals and their descendants, all characterized by harsher, abrasive, noncommercial styles associated with black metal, death metal, thrash metal, etc. A counterculture ethos that rejects mainstream music, extreme metal is influenced by a variety of musicians both a part and outside of heavy metal; it has, in turn, had a surprisingly wide influence on acts outside of heavy metal. The most infamous of these mini-waves is black metal (First Wave, 1981–86; New Wave Norwegian, 1990–present), which emerged from 1980s thrash metal, primarily (but not exclusively) in Scandinavia. Often (mis)characterized as "Satanic metal," primarily for its misanthropic, anti-Christianity stance, the sensationalized church burnings and far-right movements associated with Norwegian black metal contributed to the backlash and distrust from mainstream culture. First wave bands Venom, Bathory, and Hellhammer gave way to the second wave, which was much, much darker, including Mayhem, Darkthrone, Immortal, and Emperor.

The radical folk politics of the 1960s are alive and well—and distorted—in the numerous subgenres of black metal. National Socialist black metal, which typically blends Neo-Nazi beliefs (fascism, white supremacy/separatism, anti-Semitism, xenophobia, and homophobia) with its hostility to foreign religions (Christianity, Judaism, Islam), is a minor but increasingly worrying trend, gathering up more and more fans with the increasing popularity of right-wing, ethnocentric hate groups across the globe. Red and Anarchist black metal (RABM) generally espouses far-left and environmentalist ideologies including anarchism, Marxism, and green anarchism, and fuses black metal with anarchist crust punk (ignoring the traditional Satanic and nihilist lyrics). War metal is a more aggressive, cacophonous, chaotic black-metal style, with elements of grindcore, black, and death metal. Blackgaze, a fusion of black metal and shoegaze, emerged in the early 2000s and includes heavier elements of black metal, including blast beat drumming and high-pitched vocals, combined with melodic elements and heavily distorted guitars.

Not all black metal is sensationalist tripe, however. Successful, increasingly mainstream offshoots of black metal include symphonic black metal, which blends symphonic and orchestral elements, including keyboards/organs or full orchestral arrangements including wind, brass, percussion, and strings. Vocals may be clean, harsh, or combined; overall structure is symphonic in nature, with traditional riff-based tempo. Norwegian bands Dimmu Borgir, Satyricon, and Emperor are the established veterans here, touring with full symphonic orchestras, but the general style is increasingly popular on the international music festival circuit. Viking metal has roots in black metal and Nordic folk music and is characterized by a focus on Nordic myth, paganism, and the age of Viking exploration. Lyrics are often adapted from the *Edda* and sagas; clean and harsh vocals, anthemic choruses, and folk instruments and keyboards are characteristic. Bathory and Enslaved are considered the pioneers here; Amon Amarth is successful globally, although their lyrical content is historically inaccurate and generally misappropriated to glorify drinking and pillaging; more serious bands focusing on local heritage include Ensiferum, Moonsorrow, and Skálmöld.

Really heavy bands, the kind that horrify most nonmetal fans, are offshoots of death metal, building from the musical structure of early thrash and black metal. Slayer, Kreator, Celtic Frost, and Venom laid the foundation; since the 1990s, the genre has splintered into multiple subgenres, including technical metal (a fast, dark, musically complex offshoot that includes growling death metal vocals with epic guitar solos), blackened metal (a hybrid of death and black metal), and death'n'roll (a blend of death metal's trademark vocals and distorted guitars with elements of 1970s hard rock). The most prominent subgenre of death metal is melodic death metal, which developed in the early 1990s, primarily in England and Scandinavia. It combines elements of death metal with aspects of NWOBHM. Gothenberg (Sweden) metal is one of the most popular styles today, although they all sound relatively similar (see At the Gates, Dark Tranquility, Arch Enemy, and In Flames). While horror metal and goth rock still do a brisk business, most of the gore has gone a more visceral direction. Grindcore is one of the heavier microgenres, drawing from thrash and death metal as well as crust and hardcore. Thematically, short songs focus on gore and violence; the music is characterized by chaotic tempos, a lack of standard time signatures, blast beats, and growled lyrics. Bands like Death, Brutal Truth, and Pig Destroyer are staples here, if you have the stomach. Distinct subgenres of grindcore include deathgrind (death metal and grindcore), characterized by fast tempos and musical brutality; goregrind is dominated by visual gory scenes; lyrics typically incorporate anatomical references (see Carcass, Repulsion, and Impetigo). Pornogrind, for lovers of flesh, leans thematically toward sexual scenes and imagery, generally extreme and potentially offensive. Cock and Ball Torture is one of the stalwarts here.

Fusion isn't just a culinary trend—several decades into the life of heavy metal, musicians hoping to become the next band-wonder experiment with all sorts of hybrid styles. Alternative metal combines traditional heavy metal with melodic vocals and other unconventional sounds, structures, and approaches. The bands that brought us out of grunge include Alice in Chains, Faith No More, and System of a Down. Funk metal (late 1980s) employs the distinctive sound of funk; conventional riffing is similar to 1980s thrash metal (Red Hot Chili Peppers, Living Color, Primus, and Rage Against the Machine). Nu metal is another fusion experiment that won't die, blending alternative metal and groove metal elements, most evident in riffs and rhythms, incorporating myriad other styles like grunge, industrial, hip-hop, and funk. Turntables and sampling occasionally feature, while vocal styles range from melodic to rapping and screaming or growling/harsh vocals. Korn, Deftones, and Linkin Park are some of the more successful Nu metal bands, several of which are attempting comebacks today. Rap metal adapts the vocal and lyrical structure of hip-hop; it is often mislabeled Nu metal or rapcore (a fusion of punk and hip-hop). Rap metal occasionally uses keyboards, but does not generally include sampling or turntables. Anthrax pioneered this microgenre in the early 1980s, so we can blame them for Crazy Town, Skindred, and Rage Against the Machine. Industrial metal is the best of this group, combining elements of industrial music (synthesizers or sequencer lines, sampling, repetitive guitar riffs, and distorted vocals) and metal. Most popular in North America, industrial metal draws from a wide array of sounds and influences; think about Rammstein, Ministry, Nine Inch Nails, White Zombie, and Marilyn Manson, all still alive and making money touring and recording albums. Subgenres include industrial thrash and industrial death, which draw from the musical distortion that gives industrial its distinctive sound.

Thrash metal, a direct descendant of early speed metal, emerged in the early 1980s, and this microgenre is one that is flourishing around the world today. Fast, complex, and aggressive, the high-pitched shred guitar solos and palm-muted riffs are accompanied by double-bass drumming and aggressive vocals. The genre's Big Four (Anthrax, Megadeth, Metallica, Slayer) pioneered thrash in America, while Europe's Big Teutonic Four (Sodom, Kreator, Destruction, Tankard) introduced the sound overseas. Teutonic thrash is often considered a distinct, regional derivative. Crossover thrash is heavily influenced by hardcore punk rather than elements of standard thrash, represented by bands like Corrosion of Conformity and Suicidal Tendencies. Groove metal, also called neo-thrash, post-thrash, or power groove, uses mid- to slow-tempo thrash riffs and bluesy guitar solos, heavy drums, and harsh vocals. Pantera, Lamb of God, Sepultura, and Clutch exemplify groove metal.

For some strange reason, metalcore, a blend of hardcore punk and metal, is a contemporaneously popular subgenre. Bands like Hatebreed, Killswitch Engage, While She Sleeps, and Bullet for My Valentine, among numerous others, still sell records and dominate the American small-venue concert circuit. Subgenres of metalcore include melodic metalcore, which draws from melodic death metal, punk, and emo. Writing styles vary, but bands in this microgenre tend to favor instrumental melody, harmonic guitars and tremolo picking, and a combination of clean vocals with growling (including numerous female singers). Deathcore combines elements of death metal with hardcore punk or metalcore, creating an overwhelming cacophony of riffs, blast beats, and hardcore punk breakdowns, while mathcore uses unusual time signatures, creating a rhythmically complex, dissonant style of metal and punk; if you actually like math, check out Dillinger Escape Plan.

Metal has a softer, introspective side occasionally as well. In the 1990s, a turn toward more melodic and more regionally diverse metal provided some fresh blood. Goth metal grew out of the British Goth rock of the early 1980s and the doom-death fusion of 1990s Europe. Often conflated with early horror rock/punk-themed bands (Bauhaus, Misfits, Cramps), Goth rock/ metal evolved from post-punk and the British Goth scene. Emphasizing heavy, slower chords of doom and a gloomy, occasionally pessimistic atmosphere, vocals are deep and melodic. Moonspell (Portugal), The 69 Eyes (Finland), Fields of the Nephilim (UK), and Lacuna Coil (Italy) are the best of this microgenre. *Neue Deutsche Härte* ("New German Hardness") is a crossover style influenced by New German Wave, alternative metal, and groove metal, with elements of industrial, electronica, and techno—basically metal at da club. NDH employs the basic metal setup—bass guitar, electric guitar (tuned low, distorted), drums and vocals, along with keyboards and synthesizers. Overall, the visual aesthetic of NDH is masculine and militaristic; vocals, typically in German, are deep and clean. Rammstein is the global superstar here, but influenced a whole troop of similar sounding bands like Stahlhammer, Megaherz, and Samas Traum. This microgenre is interesting because it is one of the few non-English-language offshoots in an English-language dominated field.

One of the more interesting microgenres, diverse and strong today, is folk metal. This blend of folk music and metal includes traditional ballads and folk tales, instruments (bagpipes, flutes, harps, reels, bodrans), singing styles, and themes (mythology, history, nature) underscored with heavy guitars and drums. Emerging in Europe during the 1990s (Skyclad, Cruachan), the genre catapulted onto European charts with an infusion from Finnish metal in the early 2000s (Ensiferum, Moonsorrow, and Amorphis) that invigorated an interest in traditional forms of storytelling through music. The most important aspect of this subgenre is diversity; bands play different styles of folk music, sometimes mixed with metal, sometimes separate. Bands are large (5+ members) due to the variety of instrumentation incorporated. Many folk-metal bands sing in their native languages or medieval antecedents; see Týr (Faroe Islands), Korpiklani (Finland), Wardruna (Norway), and Eluveitie (Switzerland) for a taste of the diversity and local heritage. Subgenres within folk metal include Celtic metal (Cruachan, Primordial, Waylander), which incorporates Celtic musical instruments, tempos, and themes; another variation is Celtic punk, slightly heavier, faster music, dominated by American bands of Irish decent like the Dropkick Murphies and Flogging Molly. Pirate metal (yes, that's right) draws from pirate lore and sea shanties, fusing metal with thrash and speed metal elements; Alestorm and Swashbuckle are popular here. Medieval metal draws from medieval folk music and is primarily a German subgenre; pagan metal is distinct for highlighting pre-Christian traditions of cultures or regions.

In the "what other offshoots could there possibly be?" category, post-metal, like post-rock, includes low-tuned, distorted guitars, minimal vocals, shifting song structures, and atmospherics. Albums contain generally half a dozen songs, each extending beyond ten minutes. Lyrics are abstract and occasionally philosophical in nature. Most post-metal bands are American or Japanese, including Neurosis, Isis, and Pelican. Symphonic metal is a contemporary offshoot of neoclassical metal (still going strong) and typically refers to bands that incorporate elements of orchestral instruments in their compositions. This ranges from string sections, keyboards, and classical instruments to actual orchestras. Many symphonic metal bands are fronted by classically trained female singers, which gives bands' sound a distinct vibe and an exponentially greater vocal range (in many instances, operatic). Nightwish has been an international powerhouse for two decades, but Epica and Within Temptation are on the rise. Kawaii metal, or idol metal or cute metal, is a recent subgenre, emerging from the Japanese idol tradition of the late 2000s and early 2010s. The music fuses power metal and J-pop with elements of industrial metal (keyboards), Japanese idol aesthetics and vocals, and occasionally Japanese folk instruments. Vocals can be a mix of unclean and harmonizing pop style; most Kawaii metal bands are fronted by a squad of young girls, put together by record companies to appeal to what they assume are largely male audiences. Babymetal, Ladybaby, and Lovebites are a few examples—while the singers (few of these girls play their own instruments) are cute and "barely legal," their lyrical content is generic and about as intellectually stimulating as cotton candy.

Although the microgenres presented here give a sense of the breadth and flair that characterize the heavy metal scene today, it is necessarily only a superficial treatment. Despite the rampant media hype about pop stars in the West, and the K-Pop craze occupying the East, heavy metal is truly a global phenomenon. Scholars working in the field cover a wide array of approaches (see Nelson Varas-Diaz's *Songs of Injustice: Heavy Metal Music in Latin America* [2018] documentary project, for example), all of which underscore the longevity and lasting impact heavy metal has had, and continues to have, around the world today.

19

Mexican Neo-Surf Microgenres

Aurelio Meza

The Mexican neo-surf music scene, strongly tied to the 1990s resurgence of garage and surf in the United States, is located on a continuum between unintentional surrealism and plain fantasy. Band members and their followers wear floral print shirts and sandals, yet most live nowhere near a beach. Others delve into Wild West and frontier imagery even though the closest deserts and borders to their homes in Mexico City are several hundred miles away. Others wear Elvis-like outfits or wrestling masks while never having been to Las Vegas or a wrestling arena. Iconographic fluidity of this kind, from one culture to another, is nodal when it comes to neo-surf and its microgenres. The work of Argentinean artist and designer Dr. Alderete has perpetuated the scene's aesthetic, exemplified in his artwork for landmark albums like Lost Acapulco's *Acapulco Golden* (2004), Fenómeno Fuzz's *Martinis y bikinis* (2004), or the Cavernarios's *Camino a Varadero* (2011) (see Figures 19.1 and 19.2) as well as in posters designed for concerts, festivals, and special commissions, like a benefit night for Danny Amis (see Figure 19.3), founder of los Straitjackets and an important element in the consolidation of Mexico's surf new wave.

Some of Alderete's work features wrestling masks typical of *lucha libre* that have become a particularly resonant piece of visual iconography for the movement. These and other "authentically Mexican" elements are paired with collectively imagined beach boy outfits, rock 'n' roll Mexican dancing, and sudden shifts from moshing to wrestling and weightlifting poses, following the rhythm of a song. In the country's smoggy, crowded capital, the exoticism performed by such practices contributed to the scene's early characterization as surreal, an adjective that only partially describes the importance of the movement's visual dimension. Inspired by bands using masks onstage, including Fenómeno Fuzz, los Elásticos, Lost Acapulco, and, in their early days, los Esquizitos, both visual artists and fans have contributed to collectively shape the scene's imagery. Masks and floral print shirts differentiate this music scene from others on a visual and haptic level, if not on a musical one.

Figure 19.1 Lost Acapulco, *Acapulco Golden* (Mostrissimo Records, Mexico, 2004) [Courtesy of the artist/designer Dr. Alderete].

Figure 19.2 First LP by Fenomeno Fuzz, *Martinis y Bikinis* (Ctentaydos Records, Mexico, 2004) [Courtesy of the artist/designer Dr. Alderete].

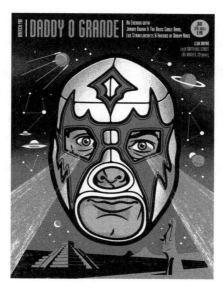

Figure 19.3 Daddy-O Grande poster for Danny Amis benefit night, featuring some of the most recurrent motifs for surf bands: wrestling masks, Rapa Nui figures, Mexican pyramids, and sci-fi imagery (Club Mayan, Los Angeles, 2011) [Courtesy of the artist/designer Dr. Alderete].

Regardless of timbre, surf is similar to punk, garage, róckabilly, and even black metal in a number of different ways. Like these rock-derived subgenres, it has inherited several blues rhythmic and harmonic techniques, such as the one-chord groove, the twelve-bar blues progression, and their accompanying repertoire of riffs and licks. Explorations into these techniques by guitarists Bo Diddley, Chuck Berry, Duane Eddy, and Link Wray influenced a new generation of musicians, among them Dick Dale and His Del-Tones. Dale is credited with bringing forth two distinctive traits of the surf guitar, both present in the hit song "Miserlou" (1962): the "wavy riff" (a *glissando* or guitar sweep on a descending scale, the finger running over the string through the fretboard from the neck's base to the nut, evoking the sound of a wave crashing against the sand) and a steady, reverb-saturated double strum. Other pioneering songs in the making of the surf sound are Dale's "Surf Beat" (1962), a sort of template for the genre's rhythmic schema, and the Beach Boys' first top-ten single, "Surfin' USA" (1963), which alters the lyrics of "Sweet Little Sixteen" by Chuck Berry (1958), in the great blues and rock tradition of adapting songs in other styles. This practice, widely exercised by the Lively Ones, the Trashmen, and Dale alike, would later on persist in punk, ska, and neo-surf.

The "rough edges" surf historically shares with punk and garage endured through the British Invasion of the Beatles and the like. From the mid-1960s on, the Sonics, the Trashmen, and the Monks influenced surf and garage in their early stages, when both seemed distinctly different from each other in terms of audience and lyrics. Later in the 1970s, the Cramps would further blend surf, garage, punk, and rockabilly (becoming the progenitors of psychobilly in the process). So by the late 1980s, when Voodoo Glow Skulls added ska to the mix, shifts toward increasingly faster tempos made sense.

South of the border, there would not be a strong surf band presence until the mid-1990s. Although lyric-less songs do exist in early Mexican garage and rock 'n' roll—like los Locos del Ritmo's "Morelia" (1960) and los Teen Tops' "Rock del río rojo" (1961)—they can only be considered instrumental surf precursors. The first artist in the 1960s to use the word "surf" in a song title was Toño Quirazco. Better known for also introducing ska to Mexican audiences, he included "Surf en Hawaiiana" in his band's eponymous first record, *Toño Quirazco y sus Hawaiian Boys* (1965). This song fundamentally observes Dale's "Surf Beats" drum rhythmic pattern. His use of a steel guitar and a slide in this and other Hawaiian Boys songs further associates their work with similar musical traditions that informed surf music: hillbilly, rockabilly, and *hapa haole* "Hawaiian" music.

While not too many precursors can be found for these genres in Mexico, there are exceptions like garage bands los Sleepers and los Monjes or northern bands los TJ's and los Rockets. In the 1970s, los Ovnis demonstrated a strong psychedelic and acid rock influence, yet by the 1980s there was no equivalent for the Go-Go's or the Stray Cats keeping surf, garage, or rockabilly rhythms alive. Nevertheless, neo-surf bands would later on pay homage to these Mexican garage pioneers. Lost Acapulco collaborated with Juanito Wau from Spanish garage band Wau y los Arrrghs!, who added his raspy voice to a cover of "Zombie" (2011), originally composed fifty years earlier by los Sleepers and foreshadowing the Cramps's style.

The 1990s witnessed a surf revival on both sides of the border, first in the United States with the advent of the Mummies, Man or Astroman? and the Tantra Monsters, among others, and later in Mexico with los Esquizitos. These bands were all formed before the release of Quentin Tarantino's *Pulp Fiction* (1994), which featured a soundtrack that catered to an audience eager for new surf material. Featuring several classic SoCal surf hits (most notably Dale's "Miserlou"), the movie was crucial for the consolidation of a surf scene. Aside from the increasing success of los Esquizitos and Lost Acapulco, during the 1990s Mexican neo-surf remained mostly underground. The number of existing bands, however, soon allowed for the creation of music festivals and collective concerts, culminating in a golden era represented by festivals that took place largely between 2003 and 2006.

One of the wellsprings of neo-surf music in Mexico City is Multiforo Alicia, a concert venue and recording studio in the downtown neighborhood of Roma, founded in 1995 and operated by Ignacio Pineda. The first surf band to play there in 1996 was none other than the founding los Esquizitos. Pineda recently mentioned he initially sought to feature artists who were not already part of the city's rock radio station programs, but within a few years Alicia became an invaluable reference in emerging music.[1] Broadcasts hosted by members of los Esquizitos (*Radio bestia*) and Lost Acapulco (*Dos horas de Brayan, Gabba Gabba, Sálvame radio*) also contributed to popularizing classic and new wave surf with wider audiences.

Despite its intense activity, the scene's early years were marked by an absence of recordings. The first ones, also the most representative of this period, were the Esquizitos's first LP and Lost Acapulco's *4* (both from 1998). According to Pineda, this delay in record production was due, on the one hand, to major labels not believing in them and, on the other, to technology gaps and limitations, as Pro Tools and the internet were still not readily available for most independent producers and emerging musicians. This was one main reason why Pineda founded Grabaxiones Alicia, a recording studio improvised in the venue's sound cabin and main stage, which nowadays utilizes a Behringer X32 digital mixing console. Pineda would eventually hire surf guitarists Omar Bustamante (Telekrimen, Cavernarios)[2] and Gabriel López (Twin Tones, Espectroplasma, Sonido Gallo Negro)[3] as sound engineers for live events and recording sessions. To date, they have produced more than a hundred records, not only by surf bands but also from other genres and subgenres roaming Mexico City's underground music scene in the 1990s—punk, ska, hip-hop, transmetal, emo, and nu metal. Some musicians would later release surf albums on their own independent labels, such as Isotonic Records, Mostrissimo, and Primitiv (all founded by different Lost Acapulco members), PP Lobo, Ctentaydos, among others.

Before many bands would have a demo of their own, some of their recordings were widely circulated through anthologies (popularly called *compilados* or *acoplados*), among them Grabaxiones Alicia's two volumes of *Surf-Mex* (2002, 2005), PP Lobo's three volumes of *Melodías intoxicadas* (2003, 2008, 2008), and the first four records in the Isotonic catalog: *Mexican Madness* (2002), *Locos Instrumentales around the World* (2003), *Instro Latin-O-Rama* (2004), and *Spaguetti & Chili Western* (2005) (see Figure 19.4). Songs by Lost Acapulco, los Esquizitos, and las Ultrasónicas (the oldest all-woman band on the scene) also appeared in the soundtrack of

Mexican films *Sexo, pudor y lágrimas* (1999) and *Perfume de violetas* (2001), exposing them to an audience beyond their usual niche. Concert festivals Vive Latino (1998–present), Surf y Arena (2004–05), Baja Surf Stomp (2015–present), and Wild O' Fest (2016–present) have been equally essential for the movement's revitalization, with a key moment occurring at the 2005 edition of Surf y Arena that gathered 100,000 people in downtown Mexico City's Zócalo Square. Through the years, both musicians and fans have wondered whether the scene's proliferation would be but a fad. Yet new bands continue to emerge (the Sonoras, las Pipas de la Paz, Megatones, the Centellas, Huma Guma) and the old school is consistently active. This was clear at the most recent iterations of Baja Surf Stomp and Wild O' Fest, which featured iconic international surf and garage bands for the first time in Mexico along with local legends and emerging new groups (see Figure 19.5).

Surf musicians have learned to associate their pieces with different styles and discourses through their use of paramusical and paratextual elements, ranging from song and album titles, poster and cover art, to samples from old films (Twin Tones's *Nación Apache*; see Figure 19.6), third-party songs (Sr. Bikini's "Saca la chela"), or even created by their collaborators (los Elásticos's "Rames"). These elements, observable in almost every Mexican neo-surf album, seek to spice up usually instrumental songs with a tinge of, say, the Wild West, space, or the beach. They have also facilitated the development of several microgenres clearly differentiated from each other by

Figure 19.4 *Spaguetti & Chili Western: A Collection of Western Instros* (Isotonic Records, Mexico, 2005) [Courtesy of the artist/designer Dr. Alderete].

Figure 19.5 Poster for the second edition of Wild O'Fest (Carpa Astros, Mexico City, 2017) [Courtesy of the artist/designer Dr. Alderete].

bands and producers (usually band members themselves) aimed at creating and targeting specific niches. This implies delving into old and new surf-related styles, learning which instruments and musical traits are more typical in them, and making it all fit under the umbrella term of "neo-surf."

Some of these revived or invented microgenres, their representative bands, and associated instruments or sound effects are space surf and terror surf, both full of theremins and synthesizers (Espectroplasma, Megatones, Telekrimen, los Magníficos); spaghetti/chili western, with their twangy silk-stringed guitars (Twin Tones, los Twangers, the Sonoras); and the pervasive fuzz and reverb in either beach surf (Fenómeno Fuzz, Perversos Cetáceos, Malibú Piña), *lucha libre* surf (los Santísimos Snorkels, los Elásticos), or garage (the Cavernarios, las Ultrasónicas, las Navajas). As for rockabilly/psychobilly (los Gatos, Eddie y los Grasosos, las Leopardas), its presence has been so pervasive, with recordings and massive concerts of their own, and musical and fan practices so markedly different from surf ones (double bass,

Figure 19.6 Twin Tones, *Nación Apache* (Grabaxiones Alicia, Mexico, 2005) (©Andrés "Huracán" Ramírez) [Courtesy of the record producer].

clothing, and hairstyles in the 1950s fashion), that it arguably constitutes a genre in its own right.

As in many cases, the best way to understand how microgenres operate is by looking at specific examples. Among those Mexican neo-surf examples, chili western is perhaps the most dazzling. Despite sharing rhythmic and harmonic traits with several genres and microgenres (cajun, country, *norteña*, Ennio Morricone's spaghetti western soundtracks), chili western has provided bands with a discursive space to engage, criticize, and perform "authentic Mexicana" simulacra as addressed to non-Spanish-speaking audiences, proposing new forms of self-representation in the process. Albums like Twin Tones's *Nación Apache* (2005) or los Twangers's *Planeta Twanger* (2008) made chili western so distinguishable from other trends that several compilations have attempted to anthologize its development, not only the aforementioned, emblematic *Spaguetti & Chili Western* but also the first volume of North Sea Surf Radio's *Latin American Surf Sampler: Valley of the Kings* (2015), released in Amsterdam and largely intended for European audiences.

Just as some microgenres like chili western are perhaps easily ascribed to bands like the Twin Tones, others may be temporarily adopted to compose a song or album. For instance, there are currently no spy surf or Christmas surf bands, although Lost Acapulco and Danny Amis have used these styles for some recordings. Perhaps the musical traits that characterize, say, spy surf are so narrow that they do not leave room for a band to devote all their output to it. It seems as if resistance from microgenre stakeholders (bands and fans) to too much change is also a driving component. This could be linked to the criticism that surf and rockabilly always sound the same. The most successful cases seem to be those that explore their chosen style without excessively mingling with other trends, as they must mind their branding. As Marie Benito shows in her documentary on los Esquizitos, for them authenticity was a matter of playing surf "*o tronar*"—that is, sticking to surf's standards. Yet their songs are among the most daring.[4]

The apparently porous borders between each microgenre seem suddenly stiffer when we consider that Espectroplasma members had to form Twin Tones first and later Sonido Gallo Negro to switch from exclusively playing space surf to chili western, then to a fusion of surf and *chicha* cumbia (a Peruvian late 1960s–1970s genre also influenced by surf). These changes in style spurned new onstage personae that used other films and different effects units, instruments, and tempos. Something similar happened to the members of Telekrimen/the Cavernarios, their former project more easily associated with terror and space surf, the latter mostly with garage.

Figure 19.7 "Zócalo Surf," photograph by Ernesto Muñiz (Mexico, 2004). An improvised luchador dances on a surfboard across the audience during a rainy concert in Mexico City's downtown Zócalo square (©Ernesto Muñiz, https://www.ernestomuniz.com/) [Courtesy of the photographer].

When asked about the scene's success, both Pineda and López agree it has endured despite largely remaining underground because it provides concert-goers with an opportunity to dance in a free style. Neo-surf fans are as witty and inventive as their idols, organizing themselves through online forums, social networks, and at concerts, most notably during their mosh-and-dance mix. This provides cultural researchers with a lesson on how some urban groups differentiate themselves at the very moment of performance (see Figure 19.7). In this light, performing Mexican surf identities on and offstage is a rehearsed behavior that participates in the processes of creating self and collective representations and in the consolidation of new communities.

Notes

1   Ignacio Pineda, interview by Aurelio Meza, Multiforo Alicia, Mexico City, June 20, 2018.
2   Omar Bustamante, interview by Aurelio Meza, Multiforo Alicia, Mexico City, June 27, 2018.
3   Gabriel López, interview by Aurelio Meza, Multiforo Alicia, Mexico City, June 28, 2018.
4   *Surf o Tronar*, directed by Marie Benito (Centro de Capacitación Cinematográfica, 2009), https://vimeo.com/47921450.

20

Fanfiction Microgenres

Elyse Graham and Michelle Alexis Taylor

In 2004, the journalist Chris Anderson predicted that, in the internet age, the marketplaces for film, books, music, and so forth would exhibit a "long tail": that is, a graph plotting consumer products against each product's market shares would have a tail considerably longer than a graph plotting the same thing for a physical store's goods. That long tail, Anderson argued, would be made possible by the relatively low overhead of making a product available online (as opposed to the cost of a store display), and it would consist of a large collection of niche products, each of which would appeal to a very specific audience. As anecdotal evidence, Anderson told the story of two books, published a decade apart: Joe Simpson's *Touching the Void* and Jon Krakauer's *Into Thin Air*.[1]

The popularity of Krakauer's book, when it was published in 1997, apparently renewed the market for Simpson's, which, published ten years prior, told a similarly tragic story of a brush with mortality in the mountains. Simpson's book, which was out of print before the publication of Krakauer's, actually went on to *outsell* it. But *Into Thin Air* didn't create that market by itself, Anderson argued: the internet, and Amazon specifically, created the market by recommending Simpson's book to anyone interested in Krakauer's; the e-retailer made this recommendation on the basis of its own monitoring of purchasing trends. In other words, Amazon invented a subgenre—let's call it the "death in the mountains plot"—not as a *form* but as a (classificatory) *function*, and the invention of the function was largely responsible for the success of those who wrote (consciously or otherwise) within the form. Anderson's anecdote demonstrates not only the way that a long tail might form within a marketplace but also how it might function: classification (i.e., a robust taxonomy) would be key to growing the economy's long tail, and conversely the key to succeeding within that economy would be understanding a taxonomy in order to manipulate or position one's work within it. One might well want, and find it newly economically viable, to write not within a macrogenre, like the romance or murder mystery, but for a subgenre or microgenre, like the "death in the mountains plot" or the "supernatural steampunk detective story."

Critics have debated the extent to which succeeding decades have borne out Anderson's predictions.[2] But at least one long tail has found ample room to unfurl: fanfiction microgenres. In recent decades, fanfiction has seen such a proliferation of microgenres that we may well say that the very proliferation of microgenres (rather than, or more than, specific microgenres themselves) characterizes the experience of reading and writing on digital fanfiction platforms.

Considering fanfiction as a kind of economy suggests, first of all, that we should think of fanfiction as a competitive space, just as we think of the marketplace. But what are fanfiction writers competing for, if not money? As it happens, in recent years a number of critics have put forth compelling analyses of creative production, in Web 2.0 spaces, as a form of "playbor" in which participants produce content in exchange for rewards, such as points, that we normally associate with game play.[3] Fanfiction microgenres are a product of that competition: each fanfiction microgenre constitutes its own niche market within which a particular "fic" may succeed or fail.

What is it about Web 2.0 platforms—not just fanfiction archives like Archive of Our Own and Fanfiction.net but also Twitter, Facebook, Instagram, and other arenas for textual playbor—that makes them so responsive to analyses that stress (in the industry's term) *gamification*? In other words, what makes activity on Web 2.0 platforms gamelike? Most definitions of a game hold that games are voluntary, rule-bound, produce relative winners and losers (i.e., have winning conditions), and take place within a magic circle, a space separated from the world of consequence.[4] That fanfiction has winning conditions is readily apparent: on major platforms, readers award stories that they like points in the form of likes, bookmarks, kudos, comments, reviews, and so forth. That they are rule-bound is the focus of our discussion here.

Like most games, fanfiction is intricately governed by rules.[5] Indeed, few other forms of fiction are subject to such extensive regulation. Fanfiction writers must ensure that their stories comply with the canon of the original work(s) on which the "fic" is based, attending to the established histories of the characters and narrative universe, the personalities of the characters, and the general properties of their world (its geopolitics, technological advancement, whether magic exists). The author may, of course, choose to depart from this canon—by adding magic or by changing a character's sexuality—in the same way that some poets write fifteen-line sonnets; but, like the fifteen-line sonnet that demonstrates its knowledge of the Petrarchan form, the story must otherwise exhibit strict adherence to the model from which it has departed. Writers must also subject their work to the conventions of the digital archival platform, which usually include filing the story within the right "fandom" and tagging it with appropriate genre(s) and tropes and which may also include a schedule for uploading new installments or chapters.

This emphasis on constraint is not a limitation of fanfiction but rather a core characteristic. Fanfiction operates on the principle that the constraints that surround fanfiction production galvanize creativity rather than stifle it. The limitations that fanfiction authors observe can be astonishingly strict: the "drabble," for example, limits a story to exactly 100 words, but the "221B" (based on Sherlock Holmes's address at 221B Baker St.) takes this form further, setting the length at exactly 221 words and stipulating that the last word must begin with the letter *B*. Another taxonomy includes story types that govern or categorize a writer's departures from the constraints of the universe of canon (in terms of setting, character history, sexuality). There are, for example, a number of categories for fics that take place within an alternative universe (AU): "crossovers," which merge "fandoms," usually by having characters from one universe meet the characters from another (e.g., Harry Potter runs into Bella from *Twilight* while on an adventure); "fusions," which place the characters of one universe in the setting of another (Elinor Dashwood takes Marianne's place in the Hunger Games); stories with new characters that take place in an already established universe; and strange, vanishingly specific minor species, like "coffee shop AUs" (a fic that takes place in an ordinary coffee shop). Other genres specify plot arcs, often implying a series of attendant tropes: the "hurt/comfort" fic (a romantic type, in which a character is comforted after being hurt physically, emotionally, or both; its tropes may include the erotic, healing touch or one character feeding another), the "curtainfic" (a mundane, domestic story, about something like shopping for curtains), and the "bodyswap," in which two characters wake up in each other's bodies (often involving the erotic discovery of another character's body, the deception and infidelity of engaging with another character's partner, and autoerotic encounters between the two bodyswapped characters). In their narrowness, their specificity, the strict constraints of expectation that the writer and reader alike bring to them, these story types constitute microgenres. For example, it is hard to imagine how much narrower a genre could possibly become than "wingfic," a story about a character sprouting wings.

What is the relationship between microgenres and the dynamics of playbor on Web 2.0? We extend two hypotheses. Our first hypothesis is that the intricate taxonomies of fanfiction are added by both the platform's designers and its users as a form of play—that they use these taxonomies as constraints that encourage playful production (and therefore further engagement on digital fanfiction platforms). By these lights, writers of fanfiction write not only *within* strict bounds of genre and formula but also *because* of them. Microgenres generate fanfiction through constraint because writers use them as prompts: they challenge writers to imagine a story that, while keeping to the canon of a fandom, nonetheless fulfills certain generic requirements. Rules produce the play of fanfiction: as Suits writes, rules "are the crux of games because … [they] generate the skills appropriate to that game."[6] Some fanfiction spaces even revolve around games of request and response, with the quality and number of stories posted measuring the success of a prompt and the number of comments posted measuring the success of a fill (i.e., a story written in response to a prompt). These requests (often called "exchanges"), which specify plot points and story lines, constitute another form of constraint. The boundaries that characterize a given microgenre delimit an arena of rules and constraints within which writers take pleasure from playing.

A second hypothesis is that, while microgenres may in some cases antecede production, they more importantly precede reading—such that microgenres govern the composition of fanfiction less than they define its reception and circulation. A writer who writes without regard for tradition or acclaim may not consider herself, in the act of writing, to be playing a game; in her view she might simply be exercising the free play of her imagination. Yet in making her fic subject to circulation on a Web 2.0 platform, she subjects her work to the great game of fandom, even if the experience of writing the fic was not, for her, competitive. In giving her story folksonomy tags (i.e., keywords used for searching that can include categories devised by the community or by individual writers, not merely by accepted taxonomic systems like the Dewey Decimal System) after its writing—identifying her story's generic commitments, tropes, and fandoms—the writer acknowledges the game after she has made her moves in it. By sharing her fanfiction on a digital platform, she accepts the tacit goal of acquiring readers, and in sharing her fic on a Web 2.0 platform, she accepts the tacit goal of acquiring the signs of those readers (likes, comments). She enters the competition.

Often the folksonomy tags attached to a story are not only vanishingly precise but clearly excessive—a phenomenon that suggests not only how important microgenres are to the experience of the site but also how important tagging is to the play of fanfiction.[7] Many stories on Archive of Our Own have over forty tags attached, and there is no tag limit. These tags are often repetitive and overlapping, noting larger generic categories that coexist with specific microgenres (e.g., a Harry Potter crossover with Twilight might be tagged "crossover," "Harry Potter crossover," "Twilight crossover," and "Harry Potter x Twilight"; it might additionally be a wingfic and be tagged "wingfic," "Twilight wingfic," and "Edward grows wings"). Excessive tagging allows a writer to appeal to the widest possible audience by reaching a plurality of extremely niche audiences (rather than, as in the blockbuster model, appealing to the widest common denominator of interest, such as "romance" or "adventure"). In other words, the sensitivity that writers display in making these tags testifies to their awareness of the importance of microgenres in the circulation of fanfiction and the activity of its readers.

Nor is the recognition of microgenres the purview of writers only; readers may also participate in the game of fanfiction by updating and maintaining its folksonomies according to the terms established by both the host archive and the existing collection of tags and microgenres. Archive of Our Own, for example, has specific taxonomical referees called "tag wranglers," editorial agents who crystalize an emerging microgenre by linking together synonymous tags and designating the "canonical" form of the tag. This canonical form becomes baked into the various ways that users may browse or search the system: the canonical tag shows up in a search autocomplete; it is a filter option in an advanced search; it is listed in the section of the site that allows users to browse fanfiction by category (e.g., a Harry Potter wingfic might be tagged "wingfic—Harry Potter," "Harry Potter wingfic," "Harry grows wings," and even, by cheekier writers, "Look at your wings, Harry!!" A tag wrangler links these tags together and designates the canonical form of the tag, the form that shows up when, for example, a user types "wings Harry Pot" into the search bar). In designating canonical tags, wranglers must work within a series of naming conventions established by the archive. Tag wranglers therefore standardize the rules of the game by identifying and naming emerging microgenres: they tame the wild proliferation of new microgenres and attendant tags produced by writers creating new voluntary constraints for their literary production.

Readers and writers of fanfiction therefore interact through microgenres not only via games of request and response, and not only via the quantitative, often point-based reward systems belonging to Web 2.0 platforms, but also via the maintenance of folksonomies, the creation and consecration of ever new constraints to govern the writing and classification of stories. In this case, readers and writers arrive at new sets of generic expectations, at the "death in the mountains plot," together and consciously: not over the course of years but over the course of months or even days. Thus, regardless of whether microgenres serve as conditions for the production of fanfiction or as post-hoc categories that galvanize the dissemination of fanfiction, microgenres are a core attribute of fanfiction that complicate and fill out the rules of play.

In their proliferation, and indeed their occasional absurdity, fanfiction microgenres testify to the game elements, especially the reliance on voluntary constraint, that belong to fanfiction as a textual culture. They also testify to the peculiar living, moving, ever-updating quality of most textual cultures in the digital ecosystem. Because digital platforms need ongoing support, preferably from an audience that clamors for its upkeep, textual spaces in Web 2.0 are designed with a conscious eye to fostering ongoing user activity—taking the "telic" out of "autotelic." The tremendous popularity of fanfiction platforms—the roughly 300,500 stories that users submitted to FanFiction. net in 2010 alone can be added to the thousands of titles that users submitted, during the same period, to sister sites such as Archive of Our Own, which since its launch in 2009 has acquired over one million titles—demonstrates the value of voluntary constraint both for generating new writing and for keeping readers perpetually browsing the moving shelves of an infinite library. Ultimately, fanfiction, with its attendant microgenres, fulfills the creative and heterogenizing promise of the long tail—however ridiculous we may think "wingfic."

Notes

1   Chris Anderson, "The Long Tail," *Wired*, October 1, 2004; Chris Anderson, *The Long Tail: Why the Future of Business Is Selling Less of More* (New York: Hachette, 2006).

2   See, for example, Anita Elberse, *Blockbusters: Hit-making, Risk-taking, and the Big Business of Entertainment* (New York: Henry Holt, 2013); Chris Anderson, *The Longer Long Tail: How Endless Choice Is Creating Unlimited Demand* (New York: Random House, 2009); Erik Brynjolfsson, Yu (Jeffrey) Hu, and Michael D. Smith, "Tales versus Superstars: The Effect of Information Technology on Product Variety and Sales Confirmation Patterns," *Information Systems Research* 21 (December 2010): 736–47.

3   Trebor Scholz, ed., *Digital Labor: The Internet as Playground and Factory* (New York: Routledge, 2013); Elyse Graham, *The Republic of Games: Textual Culture between Old Books and New Media* (Chicago: McGill-Queen's University Press, 2018).

4   This is another way of suggesting that games are played by amateurs, who engage with the game for noninstrumental or, as Bernard Suits terms it, "autotelic" purposes (Bernard Suits, "Tricky Triad: Games, Play, and Sport," *Journal of the Philosophy of Sport* 15, no. 1 [1988]: 1–9).

5   Bernard Suits defines a game as "rule-governed interplay," "a voluntary effort to overcome" the "unnecessary obstacles" that constitute the rules (ibid.).

6   Ibid., 5.

7 By 2012, Archive of Our Own reported that over 140,000 "canonical" tags were in use in its database, meaning that there are over 140,000 recognized categories to which a story might belong. (While many of these categories are microgenres, tags also categorize stories according to tropes, characters, and fandoms; however, microgenre tags are of particular interest here.)

21

Machine-Classified Microgenres

Jonathan Goodwin

Microgenres are digital. The prefix *micro* remains associated with the computer, long after familiarity has removed it from everyday use. And the most familiar examples of microgenres are from video- and music-streaming services. But what does this digitally inflected concept tell us about literature? If the "folksonomies" seen on TV Tropes and Wikipedia show us just how small genres can be, are machine-assisted techniques useful for identifying and validating them? Literary scholarship has begun to explore these issues. I will review some of its intriguing findings and show how a machine-classifier handles microgenres.

Microgenres and other niche interests thrive on the internet through the "long tail" phenomenon.[1] By allowing for cheap storage of large amounts of inventory or at least efficient distribution of it across a wide range of merchants, internet commerce allows people to find rare products far more efficiently than in the past. The efficient communication and relatively cheap barriers to access also mean that people who enjoy highly specific content can discuss its finer points on online forums in great detail. Perhaps connoisseurship has been demystified to some degree through all of this connection of interests and tastes. The implications of the broader economic shift run from the profound to the trivial, and microgenres of commerce and art flourish as never before. But how can we keep track of all of them?

What follows is a very brief overview of the techniques used by some scholars to train computers to identify textual genres. Special attention will be paid to the level of granularity achievable via such techniques. Two well-known commercial microgenres projects, Netflix and the sound map created by engineers at Spotify, rely on proprietary information. What we know about the Netflix story was originally revealed by reverse engineering.[2] Machine learning techniques were certainly used as part of the process. Much of this type of statistical analysis involves the familiar problem of taking high-dimensional data, a set of things with many different features, and reducing them by isolating the ones that explain most of the variance. Such procedures are at the heart of inferential statistics, and they sometimes also come under suspicion. One such technique, factor analysis, was used during the early days of intelligence testing, for example, in the service of arguments whose cultural bias is now plain, and contemporary statistical classifiers are used in criminal sentencing and credit applications in ways that reveal similar cultural biases.[3]

Ted Underwood has used a form of classification known as logistic regression to identify broad genres in literary history. Underwood's essay is mostly concerned with the changes in specific genres over time and also how strongly one genre can be distinguished from another. Such relatively simple classification techniques may disturb some literary scholars, who associate generic identification with a high degree of expertise, but Underwood argues that adopting a supervised approach to classification helps allay those fears. By "supervised," he means that he provides the algorithm a human-composed training set of texts that bibliographers or other scholars have identified as being of the same genre.[4] This human-identified set is then used to compare against other texts. The ways in which genres do and do not cohere can then be analyzed, usually by comparing the machine-generated version with our intuitions.

Another interesting feature of how this particular algorithm works is that it is based on word frequencies. The texts themselves are reduced to word-frequency lists beforehand. This format is known as a "bag of words," an admittedly unlovely phrase. But there is a reason why this simple format is used. Words carry meaning, even stripped of their original context. Underwood notes that words associated with science fiction include measurements of magnitude, particularly of great distances and size. It is easy to see why this would be true, but—and this is an important point—it is not necessarily the type of observation that would have come to mind before the computerized classification was done. It is not that its novelty is astonishing, just that it would not likely have seemed plausible enough to try to check by hand. So: both plausible and counterintuitive or difficult-to-anticipate observations, those that are generative of further critical insights, are reasonable expectations from these models. I want to take this observation and demonstrate it by exploring how Underwood's technique can be used to identify genres smaller than the more traditional ones he considers such as detective fiction and horror.

What counts as a microgenre? How small does it have to be? To take one example that I will describe in more detail below, the Southern Gothic is a mixture, plainly, of the Gothic and the Southern (U.S., though perhaps not exclusively). Further subdivisions could be explored by region or state, or perhaps by thematic divisions of the Gothic itself. And genre is accretive; there seem to be few a priori limits on the number of genres any given text can contain, though the more it has, the more it becomes unified under the heading of "pastiche" or other form of satire or comedy. It is difficult for me to think of a minor or microgenre that cannot be said to be composed of other, larger generic categories. Some of the sharpest work that I have read when it comes to firm generic decisions is Darko Suvin's on Victorian science fiction.[5] I have tested several of his claims about books that are commonly considered to be Victorian science fiction that should not be, according to his theories, and I found applying Underwood's approach to genre classification agreed with Suvin's about 80 percent of the time.[6]

Before moving into these more detailed analyses, I want to briefly consider how cultural critics have used the term "microgenre." You could be forgiven for assuming it was a very recent coinage, but it has been used by critics for decades. Fernando Galván employs it as another word for *topos* to refer to travel writing; Michel Beaujour deploys it for literary self-portraits. Emily Apter describes "cabinet fiction" as a microgenre, and Anne Clark Barnett uses it to refer to medieval narratives of nuptial and Passion contemplation.[7] Examples can be multiplied, as it represents both a common phenomenon and an easily replicated word-making pattern in both English and French. (The earliest examples I have found were in French writing.) Steven Berlin Johnson, in his aptly titled *Everything Bad Is Good for You*, notes "think of this as a new microgenre of sorts: the mind-bender, a film designed specifically to disorient you, to mess with your head. The list includes *Being John Malkovich, Pulp Fiction, L.A. Confidential, The Usual Suspects, Memento*."[8] I cite Johnson's example here, because he is using the term *microgenre* to relate films that have no obvious connection other than the fact that they are from the same era and nationality and also have a similar narrative effect, an intent to confuse the viewer. Another approach is Bob Rehak relating microgenres to accelerated or slowed time scales in his discussion of "bullet time" in *The Matrix*.[9]

If we accept that microgenres have been used for quite a while without much formal attempt to distinguish them from genres of greater size, other than a vague and relative appeal to scale, then it is clear that attempting to establish a definite boundary for them is pointless. If there is no need to have a theory of what constitutes the microgenre level, then of what use is it as a critical category? One reason is simply to provoke discussion. Non-academic discussion of genre often involves argument over what category a certain work should be placed in according to an appeal to commonly accepted standards. Witness the scene in *The Sopranos* in which the potential investors for *Cleaver* (is the film-within-a-tv-series a microgenre?) discuss what is and is not a slasher movie. Silvio Dante notes that a film that does not feature teenagers being attacked ("couple of kids naked in a lake" is his exact phrasing) is not a slasher film per se, even if it involves a great deal of slashing (cleaving). Many debates of this type can be found on discussion forums and sites like TV Tropes. And what about Wikipedia, whose theory of categorization reaches a wide audience? There is a Wikipedia page on microgenres that focuses, as of the time of this writing, almost exclusively on music.

A glance at the talk and revision pages of the Wikipedia entry on Southern Gothic reveals much recrimination and disputation of sources and authority. One iteration of the page was done as a class project, and the legitimacy of that enterprise is called into question. Actual discussion of what makes something Southern Gothic is lacking. There are questions about geography, certainly, and a few discussions of gothic mood and psychology. The presence of *To Kill a Mockingbird* on the list invites some debate, as well it should. The TV Tropes discussion of Southern Gothic seems a bit better informed by the scholarship, alluding to the sense of social and architectural decay being the primary elements. I would expect that the sense of genre would be sharper on a website that is devoted to classifying it, but the list of texts that meet the criteria in both film and literature is much smaller than on the corresponding Wikipedia page.

Even such a questionable list of texts as the Wikipedia entry on Southern Gothic coheres as a genre with a high degree of reliability. How do I know this? The procedure is simply to take a list of texts designated as "Southern Gothic" by some source or another, download them, and then test the coherence of the set against a random group of texts selected for comparison.[10] The problem with using this technique for microgenres is, well, that microgenres are small. Southern Gothic is large enough to come up with fifty to one hundred unambiguous examples, though if you limit yourself to one-per-author it becomes more difficult. (An author's personal style often sends a stronger signal to classification algorithms than genre.) But what of Louisiana Gothic? New Orleans Gothic? Acadian Gothic with Lovecraftian elements? I hope you see the problem. As the number of available examples decrease, so does the reliability of any algorithmic method of detection. I am oversimplifying what is a complex issue in statistical classification, but the general point stands. But how did Netflix engineer "mind bending cult horror movies from the 1980s?" The answer is simple combination. The date is obvious, marketing information would provide the horror label, user feedback would supply cult and mind bending. *The Atlantic* article supplies more detail on the exact mechanism that was used here, but that is not the point. What is relevant is that the process combined supervised human classification from a variety of sources with algorithmic classification techniques.

For me, the main benefit of machine classification of genre is in discovery. It is possible to define a training set of texts that you reliably believe to be in a certain genre, have the classifier confirm their consistency, and then use that training set to match against a wide number of other texts. It is an inefficient way to find new examples of the Southern Gothic: of that there is no doubt, but it is an interesting and generative one. Let us see what happens when we trawl a larger group of texts with our Southern Gothic data set. Before I tried it with Southern Gothic, I chose a more generically consistent erotica group, which consistently cohered against a group of 272 novels published in the 1990s that were cataloged as "Domestic Fiction" in the Library of Congress subject heading. Novels that were identified as strongly "Southern Gothic" in the Domestic Fiction of the 1990s set included Rilla Askew's *The Mercy Seat*, a historical fiction set in Oklahoma in the nineteenth century; Robert Morgan's *The Hinterlands*, a novel set in the Appalachians with fantasy elements; and two texts that turn out not to be first published in the 1990s— Charles Major's *Uncle Tom Andy Bill* and Richard Wright's *Lawd Today!*.[11] Both have clear Southern content in terms of dialect, but the Gothic signal is mostly absent. What does this mean for our theory of computer-detected microgenres?

To answer this question, I will take a closer look at how these genres were detected and evaluated by the classifier. What words were most associated with Southern Gothic? Against a random training set, the words selected as most associated with Southern Gothic included "porch," "whiskey," "preacher," and "honor."[12] Both "sleep" and "asleep" were even more strongly associated with these texts, though the precise level of association is probably not terribly significant. The first words I quote above fit my sense of what Southern Gothic novels would contain, but the emphasis on sleep might be worth exploring. Another approach is to model one genre against another. If you compare Southern Gothic to erotica, which Southern Gothic novel is the naughtiest? At least in this training set, the honor goes to Charlaine Harris's *Living Dead in Dallas*, a vampire novel that involves a sex party. (Recall that my list of Southern Gothic novels was derived from the Wikipedia list.) The least erotic, or most strongly Southern Gothic, is Cormac McCarthy's *Child of God*, a novel whose necrophilia is indeed anti-erotic, despite its heavy sexual content.

Perhaps we cannot expect machine classification to reliably identify a truly *micro*-genre. We can expect it to find broader classifications, though in both cases, the discrepancies often show us things that we might not have seen otherwise. By formulating a theory of a microgenre and testing it using machine classification, we can see what an otherwise disinterested process thinks about our theory. What distinguishes this microgenre in our minds is often not going to be what distinguishes it from a classifier's point of view. The strong signal of erotica comes from its frequent use of sexualized words and body parts that do not appear with the same regularity in other fiction. That much seems obvious, and the experiment demonstrated it. But a genre like Southern Gothic, on the other hand, is inherently more nebulous and more difficult to distinguish from Southern literature overall. That the procedure did not do a particularly good job of distinguishing the gothic parts of it does not surprise me, but the false positives and boundary cases presented interesting material for interpretation. In any case, I don't aim to criticize work like Underwood's that makes broader historical claims about genre formation based on these techniques. My emphasis on more playful and frivolous uses of the technology is not meant to undermine more sober claims. I believe in the value of machine classification as a conversation starter, a great classroom exercise.

Unfortunately, it takes a great deal of effort at present to perform these types of experiments with machine classification of genre. If you want to examine a large body of fiction, there are no preexisting tools with graphic interfaces that work on any platform. It would be relatively easy to create some of these, and I hope that some will become available soon. The type of work that it requires often is difficult to anticipate with a graphical tool, however. If, however, you have some experience with this type of programming or have a good support staff, I highly encourage this form of genre exploration. As of the time of this writing, the HathiTrust is now making available many contemporary texts that students in particular might want to explore this way. The digital exploration of textual microgenres has only just begun.

Notes

1　See Chris Anderson, *The Long Tail: Why the Future of Business Is Selling Less of More* (New York: Hyperion, 2006).

2　See Alexis C. Madrigal, "How Netflix Reverse Engineered Hollywood," *The Atlantic*, January 2014, https://www.theatlantic.com/technology/archive/2014/01/how-netflix-reverse-engineered-hollywood/282679.

3　Stephen Jay Gould, *The Mismeasure of Man* (New York: Norton, 1981); Cathy O'Neil, *Weapons of Math Destruction: How Big Data Increases Inequality and Threatens Democracy* (New York: Crown, 2016).

4　Ted Underwood, "The Life Cycles of Genres," *Cultural Analytics*, 2016, https://doi.org/10.7910/DVN/XKQOQM. An unsupervised approach to the large-scale analysis of genre is used by Matthew Wilkins, "Genre, Computation, and the Varieties of Twentieth-Century U.S. Fiction," *Cultural Analytics*, 2016, https://doi.org/10.31235/osf.io/e7wy6

5   Darko Suvin, "On What Is and Is Not an SF Narration; with a List of 101 Victorian Books That Should Be Excluded from SF Bibliographies," *Science Fiction Studies* 5, no. 1 (1978): 45–57; "Seventy-Four More Victorian Books That Should Be Excluded from Science Fiction Bibliographies," *Science Fiction Studies* 7, no. 2 (1980): 207–12; *Victorian Science Fiction in the UK: The Discourses of Knowledge and Power* (Boston: G. K. Hall, 1983).

6   Jonathan Goodwin, "More Suvin," October 14, 2016, http://jgoodwin.net/blog/more-suvin.

7   Fernando Galván, "Travel Writing in British Fiction: A Proposal for Analysis," in *British Postmodern Fiction*, ed. Theo D'Haen and Hans Bertens (Amsterdam: Rodopi, 1993), 79; Michel Beaujour, *Poetics of the Literary Self-Portrait*, trans. Yaro Milos (New York: New York University Press, 1992); Emily Apter, *Feminizing the Fetish: Psychoanalysis and Narrative Obsession in Turn-of-the Century France* (Ithaca: Cornell University Press, 1991), 39; Anne Clark Barnett, *Male Authors, Female Readers* (Ithaca: Cornell University Press, 1995), 4.

8   Steven Berlin Johnson, *Everything Bad Is Good for You* (New York: Penguin, 2006), 129.

9   Bob Rehak, "The Migration of Forms: Bullet-Time as Microgenre," *Film Criticism* 32, no. 1 (2007): 129.

10 The HathiTrust makes word count data, which this procedure uses, available to researchers of even in-copyright texts.

11 The problem this reveals, of inadequate or misleading metadata, bedevils much research of this type.

12 The code and some of the training data are taken from Ted Underwood's repository in support of his "The Life Cycles of Genres" essay.

Index

Abert, James William 61, 66
Adventures of Lucky Pierre, The
    (Lewis) 93, 96, 98–9
Ainsworth, William Harrison 34
Aladdin and the Wonderful Lamp
    (Franklin) 82
Alderete, Dr. 171–3, 176–7
algorithms 1, 190, 192
All the Year Round (periodical) 43
Amazon 1, 155, 158, 181
Amer (Cattet and Forzani) 111
Anderson, Chris 181–2
Anderson, Laurie 126
Anderson, Laurie Halse 37
anthologies 3, 9–10, 175, 178
Antipater of Sidon 11, 13
anxiety, role in creating microgenres
    6, 16, 39–44, 113–19
Apter, Emily 191
Argento, Dario 107, 111
As Good As It Gets (Brooks) 56
Askew, Rilla 193
audiences 42, 106, 108, 147, 155,
    178–9, 185
Ausonius 10, 13

Bad Mother (Waldman) 148
Balzac, Honoré de 51
Barnes, Peter 37
Barnett, Anne Clark 191
Bartlett, John Russell 66
Basic Instinct (Verhoeven) 111
Bataille, Gaillard de la 26
Bava, Lamberto 111
Bava, Mario 103, 111
Bay of Blood, A (Bava) 110
Beaujour, Michel 191
Beck, Martha 150
Beerbohm, Max 77
Behn, Aphra 16, 19–20

Belkin, Lisa 149
Bell, Bare, and Beautiful (Lewis) 99
Bell, Virginia 99
Belleau, Rémy 16
Benito, Marie 179
Bérubé, Michael 151
Beys, Charles 16, 18
Bibo, Walter 95
Bird with the Crystal Plumage, The
    (Argento) 107
Blade Runner (Scott) 43
Blaze Starr Goes Nudist (Wishman)
    98
Blood and Black Lace (Bava) 103, 110
Blood Feast (Lewis) 98–9
Bloodstained Shadow (Bido) 105
Boin-n-g!! (Lewis) 98–9
Boone, Danny, Jr. 89
Braddon, Mary Elizabeth 39, 41–2
Bradford, Mark 136, 143–5
Braudy, Leo 16
Breeder (Gore and Lavender) 148
Bromley, Henry 73
Brooks, Max 157
Brown, Charles Brockden 35–6
Browning, Robert 77
Bugsy Malone (Parker) 83
Bull, Richard 73
Burden, Chris 121
burlesque 100
Burton, Robert 74

Cage, John 126
Camus, Albert 37
canonical and non-canonical works
    4, 25, 185
Cantenac, Jean Benech de 16, 19
Captivity (Joffé) 111
Carlyle, Thomas 50, 51
carpinteros, los 136

Case of the Bloody Iris, The
(Carnimeo) 103–4
Casetti, Francesco 128
Castle (television series) 40
Cather, Willa 64
censorship 17, 53, 94
Motion Picture Association of
America rating system 94, 97
Motion Picture Production Code
(Hays Code) 83, 93–4, 100
Chabon, Michael 148
Chaffin, Tom 65
Charles II (King of England) 17–19,
22
Child, Lydia Maria 5, 33–4
Chong, Kevin 37
Christie, Agatha 103
Clarendon, Edward Hyde, Earl of 73
classification 1–2, 6, 12, 163–70,
181–6, 189–94
Cleland, John 26
Cohen, Ralph 3
Cole, Thomas 34–5
Coleridge, Samuel Taylor 50, 51
comic books 44
community, role of in creating
microgenres 5, 6, 26, 180
Cook, James 157
Cooper, James Fenimore 62
Corkran, Henriette 53
Corinne, or Italy (de Staël) 50, 52
Countdown to Looking Glass (Barzyk)
113, 115–18
Covered Wagon, The (Cruze) 81
Crary, Jonathan 129
"Creating a Mind" (Meade and
Halifax) 40
Crichton, Michael 36
critics and reviewers 33, 65, 115, 151

Dana, Richard Henry 63
Darling, Jesse 136
Darnton, Robert 27
databases 39, 158, 194
Davidovich, Jaime 122, 126–7, 129

Day After, The (Meyer) 113, 115–16,
118
Death Walks on High Heels (Ercoli)
105–6
Deep Red (Argento) 107, 109
Defoe, Daniel 32, 37, 157
Delirium (Bava) 111
Demetrius of Bithynia 13
DePalma, Brian 111
detective fiction 39, 103–4, 190
Diary of a Nudist (Wishman) 96
Dickens, Charles 43
Diderot, Denis 25, 27
digital culture 1, 76–7. *See also*
Internet
Dimock, Wai Chee 2
Dixon, Edmund Saul 39, 42
DJ Shadow 76
Downe, Allison Louise 99
Doyle, Arthur Conan 103
duCille, Ann 83
Du Maurier, George 53

Earthquake (Robson) 116
Emerson, Ralph Waldo 64
Emory, William 66
erotica 6, 15–22, 93–100, 193
Etherege, Sir George 16, 18–19
experimentation 51, 121, 163

Fanfan (Franklin) 82
fanfiction 2, 4, 5, 155–61, 181–6
feminism 4, 6, 99, 121, 149–50
Fenn, William W. 55
Fifth Cord, The (Bazzoni) 107
Flagg, Edmund 63
Follett, Ken 37
Forbes-Robinson, Frances 55
*Forbidden Photos of a Lady Above
Suspicion The* (Ercoli) 109
Fougeret de Monbron, Louis Charles
26
Frémont, John C. 61, 63–6
Freud, Sigmund 55
Friday the 13th (Cunningham) 110

Friedman, Dave 93, 97–8, 100
Front Page, The (Milestone) 82
Frye, Northrop 3

Galván, Fernando 191
Garber, Marjorie 83
Garden of Eden (Nosseck) 95
Gardiner, Baron 53
Gautier, Théophile 51
Geminus 10
gender and sexuality 6, 15–22, 25–9,
      93–100. *See also* feminism
   homosexuality 55, 58, 144
   motherhood 25, 28, 147–52
   representations of women 48, 52–3
   sexual assault 41
Genette, Gérard 77
Gilliam, Terry 4, 79
Gilmore, Kate 136, 140
Gingrich, Newt 117
Girl Who Knew Too Much, The (Bava)
      103, 107, 110
Glad Rags to Riches (Lamont) 88
Goethe, Johann Wolfgang von 48, 51
Goetzmann, William 63
Goldhill, Simon 13
Goldilocks and the Three Bares (Lewis)
      99
Gordaneer, Alisa 151
gothic fiction 1–2, 47, 49–50, 107,
      190–4
Granger, James 71–3
Grant, Michael 37
Greene, Graham 84
Gregg, Josiah 63
grindhouse theaters 6, 94, 103, 109
Gubar, Marah 81, 83
Gusterson, Hugh 114
Gutzwiller, Kathryn 12, 13

Halloween (Carpenter) 110–11
Halloween (Zombie) 111
Happy Birthday to Me (Thompson)
      110
Hardman, Joseph 51

Harraden, Beatrice 53
Harris, Charlaine 193
Harrison, Rachel 136, 138, 141
Harry Potter novels 161, 183–4
Hatch, Kristen 82–3
Hawthorne, Nathaniel 50
Her (Jonze) 56
Hideout in the Sun (Wolk) 98
historical fiction 1, 31, 35–6
Hitchcock, Alfred 103, 106
Hodges, Nathaniel 32
Hoffmann, E. T. A. 49–50
Hohauser, William 127
Holt, Nancy 121
horror film 4, 6, 98, 103–11
   slasher films 98, 103, 110–11,
      191–2
Hostel (Roth) 111
Household Words (periodical) 43
Human Centipede, The (Six) 111
Humboldt, Wilhelm von 48
Hurlic, Philip 86
Huxley, Aldous 43
hybrids, generic 62, 64, 163–70, 173–4

Ibsen, Henrik 77
Immoral Mr. Teas, The (Meyer) 96–9
Internet 1, 4, 129, 149, 151, 175,
      181–6, 189–94
   blogs 147, 150, 156
   memes 4
   social media 123, 180, 182
   streaming services 1, 189
   Wikipedia 192
Irving, Washington 50, 62–3
Ives, Joseph C. 63, 66

Jack and the Beanstalk (Franklin) 82
Jackson, Donald and Mary Lee Spence
      64
Jackson, Heather 72
Jackson, Holbrook 74–6
James, Henry 55
Jensen, Wilhelm 55
Johnson, Gary 98

Johnson, Steven Berlin 191
Jones, T. K. 114
Joyce, James 55
Julian of Egypt 10, 13

Kelley, Mike 124
Kendall, George Wilkins 65
Kenealy, Arabella 39, 41, 44
Kerwin, William 99
Kid 'in' Africa (Hays) 89–90
Kid in Hollywood (Lamont) 84
Kid's Last Fight, The (Lamont) 85
King, Stephen 36
King of the Hill (television series) 40
Knight, Jeffrey Todd 76
Koven, Mikel 104
Krakauer, Jon 181

Laclos, Pierre Choderlos de 25
Lamott, Anne 147
LaRose, Rose 100
Laura (Preminger) 56
Lavery, Hanna 16, 18
Lease, Maria 99
Lee, Vernon (Violet Paget) 52, 53
Leonidas of Tarentum 10, 13
Lewis, Matthew 49
Lewis and Clark 62
Lewis, Barbara 93
Lewis, Herschell Gordon 93, 98, 100
Lin, Maya 136
London, Jack 36
Longfellow, Henry Wadsworth 64
Louis XIV (King of France) 17
Ludgate Magazine 44

macrogenres 1–3, 181
Madden, Deanna 36
Mahon, Barry 99
Major, Charles 193
Mallarmé, Stéphane 77
Mann, Thomas 36
Manns, Sara 151
Männlein-Robert, Irmgard 12–13
Marcus Argentarius 11

Márquez, Gabriel García 36–7
Mason, Connie 99
Matrix, The (Wachowski) 191
McCarthy, Cormac 193
McCarthy, Eugene 117
McCarthy, Paul 122, 124–5, 129
McDonough, Jimmy 98
McMahon, Paul 127
medicine and literature 31–7, 39–44, 150
memoir 2, 6, 26, 147–52
Meyer, Russ 93, 98, 100
microgenres
    death of 14, 39, 47, 55, 97, 118
    definition of 1, 135, 189–91
    as marketing categories 2, 4, 5, 12
    creation of 4, 40, 49, 63, 163, 181
    relationship to politics 16–20, 33–4, 113–19, 166
Miller, Joaquin 64
Molloy, J. Fitzgerald 55
Montaigne, Michel de 15
Morangle, Payot de 16
Morgan, Robert 193
Morgan, Winter 159
Morrill, Angela 148
Mr. Peters' Pets (Crane) 95
musical subgenres 1, 6, 163–80
My Bloody Valentine (Mihalka) 110
Myron (sculptor) 10
Mystery. *See* detective fiction

Nelson, Maggie 125
Nerval, Gérard de 51
Netflix 1, 189, 192
Nevins, Allan 64
Newnes, George 43
Newton-Robinson, J. 55
Night to Dismember, A (Wishman) 98
9/11 Commission Report 61
Nolan, Cady 133–5, 141
Nude on the Moon (Brooks) 96, 98

Olsen, Tillie 150
O'Neill, John H. 16–17

O'Sullivan, John 66
Ouida 52–4
Outpourings of an Art-Loving Friar
	(Tieck and Wackenroder) 49
Ovid 15, 47

Page, Bettie 99–100
Paik, Nam June 121
Parker, Alan 83
Parkman, Francis 63
Pater, Walter 52
Paulding, James Kirke 61
Pegram, Chelsea 136
Peltz, Lucy 73–4
Penn, Mary E. 52–3
Pennant, Thomas 73
Periwig Maker (Schäffler) 37
Petronius 15
Pfaff, Judy 136
Philippoteau, Philip 143
Philippus of Thessalonica 10
Philyaw, Deesha 151
Picture of Dorian Gray, The (Wilde) 4,
	47, 53–5, 59–60
Pie-Covered Wagon, The (Lamont) 81,
	86, 88
Pike, Zebulon 62
Pineda, Ignacio 175
Plato 33
Playboy (magazine) 97
Pliny the Elder 11–12
Poe, Edgar Allan 33–4, 47, 50
poetry 6, 9–22
Polly Tix in Washington (Lamont) 86
Powell, John Wesley 67
Portrait of Jennie (Dieterle) 56–7
Price, Seth 136, 141–2
Propertius 11–12

Quaintance, Richard E. 16

race and racism 6, 86–90, 144, 151,
	166
Rachilde 53–4
Rapp, Rayna 150

Reagan, Ronald 113–14, 127–8
Rebecca (Hitchcock) 56
Régnier, Mathurin 16
Rehak, Bob 191
Richardson, Benjamin Ward 41
Richardson, Samuel 157
Robinson, Bill "Bojangles" 86
Robinson, Jesse 136
Rochester, John Wilmot, Earl of
	15–17, 20–2
Roiphe, Anne 149–50
Rossetti, Dante Gabriel 51–2
"roughies" 97–8
Rousseau, Jean-Jacques 28–9
Rowland, Cameron 136
Ruby Sparks (Dayton and Faris) 56
Runt Page (Nazarro) 81, 84
Ruskin, John 50–1

Sachs, Tom 136
Sade, Marquis de 4, 25–6, 29
sampling 76, 176
Sand, George 52
satire 17, 22, 27, 122, 128, 142, 191
Saw (Wan) 111
Schell, Jonathan 115
Schiller, Friedrich 48
Scott, Walter 1, 49
Scream (Craven) 110
Segalove, Ilene 127
Serra, Richard 121
Sevareid, Eric 117
Seven Blood-Stained Orchids (Lenzi)
	108
Shelley, Mary 36, 39
Sibony, Gedi 136
"Silenced" (Meade and Eustace) 42
Simpson, James 63
Simpson, Joe 181
Smith, Michael 122, 128–9
Soavi, Michele 111
Sonney, Dan 97
Sopranos, The (television series) 191
South Park (television series) 79
Squire, Michael 13

Staël, Germaine de 50
Stagefright (Soavi) 111
Starr Report (1998) 61
Stevenson, Robert Louis 39
Stewart, George R. 36
Stockholder, Jessica 136–7, 141
Stories of the Sanctuary Club (Meade
    and Eustace) 43
Strand Magazine 43
Strange Color of Your Body's Tears, The
    (Cattet and Forzani) 111
Strange Vice of Mrs. Wardh, The
    (Martino) 106
Susannah of the Mounties (Seiter) 86
Suvin, Darko 191
Sweerts, Michael 31–2
Symons, Arthur 55

Tarantino, Quentin 111, 174
Taylor, Bayard 62
technology, role in creating
    microgenres 5, 56, 122–4, 130,
    150, 158
television 5, 113–19, 122–30
Tenebrae (Argento) 107, 109–10
Temple, Shirley 6, 81–90
Testament (Littman) 113, 115–18
Thar She Blows! (Kanter) 96
Thompson, Clive 157
Thompson, Sherry 150
Thoreau, Henry David 64
Threads (Jackson) 113, 116, 118
Thucydides 31, 35
Tieck, Ludwig von 49–50
Titanic (Cameron) 56, 58
Tolstoy, Leo 77–9
Torso (Martino) 110
Towering Inferno, The (Guillermin)
    116
translation 17, 26, 169
travel narratives 61–8, 157

Treasure Island (Franklin) 82
Truman Show, The (Weir) 122
Tse, Shirley 136
Twilight novels 183–4
Two Thousand Maniacs! (Lewis) 98

Underwood, Ted 2, 190–1, 194
Ursata, Andra 136

Varas-Diaz, Nelson 170
vaudeville 81–2, 129
Vertigo (Hitchcock) 56, 58
video 110, 122–30
video games 155–61, 182
Voltaire 27

Wald, Priscilla 37
Waldman, Ayelet 148–51
Walker, Alice 148, 150
Walker, Rebecca 148–9
Walker, Stacey 99
War Babies (Lamont) 81, 85
War Game, The (Watkins) 116
Washburn, Phoebe 136, 139
Waters, John 96
Wee Willie Winkie (Ford) 86
Wharton, Edith 55
What Price Glory (Walsh) 81
Whitman, Walt 64
Whittier, John Greenleaf 64
Wideman, John Edgar 37
Wilde, Oscar 4, 41, 47, 52–5
Wishman, Doris 98
Wolfe, Sean Kay 160
Woolf, Virginia 55–6, 150
Wright, Richard 193
Wynne, M. E. 37

Yeager, Bunny 99
Year of the Plague (Cazals) 37